Arm V

Bitton Station

20 March 2015.

Derby and the Midland Railway

Derby and the Midland Railway

Peter Billson

The Breedon Books
Publishing Company
Derby

First published in Great Britain by
The Breedon Books Publishing Company Limited
Breedon House, 44 Friar Gate, Derby, DE1 1DA.
1996

I am grateful to various people for assistance with points in furthering this book. I am also grateful for the ready assistance given by the following - The National Railway Museum, Derbyshire Record Office, Derbyshire Local Studies Library, Nottinghamshire Record Office and Local Studies Library, Leicestershire Museums and Record Office; Derby Museum and Industrial Museum.

Picture Credits

The author and publishers are grateful to the following for their permission to reproduce photographs and illustrations in this book:
National Railway Museum: cover centre, frontispiece, 43 top, 44 top, 50, 73 top, 85, 87 top, 101 top, 103 top, 105, 107 lower, 108 top, 109 lower, 110 top, 111 top and lower, 112 top and lower, 113 top, 118 top and lower, 119 top, 122 top, 123, 125, 128 lower, 129 lower, 130 lower, 131 top and lower right. Derby Museums: 11 lower, 20 lower, 23 lower, 30 top, 37 centre, 39, 41 top and lower, 42, 46 lower, 47 top and lower, 48 top and lower, 57 lower, 61, 79 left, 106 top, 108 lower right, 116 lower right, 124 top and lower, 134 top and lower, 136, 137 top, 138 lower, 139, 140. Derbyshire County Library, Local Studies: 15 lower, 16 top, 17, 18 top and lower, 19 left, 20 top, 24 top, 32 bottom, 35 top, 36 lower, 38, 52, 64, 66, 67, 75, 84 right, 96, 100 top, 116 lower right, 117, 138 top. Nottinghamshire County Council: 25 lower, 68 top, 73 bottom, 92 top and centre. Leicestershire Museums: 27 bottom. Derbyshire Archaeological Society: 96. Midland Railway Trust: 42 lower. Royal Commission Historic Monuments England (per Laurence Knighton): 45 centre, 55, 57 top, 59 top and lower, 87 lower, 103 lower, 104 top and lower, 126 top, 127 centre and bottom. Midland Hotel, Derby: 82, 84 left. Laurence Knighton: 127 top. David White: 40 bottom right. Alan Morrison: 14 top. Malcolm Burrows: 14 lower. Don Newing: 33, 142 top. Mark Higginson: 52 top and centre right, 53 top. John Heath: 37 top, 116 top, 120, 126 centre, cover left bottom.

ISBN 1 85983 021 8

Printed and bound by Butler & Tanner Limited, Selwood Printing Works, Caxton Road, Frome, Somerset.

Colour separations by Colour Services, Wigston, Leicester.

Jacket printed by Premier Print, Nottingham.

Contents

To Brenda for her support

and
in commemoration of
Thomas Bainbridge (1831-1898)
Porter – Midland Railway, Nottingham – 1860s.

and
John Britland Sutton (1866-1940)
Coppersmith – Midland Railway Works, Derby – *c.*1887-1931.

A classic Midland Railway Express train just out of Milford Tunnel, Duffield in 1904. Posed photograph used for publicity purposes showing a fairly new Johnson compound 4-4-0 locomotive no. 2633 – probably photographed by Scotton junior.

Preface

Men without learninge, and the remembrance of things past, falls into beastlye sottishness.
William Dugdale, 1655

IN WRITING this book I am consciously grateful for leads given by others who have helped pave the way by their own researches and accounts.

This book has its origins in research started in January 1978 following the publication by the Derby City Council of a 'Notice of Intent to Demolish' the Brunswick Inn, a listed building. It also transpired that the city council, the then owners of the adjacent railway houses, intended to demolish them also for a new road and for a car-park. The Derby Civic Society's interest was aroused and for my part I undertook to establish the origins of the Inn and the houses.

The latter had hitherto been generally accepted to have been built by the Midland Railway for its employees. I was able to establish that they were earlier, having been built by its forerunner the North Midland Railway in 1841-42 as a group with the Brunswick Inn. A 'save' campaign by the Derby Civic Society eventually led to the Derbyshire Historic Buildings Trust being brought in and the City Council being persuaded to sell the houses and Inn. The Trust's brave step of taking on the rehabilitation of the houses resulted in a fine scheme that achieved local and national acclaim. My submissions in 1978 for the houses and the Midland Hotel to be designated listed buildings within a Railway Conservation Area were rewarded by decisions of the Department of the Environment in late 1979 and October 1980 respectively, with the City Council confirming a conservation area in March 1980. Ironically, strong representations to stop British Rail demolishing the historic Midland Railway Station, the heart of that splendid Derby company, and the newly created 'Railway Conservation Area', were ignored by British Rail and not supported by either the Department of the Environment (now renamed the Department of National Heritage) nor even Derby City Council. It was finally demolished in 1985.

My interest in the beginnings of the company and the relationship to Derby have culminated in this account. I was additionally encouraged, particularly in respect of the Castlefields aspects, from reading a quotation in Gillian Tindall's perceptive book *The Fields Beneath* – an account of her own London suburb of Kentish Town (which also happens to have a Midland Railway connection). This relates how one day she came across a row of unremarkable mid-Victorian houses, and in the sooty yellow bricks over the lintel of one of the houses had been cut the memorable inscription:

'The Fields Lie Sleeping Underneath'

Peter Billson
Allestree, Derby
April 1996

Introduction

As to the town in general it is a very desirable place to live in, having as much benefit of all the Four Elements as any other town in England: coal for fire being got within four miles from the town in several places, as Smaly, Denby etc., and brought thither and laid down at 4d per hundred weight, or under.

William Woolley, *c.*1712

FEW people viewing the late Victorian Midland Station at Derby just before its final demolition in 1985 by British Rail, realised the significance of what lay before them. Later additions and Charles Trubshaw's splendid forward extension of 1893 concealed most of Francis Thompson's great 1840 station, but the original building remained largely intact behind the later frontage. All the building elements from 1840 to 1893 were steadily deteriorating through neglected maintenance during the British Rail years of ownership. The brickwork was dulled from railway smoke. The windows and paint work depressingly dingy. It was difficult to imagine that behind all this was a marvel of early Victorian Britain – that we were in the presence of what an eminent authority called "the first really great Victorian station". Since the sweeping away of the great Midland Station and the present ongoing demolition of the old Midland Works only the original 1840 workshops of the North Midland and the Midland Counties Railways now survive as testimony to the heart and origins of a great railway. The Midland Railway Company – from 1844 to 1923. In 1994 we celebrated its memorable creation 150 years ago.

This book is a commemoration of the creation of the Midland Railway, with a picture of the circumstances leading to it, and an outline of its general development. For a more detailed history of the Midland Railway, its locomotives, stock and lines there are already numerous books on the subject, and several specialist histories by Williams, Stretton, Hamilton-Ellis, Barnes and Radford, although a definitive account has yet to be written.

The Midland Railway Company came into existence on 10 May 1844 when the Midland Railway Consolidation Bill had passed all its Parliamentary stages and received the Royal Assent. It was not an original railway but was created from the amalgamation of three existing early companies which all connected at Derby – these were the Midland Counties Railway, The Birmingham & Derby Junction Railway, and the North Midland Railway. It was the first merger of consequence of railway companies and it created the then largest railway in Britain under single management, with a total main line route mileage of some 180 miles.

From these beginnings the Midland Company grew steadily during its near 80 years of existence until by 1922, the last year of its independent existence, it was the third largest railway in the country after the Great Western and, the London & North Western Companies. During that period its offices at Derby grew more and more extensive, and its locomotive, carriage and wagon building and repair workshops, with other necessary support facilities expanded to a great commercial enterprise. During its development and expansion it absorbed some 40 smaller railway companies across the country and entered into joint ownership of several others. It became the major employer in Derby in its time and contributed substantially to the expansion of the town. It was a municipal participant in the transformation of Derby from a genteel country town into a modern industrial city. There is every reason to regard Derby as the first of the great English railway towns.

The Midland Railway has been described as a magnificent railway. This may in present time seem a highly colourful claim, but the Midland did have two spectacularly scenic routes through and over the Pennines – the route to Manchester and the stunning line from Settle to Carlisle. Over its last 50 years it provided very comfortable accommodation for passengers on its trains and, for the third class the most comfortable of any railway. It surprised its competitors by introducing third-class coaches on all trains in 1872, instead of making this class travel on special trains with slower schedules and poorer carriages. The Midland followed this major change with the even more radical one three years later of abolishing all second class, and upgrading its ordinary or third-class accommodation. In 1874 the Midland Company introduced the luxury of American Pullman cars to Britain – shipping these in kit form to their railway works at Derby; there they were assembled and put on the line. The first three cars were two sleepers and a saloon. The Midland were a little belated in introducing dining cars, but in 1882 they converted two Pullman cars into 'hotel cars'. Each seated 21 first-class diners in handsome surroundings. These beginnings would develop into splendid multi-course meals cooked on board, with fine wines provided from the company's extensive cellars at the Midland Hotel, Derby and at St Pancras. Until later, with the advent of corridor carriages, more modest food for travellers could be obtained in good luncheon baskets from the refreshment rooms at each of its main stations.

Its trains were fast, frequent, well timed and immaculate. From 1887 they were distinguished by the memorable and splendid crimson lake livery colour of 'Midland Red'. Its locomotives shone with pride. The Midland was always a small engine line – although this was not noticeably so in the nineteenth century compared with its rivals, it became more so in the twentieth century. Double heading locomotives was common, but if not economic the Midland Company seemed to thrive on it. It set itself high standards – in the locomotive department, probably the most vital section, its mechanical engineers, Kirtley, Johnson, Deeley and Fowler ensured a particularly high quality.

The Midland Railway started off its existence with a collection of architecturally fine stations on the former North Midland Railway line designed by the respected Francis Thompson, including the great station at Derby. There were also distinguished station buildings at Leicester and Nottingham on the former Midland Counties line. The Midland would continue this tradition of good architecture and good provisions for its passengers through the work of its own staff architects John Holloway Sanders and Charles Trubshaw and, in its employment of outside architects like Charles Driver, Edward Walters, and Sir Gilbert Scott.

The Midland was also an extremely busy goods carrying concern with big marshalling yards and extensive freight trains, which together with coal transportation were essential to its economy. It was memorable, in contrast to its more showy glories, for its long trains loaded with enormous quantities of Midlands coal, making a constant procession from Toton via Trent Junction to the vast marshalling yards at Cricklewood for London, and eastward via Peterborough for East Anglia – also to the west via Birmingham. This was a continuation of business that started on the day the North Midland Railway opened for traffic on 11 May 1840, when it was reported that "a very considerable quantity of coals were conveyed along the line on the day of opening".

The Midland was especially memorable for the series of most elegant single driving wheel express engines introduced by Samuel Johnson from 1887, then his neat and sturdy 4-4-0 class from 1900 followed by the fine 4-4-0 compounds from 1902, with Richard Deeley's refined versions coming out from 1905-06. Henry Fowler's standard 0-6-0 superheated goods engines appeared in 1911 but large-scale construction did not occur until 1917. These engines were destined to be one of the largest quantities of the class built in England, continuing to be built well into the subsequent LMS era. It is a curious fact that the Midland Railway never built any larger goods engines than Fowler 0-6-0's for its own heavy freight trains, although it did produce a pure Midland design large 2-8-0 by Fowler in 1914, for hauling freight trains over the steep grades of the jointly owned Somerset and Dorset Joint Railway main line. The largest engine to come out of the Midland Railway's Derby works was Fowler's 0-10-0 locomotive of 1919, known affectionately as 'Big Bertha', a sole example built specifically for banking heavy trains up the steep Lickey incline at Bromsgrove on the Birmingham-Bristol line.

In 1867 the Midland Railway achieved its own London terminus with William Barlow's magnificent arched train shed at St Pancras Station, with great iron roof ribs made by the Butterley Company. This stunning piece of engineering was complemented in 1873 with the opening of Sir Gilbert Scott's masterpiece of the St Pancras Hotel, placed in front to Euston Road. The Midland's eventual arrival on the London scene was calculated to outface its rivals, especially those nearby, the Great Northern at King's Cross and the London & North Western at Euston. It made its appearance with a masterly statement of grandeur and an innate confidence in its reputation as a magnificent railway.

Origins of the Midland Railway

I cannot say I liked it, the speed was too great to be pleasant, and it makes you rather giddy, and it certainly is not smoother and easier than a good turnpike road. When the carriages stop or go on a very violent jolting takes place, from the ends of the carriages jostling together.
Early Railway Travel, Anon

IT IS commonly stated that the Midland Railway originated from the weekly meeting of the Erewash Valley coalmasters at the Sun Inn, Eastwood, Nottinghamshire on the 16 August 1832. While that and other meetings of the coalmasters in 1832 did lead to the creation of the Midland Counties Railway in 1836, and which in turn led to that railway becoming one of the constituents of the Midland Railway in 1844, in reality the origins go back further.

Until the eighteenth century Derby was principally a market town and, the social centre of the shire for the gentry. There were old established industries such as flax working, weaving, soap making, tanning and milling on a modest scale, which enabled Derby and similar towns to be largely self supportive. Within these activities a degree of industrial organisation on the workshop principle had evolved, but most trades were still individual and of cottage industry scale. The building of Thomas and John Lombe's large, water-powered silk mill in the town in 1718 marked a significant step in its eventual industrial advancement.

Even so, the rate of industrial development in the town during the eighteenth century was slow. There was a steady development of the silk industry, and the Derby Porcelain manufactory was established on Nottingham Road by mid-century. But, no other factories of particular consequence were built until William Strutt erected his big cotton mill in 1793 on the Markeaton Brook, in the area now called Osnabrück Square. By the early nineteenth century numerous silk factories had sprung up. There were now also a number of cotton mills specialising in narrow fabrics and tapes. The iron trade had developed and become significant, with three major foundries manufacturing a wide range of domestic and other products. There were steam engine builders and engineering machine makers of lathes, planers and printing presses. By the 1840s these foundries were also manufacturing a range of products for the expanding railways - locomotive, tender and carriage wheels, general castings for railway engines, bridges, cast and wrought-iron roof members, iron columns, turntables, and more.

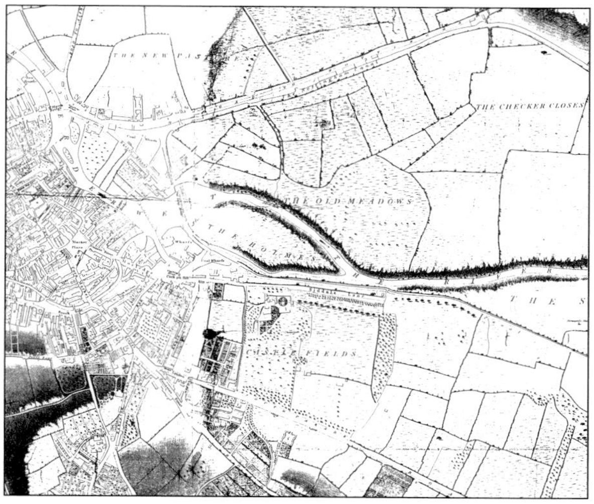

The development of industrial mechanisation in England accelerated towards the end of the eighteenth century with major developments in power spinning and weaving of textiles. Production of pig-iron tripled, and wrought iron for construction became readily available. The stationary steam engine was perfected, eventually enabling factories and manufacturers to free themselves from being tied to riversides, stream sites, and the vagaries of water flow for power.

Canal building began in earnest in the 1750s. The motivation being the need to provide better, faster transport, with greater capacity to move the raw materials for industrial activity. Also for the transportation of finished goods, swiftly and safely to the customers. River transport had many limitations, but the introduc-

Town of Derby and its environs William Rogerson - Land Surveyor - September 1819.

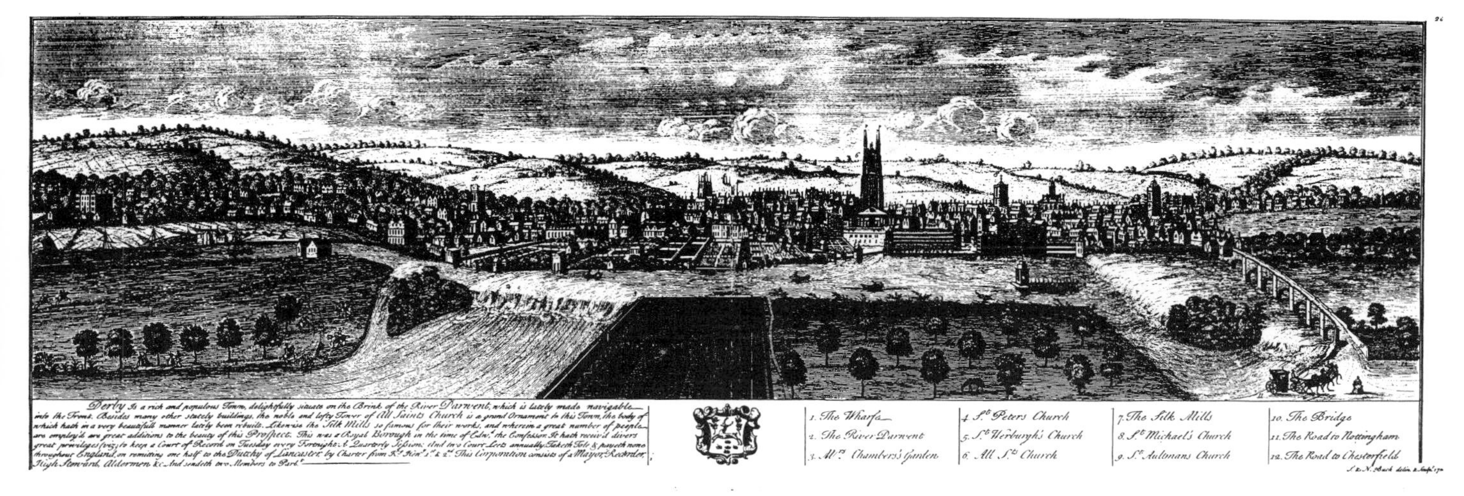

East Prospect of Derby – Castlefields House, the Derwent Navigation and The Holmes can be seen to the left – J&N Buck 1728.

tion of canals, and a general improvement in road construction through the turnpike system, interacted to spur industrial growth.

The East Midlands – Nottinghamshire and Derbyshire along the Erewash Valley, and North Leicestershire, had extensive resources of the important basic minerals – coal, ironstone, limestone. It also had river water navigation which served as a basis for development. The River Trent had been made navigable up to Burton upon Trent and up its tributary the River Derwent to Derby by 1721. But this navigation with its shoals and rapids was soon proving inadequate to cope with the demands of the steadily increasing output of coal from the Erewash Valley and North Leicestershire coal pits. This demand caused the construction of the Erewash Canal from the Trent up to Langley Mill – opened in 1779. The canalisation of the River Soar from the Trent to Loughborough was improved in 1780 by the construction of broad locks on the Loughborough Navigation. Barges could now easily make the through trip from the Erewash Valley collieries down to Loughborough, from where the coalmasters' coal was conveyed on to Leicester by road carts.

The Cromford Canal was promoted in 1787 as an extension of the Erewash Canal up to Pinxton to connect to more coal pits. In the following year Richard Arkwright became involved, seeing that if the canal was extended to Cromford his mills and other industries could be connected into the system. The Cromford Canal was eventually opened in 1794.

Navigation connections to Nottingham and Derby were improved when the Nottingham Canal to Langley Mill was completed in 1796, and the Derby Canal in the same year. The Act of Parliament for the Derby Canal also provided for "making Railways... to several collieries in... Denby, Horsley and Smally..." and this was fulfilled by the construction of a horse-drawn mineral tramway, called the Little Eaton Gangway, opened in 1795. By 1830 costs of conveying the coals into Derby were rising, against those of carters using the adjacent improved Alfreton Road. In November 1830 the company invited George Stephenson to survey the line and provide an estimate for the costs of converting the line to a steam railway and extending it to Little Chester, Derby. Stephenson did this promptly, but although the report was given to the committee in February 1831 showing alternative scheme costs of around £13,250.0.0., nothing came of the proposal. That is, until the gangway became largely superseded by the parallel standard gauge branch railway built by the Midland Company from Little Eaton to Ripley in 1856, to tap the several collieries on this western edge of the Erewash coalfield. Even so, the gangway continued to operate until 1908.

Little Eaton Gangway of 1795 seen in July 1908, with arrival of the last train of loaded coal wagons at the Little Eaton wharf of the Derby Canal.

Among other interesting branches on this canal-based transportation system was the Mansfield and Pinxton Railway, a predominantly mineral line opened in

Portland Wharf warehouse at the Mansfield terminus of the Mansfield & Pinxton Railway, a bullock-drawn (later horses) tramway opened 13 April 1819 to carry coal and stone.

Portland Viaduct at King's Mill near Mansfield. An early viaduct built in 1817 to carry the Mansfield & Pinxton Railway.

1819, from Portland Wharf yard, Mansfield to Pinxton Wharf on the Cromford Canal. This wagonway was engineered by Josias Jessop, who also happened to own a coal pit at Kirkby on the route and realised the potential of direct access to the canal. The wagons on this line were at first pulled by bullocks, but later these were replaced with horses. It continued to run in this form until taken over in 1848 by the Midland Railway, after which it was modified for conversion to standard gauge track operated by steam locomotives from after 1849.

The Cromford and High Peak Railway was opened in two sections, in 1830 and, fully in 1831. This line ran from High Peak Junction to the Cromford Canal then up over difficult high limestone country, before terminating at Whaley Bridge canal basin in the extreme north-west corner of Derbyshire. The line had several steep inclines operated by means of stationary steam engines with cables pulling up the wagons – horses pulled the wagons along the level track lengths between the inclines. Locomotives were only gradually introduced from 1833, but it was not until the late 1860s that all the level sections had them. The Cromford and High Peak was eventually to come, not into Midland Railway control as might have been expected, but instead into London & North Western Railway ownership being leased to the L&NWR in 1862 and amalgamated with it in 1887. As early as January 1840 there had been a meeting at Matlock Bath, where it was reported that the North Midland Railway directors intended to establish a first class station at Ambergate. And, shortly afterwards it was reported that there was to be an application to Parliament for a branch to run up the Derwent Valley to join the High Peak Railway. In the event this did not happen until the Midland Railway era, when that company made a physical connection at High Peak Junction, between Cromford and Whatstandwell in February 1858. This was to a line constructed north up the Derwent Valley from Ambergate to Rowsley under the rather pompous name of the Manchester, Buxton, Matlock & Midlands Junction Railway, originally a joint venture between the Manchester & Birmingham Railway and the Midland Company for the latter to gain access to Manchester. This line was the beginning of what later became the Midland Company's splendid Peak mainline route to Manchester when extended northward from Rowsley in 1862, with the service opening through to Manchester in February 1867. The Manchester, Buxton, Matlock & Midlands Junction Railway section was finally absorbed into the Midland Railway in 1871.

Midland Counties Railway

But to return to the reasons for the creation of the Midland Counties Railway in the 1830s. Following the opening of the Soar Navigation to Loughborough in 1778, improved access to the important manufacturing town of Leicester became the objective of both the north-west Leicestershire and the Erewash Valley coalmasters. Twelve years later, after a bitter Parliamentary struggle, the construction of a broad waterway from Loughborough to Leicester was authorised, together with a simultaneous arrangement for a branch canal across Charnwood to the north Leicestershire pits. These two waterways were both opened in 1794 and, following the opening of the Nottingham Canal and the Derby Canal in 1796 the three important midland towns of Nottingham, Derby and Leicester all became linked directly by good water transport to the vital coal and mineral supplies in the two coalfields.

In this heyday of the canals Derby was a thriving inland port rivalling nearby Shardlow. In the Morledge area of the

George Stephenson (1781-1848) – railway engineer and visionary who made the railway revolution possible. Joint engineer with son Robert for the North Midland Railway and the Birmingham & Derby Junction Railway.

town were four large basins with several bays off, all to handle the volume of goods manufactured and marketed through the town; together with extensive coal wharves.

Following the linkage of the three towns there was inevitable fierce price competition between the two groups of coalowners. This however was only to be short-lived, for in 1799 there was a disastrous collapse of earthworks on the Charnwood Canal which led to the end of its use. Coals could again only be carted out from the North Leicestershire pits with difficulty by road transport. As a consequence the Erewash Valley coalmasters gained a clear transport and financial advantage over their rivals which would last for the next 30 years.

It was not until 1828 that any real turn in events came about. During a visit to Durham in 1828, William Stenson one of the Leicestershire coalowners saw the operational capacity of the recently opened Stockton and Darlington Railway with its rudimentary steam powered locomotives. Duly impressed and realising that such a railway could overcome their own disadvantage, the Leicestershire men, represented by John Ellis, his son Robert, William Stenson, and two local surveyors Harris and Whetstone, travelled to consult George Stephenson who was then working on the construction of the Liverpool and Manchester Railway. Soon after this meeting, Stephenson with his son Robert visited Leicestershire to meet the coalmasters and inspect the proposed route. Stephenson in turn was impressed by the proposals and seeing further commercial opportunities in the area for himself, agreed to become involved. The Leicester & Swannington Railway was surveyed, promoted and eventually obtained the Royal Assent in May 1830 after its passage through Parliament. By the end of that year construction works were in progress. There were difficulties with the contractors during the works and problems with the construction of Glenfield tunnel, not least when the contractor Daniel Jowett was killed by accidentally falling down a working shaft. The railway was finally opened on 17 July 1832, and by the end of that year Leicestershire coal from Whitwick, Ibstock and Bagworth Collieries was regularly being delivered to Leicester at a price below that from the Erewash Valley.

These events caused a break in the Erewash coalmasters near monopoly of the coal trade in the East Midlands. Erewash Canal Company share values slumped, and it marked the beginning of a decline in local canal transport.

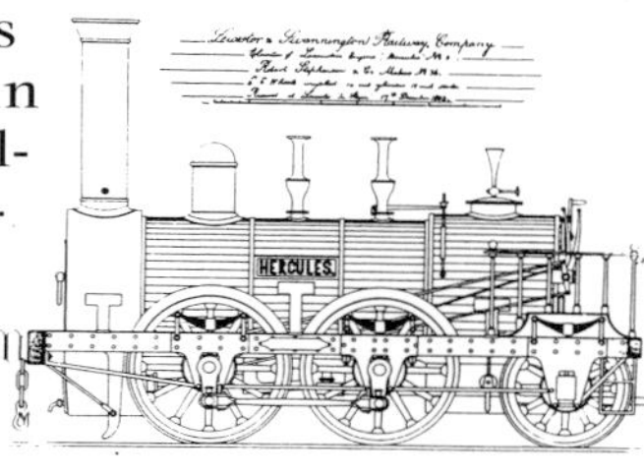

Leicester and Swannington Railway – 0-4-2 locomotive 'Hercules' built by Robert Stephenson & Co., of Newcastle – delivered 17 December 1833.

Facing the bleak prospect of the considerable loss of their Leicestershire trade, the Erewash coalowners arranged a special meeting to discuss the problem. This was held at the George Inn, Alfreton on 27 August 1832 with Edward Miller Mundy of Shipley Hall in the chair. There had clearly been some prior discussion following the opening of the Leicester and Swannington in mid-July, and it has long been asserted that this was at one of the regular meetings of the coalmasters on the well-known date of 16 August 1832 at The Sun Inn, Eastwood. Whatever was discussed at that meeting is now uncertain, but at the Alfreton meeting on 27 August the Erewash men agreed the resolution that – "There remains no other plan for their adoption than to attempt to lay a railway from these collieries to the town of Leicester."

Such was the beginning of the Midland

The George Inn, Alfreton an old coaching inn where the Erewash coalowners met on 27 August 1832, and resolved "to attempt to lay a railway from these collieries to the town of Leicester".

Edward Miller Mundy MP (1774-1849) of Shipley Hall, coalowner who chaired the Erewash coalmasters meeting at Alfreton on 27 August 1832 when it was resolved to build a railway.

Counties Railway (and not the Midland Railway as commonly believed). The concept for the scheme was then made public for the first time through the agency of local newspapers. A provisional committee was appointed at a meeting on 4 October to further the proposal to make an end-on connection at Pinxton wharf to the existing Mansfield and Pinxton horse-drawn railway and to then lay a line down the Erewash Valley and on to Leicester.

The project was confirmed at another meeting on 15 October 1832 when promises of substantial subscriptions were made, and the intended name of The Midland Counties Railway was first used. A prospectus was published early in 1833, printed by George Coates of Alfreton. Parliamentary notices were not deposited until November 1833 and by then the concept for the railway had been modified and developed. The project was now for further extension of the railway with connections to Nottingham and Derby as well as Leicester. And further, with a prospect of extension from Leicester to connect on to the proposed London & Birmingham Railway's line at Rugby, clearly inspired by the Parliamentary Approval and Royal Assent given to that railway scheme a few months before on 6 May 1833.

Surveys had already been carried out some years before in 1825, for a far-sighted but prematurely ambitious scheme called the London North Railroad. This was launched in 1824 with the then huge projected capital of £2,500,000, with the stated intentions of connecting London, Birmingham, Manchester and Hull. The scheme proposed two alternative routes – the first via Cambridge,

The Sun Inn, Eastwood which has long enjoyed a reputation for being the place where the Erewash coalmasters met and decided to build a railway on 16 August 1832.

Peterborough and Oakham to near Loughborough with branches onward to Derby and Nottingham – the second to go via Northampton to Leicester and Derby with a branch to Nottingham. There were to be other branches from Northampton to Coventry and Birmingham and, from Derby to Manchester with another branch from Derby to Sheffield and on to Leeds. Extensions onward to the port of Hull were another option. The provincial London board sported an impressive array of the peerage as president and vice-presidents, with more notables among the directors. Locally there was Lord Scarsdale of Kedleston Hall, Joseph Strutt of Thorntree House, Derby (who is better known for his benevolent gift of the Arboretum to the town in 1840). Sir Charles Henry Colvile of Duffield Hall, the bankers Ichabod Wright of Nottingham, and his grandson John Wright of Lenton Hall, Nottingham, one of the founding partners of the Butterley Company. George Stephenson was listed as the engineer to the railway.

Due to the great scale of the project the promoters eventually decided to try to build it in sections, the first of these to be a link between the existing Cromford and High Peak Railway and the Mansfield & Pinxton, with a line then running on to

At a Meeting of Subscribers to the ***RAILWAY*** *from* ***PINXTON*** *to* ***LEICESTER****, held this 4th day of October*, 1832,

EDWARD MILLER MUNDY, ESQUIRE,

In the Chair;

It was Resolved,

That a Provisional Committee be formed to superintend the affairs of the proposed Railway, and that the Members of the late Committee of Proprietors and Lessees of Collieries of the Counties of Derby and Nottingham, being Subscribers thereto, be requested to continue their services, until Directors and other Officers are appointed, with authority, in the mean time, to add to their number, and to take such preliminary measures as may be necessary for disseminating a knowledge of the great public advantages involved in the undertaking, as well as for obtaining the sanction of Parliament for the Construction of the proposed Railway at the earliest possible period.

E. M. MUNDY, Chairman.

Resolution to form a Provisional Committee to superintend building a railway from Pinxton to Leicester – dated 4 October 1832.

Alfreton, October 15th, 1832.

The Committee appointed by the foregoing Resolution, in compliance with the wish therein expressed, have prepared the following general explanation of the origin, objects, and advantages of the Railway from Pinxton to Leicester, with its contemplated extensions to Nottingham and Derby, which they propose to denominate the MIDLAND COUNTIES RAILWAY, and trust that the facts and observations they have subjoined will be conducive to the end desired, of disseminating a knowledge of the great public benefits which are contingent on its execution.

Report and proposal to name the railway from Pinxton to Leicester as the Midland Counties Railway – 15 October 1832.

MIDLAND COUNTIES

RAILWAY.

PROSPECTUS

OF THE PROJECTED RAILWAY FROM

PINXTON TO LEICESTER,

WITH

REPORTS

ON THE ESTIMATED COST OF THAT UNDERTAKING, AND ON THE APPLICATION OF LOCO-MOTIVE STEAM POWER TO RAILWAYS GENERALLY.

ALFRETON:

PRINTED BY GEORGE COATES.

1833.

Cover page of the prospectus for the Midland Counties Railway – printed by George Coates of Alfreton 1833.

Leicester.

The survey, plans and estimates for this section were made by Josias Jessop, who had already engineered the C&HP Railway and the M&P Railway. Josias was the second son of William Jessop the noted engineer, who among other things had constructed the Cromford Canal and was another founding partner of the Butterley Company. The London Northern Railroads project eventually faltered but its vision and essence were to be furthered and achieved in other later schemes.

The Midlands Counties Railway promoters initially adopted the survey proposals of Josias Jessop for the London Northern Railroad, but then commissioned George Rennie to scrutinise it. After recommendations for a re-survey Charles Vignoles was appointed engineer for the line in 1835. Modified plans were then submitted to Parliament in the November of that year. The scheme had a rough passage through its Parliamentary stages. There had been strong opposition, initially from the Leicester and Swannington Company, and also from the canal companies, since it threatened their vested interests. Then at a later stage when the proposed North Midland Railway appeared on the scene, that company with its influential financial backers proved a formidable opponent.

Its chief concern being that the Midland Counties had introduced a further variation in its scheme with a proposal to extend its Erewash Valley line northward

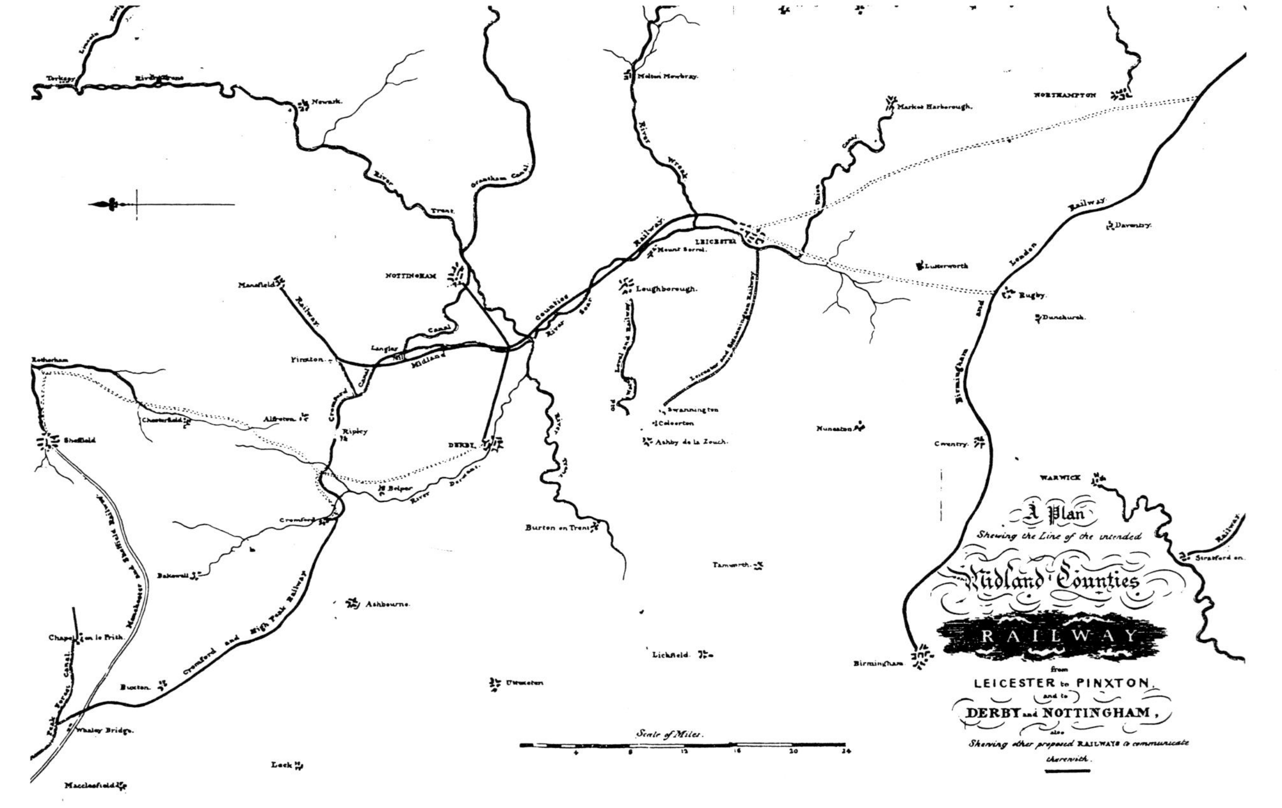

Plan showing line of intended Midland Counties Railway accompanying prospectus of 1833. E.Wild, engraver, Nottingham.

MIDLAND COUNTIES RAILWAY.

UNDER THE PATRONAGE OF THE RIGHT HONORABLE THE VISCOUNT MELBOURNE.

PROVISIONAL COMMITTEE.

LEICESTERSHIRE.	*NOTTINGHAMSHIRE.*	*DERBYSHIRE.*
COLONEL CHENEY, C. B.	LANCELOT ROLLESTON, Esq.	EDWARD MILLER MUNDY, Esq.
CHARLES WILLIAM PACKE, Esq.	JOHN MUSTERS, Esq.	WILLIAM PALMER MOREWOOD, Esq.
MATTHEW BABINGTON, Esq.	JOHN WRIGHT, Esq.	WILLIAM LEAPER NEWTON, Esq.
THOMAS EDWARD DICEY, Esq.	JOHN COKE, Esq.	JOHN BODEN, Esq.
WILLIAM HEYRICK, Esq.	FRANCIS WRIGHT, Esq.	EDWARD SORESBY COX, Esq.
JOHN HILL, Esq. M. D.	WILLIAM TRENTHAM, Esq.	JAMES OAKES, Esq.
JOSEPH NOBLE, Esq. M. D.	THOMAS BARBER, Esq.	DOUGLASS FOX, Esq.
JOHN BRIGHT, Esq.	SAMUEL PARSONS, Esq.	SAMUEL FOX, Jun. Esq.
JAMES BROOKES, Esq.	RICHARD KENSHAW, Esq.	HENRY CHAPMAN, Esq.
JOHN NEDHAM, Esq.	H. B. CAMPBELL, Esq.	MR. JOHN WRIGHT.
Mr. TOONE.		MR. JOHN SANDARS.
MR. HACKETT.		MR. WILLIAM BAKER.
MR. C. B. ROBINSON.		MR. BYNG.
MR. ALFRED BURGESS.		MR. TUNNICLIFFE.

BANKERS.

Leicester—Messrs. MANSFIELD, & BABINGTON.
Nottingham—Messrs. I. & I. C. WRIGHT, & Co
Derby—Messrs. CROMPTON, NEWTON, & Co.
Mansfield and Chesterfield—Messrs. MALTBY & ROBINSON.
Rugby—Messrs BUTLIN & SON.
London—Messrs. SMITH, PAYNE & SMITH.

SOLICITORS.

Nottingham—Messrs. LEESON & GELL.
Leicester—Messrs. BERRIDGE, BERRIDGE, & MACAULAY.
Derby—Messrs. MOUSLEY & BARBER.

ENGINEERS.

GEORGE RENNIE, Esq.——WILLIAM JESSOP, Esq.

SECRETARY.

Mr JOHN FOX BELL, *Leicester.*

Capital £600,000, in 6000 Shares of £100 each.—Deposit £2. per Share.
Application for Shares to be made at the respective Banks, or (if by letter, post paid,) to the Secretary.

PROSPECTUS.

THE passing of the Act for the formation of a Railway between Birmingham and London, the line of which is intended to approach within about eighteen miles of the Town of Leicester, having, thus far, matured the design of a Railway connection between the Midland Counties and the Metropolis, and provided for the execution of the larger and the more expensive portion of this great national undertaking, it remains only for the Towns of Leicester, Nottingham, and Derby to establish a communication with each other, and with the central line, at its nearest and most convenient point, near Rugby, to secure to themselves, and to their wealthy and populous neighbourhoods, a full participation in the new and copious sources of prosperity thereby opened to them.

There is, perhaps, no part of the United Kingdom to which the benefits of Railway intercourse are yet unapplied, so rich and various in its combinations of advantage, as the district comprised within the views of the Midland Counties Railway. It occupies a position in the direct line of communication between Manchester and London, and along which the principal Coaches, and the Mail already travel. It bears, also, the same relation to the manufacturing Towns of Yorkshire; the Leeds Mail, and numerous Coaches, from these, taking the route of Nottingham to London. The distance through Nottingham, or through Derby, from the South-western part of Yorkshire, being the same, the public will thus have the choice of a double communication with London, as business, or other motives suggest. But, the completion of a Railway from Sheffield to Derby, through the vallies of the Rother, Amber, and Derwent, which has of late engaged much attention, would consummate the work of the Midland Counties Railway, by directing upon it, in addition to the Coach Travelling, the principal manufacturing traffic of Yorkshire, and the contiguous parts of Lancashire, and thereby render it, at once, the most useful, and the most prosperous of all similar enterprises. Of the pre-eminent value of such improved means of intercourse to Yorkshire, no adequate estimate can be formed by those who omit to bear in mind, that this immense County, which comprises within its surface so much of the manufacturing and mining wealth of the Empire, is, even yet, excluded from the advantage of any *direct* communication with London, or with the interior, by Canal, consequently, unlike Liverpool and Manchester, which before the establishment of the celebrated Railway bearing their names, had the benefit of a very effective intercourse by water, the Towns of Yorkshire would thus suddenly emerge, as to such an object, from the state common to the whole of England, prior to the existence of Canals. The work destined to accomplish this, may truly therefore claim for itself, the reputation of being more useful than any which has preceded it, and considering that its execution has been reserved for a period, when the great, and costly experiment of the Liverpool and Manchester Railway, has demonstrated, not only the grounds of success in such undertakings, but the errors to be avoided in them, it may, from the joint operation of diminished cost, and ample revenue, be described with much probability, as the most happy and productive of all yet executed, or in contemplation.

The Towns of Nottingham and Derby being situated upon rivers, which communicate with each other, and the waters of these being met by the Soar, a river flowing Northward, from the southern part of Leicestershire, the vallies occupied by these streams, (which have a fall of only five feet in a mile) constitute natural indications of the direction the Midland Counties Railway should follow. The course of this Railway from Nottingham is along the Northern bank of the Trent, meeting the road from Derby at a point convenient for crossing that River, and for effecting the junction of the two Towns. Proceeding Southward, it enters the valley of the Soar, which it pursues to Leicester, and

A further prospectus of the Midland Counties Railway listing members of the Provisional Committees, with other details including a capital value of £600,000, later 1833.

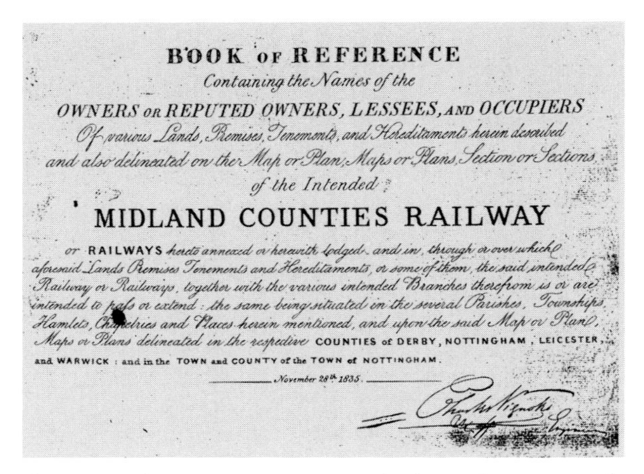

BOOK of REFERENCE

Containing the Names of the

OWNERS or REPUTED OWNERS, LESSEES, and OCCUPIERS

Of various Lands, Premises, Tenements, and Hereditaments herein described and also delineated on the Map or Plan, Maps or Plans, Section or Sections, of the Intended

MIDLAND COUNTIES RAILWAY

or RAILWAYS hereto annexed or herewith lodged, and in, through or over which aforesaid Lands Premises Tenements and Hereditaments, or some of them, the said intended Railway or Railways, together with the various intended Branches therefrom is or are intended to pass or extend: the same being situated in the several Parishes, Townships, Hamlets, Chapelries and Places herein mentioned, and upon the said Map or Plan, Maps or Plans delineated in the respective COUNTIES of DERBY, NOTTINGHAM, LEICESTER, and WARWICK: and in the TOWN and COUNTY of the TOWN of NOTTINGHAM.

November 28th 1835.

Title page of a Book of Reference containing names of owners, lessees and occupiers of lands required for building the Midland Counties Railway – dated 28 November 1835.

from Pinxton up to join the North Midland Railway tracks at Clay Cross or Chesterfield. The NMR financiers and their engineer George Stephenson perceived this as a threat to the southern length of their own proposed line down to Derby, with the risk of jeopardising their scheme which was also under Parliamentary review. To save the NMR scheme the financiers effectively forced the removal of the whole of the Erewash Valley line from the Midland Counties project before the rest obtained Parliamentary Approval.

Royal Assent for the Midland Counties Railway was eventually granted on 21 June 1836 in the final year of the reign of William IV. With the abandonment of the Erewash Valley section, the original *raison d'être* for the railway was abandoned in favour of wider objectives, and the Erewash coalmasters were left with their problems.

By 1836 there was upwards of 500,000 tons of coal being conveyed on the Erewash Canal each year. Cheated of their expected railway the coalowners were not prepared to let the matter rest. Their original need had intensified – the canal companies enjoyed a monopoly and transportation was slow. Led again by Edward Miller Mundy they made another

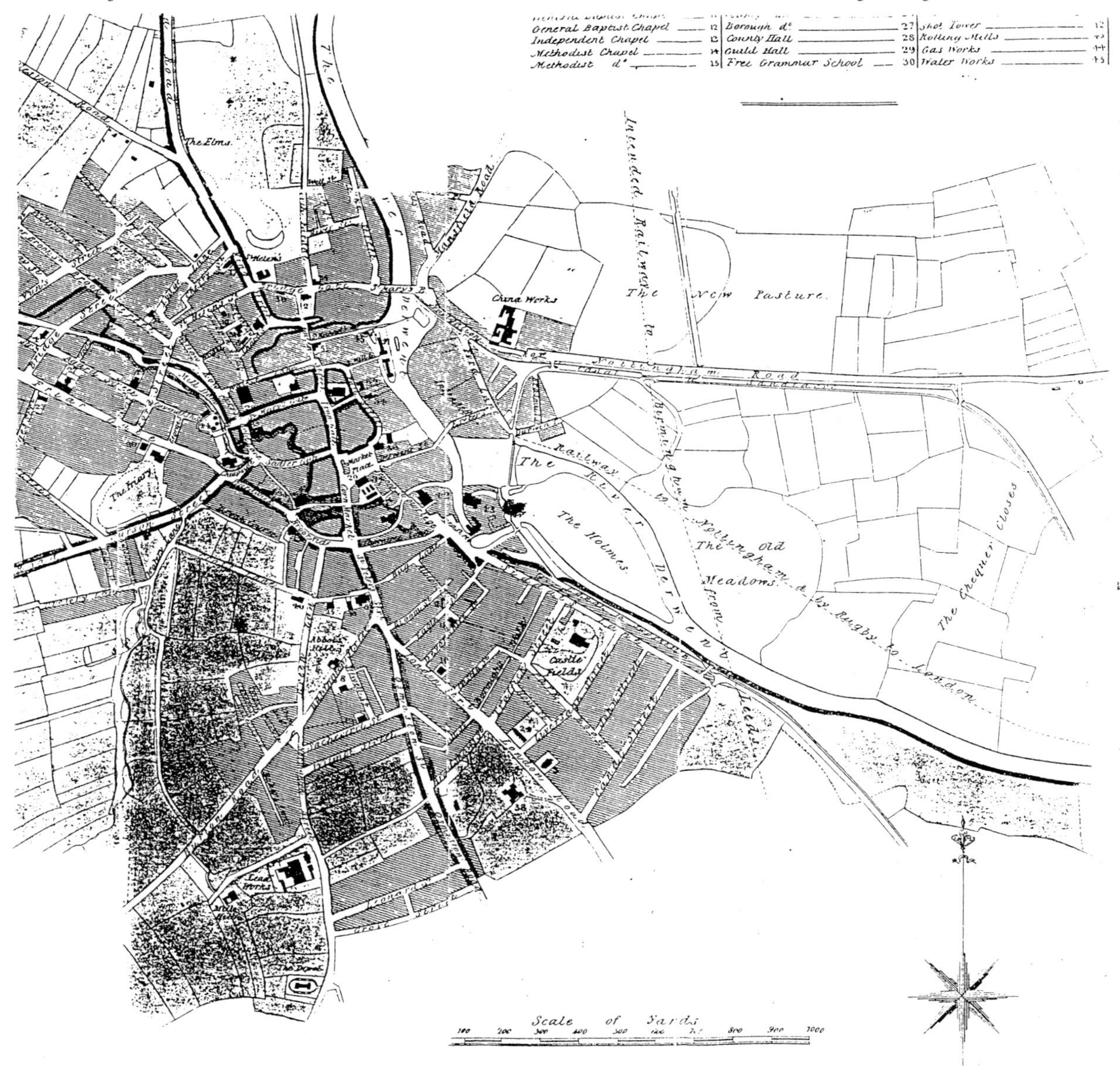

New map of the Borough of Derby showing intended railway lines to Nottingham, Birmingham and Leeds. L.T. Swanwick, land surveyor, 1835.

ANNO SEXTO

GULIELMI IV. REGIS.

****

Cap. lxxviii.

An Act for making a Railway, with Branches, commencing at the *London* and *Birmingham* Railway in the Parish of *Rugby* in the County of *Warwick*, to communicate with the Towns of *Leicester*, *Nottingham*, and *Derby*, to be called " The Midland Counties Railway."

[21st *June* 1836.]

WHEREAS the making a Railway, with proper Branches, Works, and Conveniences connected therewith, for the Conveyance of Passengers, Goods, and Merchandize, from the *London* and *Birmingham* Railway in the Parish of *Rugby* in the County of *Warwick* to the Towns of *Leicester*, *Nottingham*, and *Derby*, and Places adjacent thereto, thereby affording Facilities for Railway Communication with the important manufacturing Towns to the Northward of such Places respectively, will prove of great public Advantage, by opening an additional, cheap, and expeditious Communication between the Metropolis and the large manufacturing Counties of *Leicester*, *Nottingham*, and *Derby*, and will at the same Time facilitate the Means of Transit and Traffic for Passengers, Goods, and Merchandize between the above-mentioned Towns and Places and the adjacent Districts, and the several intermediate Towns and Places: And whereas the several Persons herein-after named are willing, at their

[*Local.*] 32 *A*

Far left: **Front page of the Act of Parliament 21 June 1836 for the Midland Counties Railway.**

THE

North Midland Railway,

UNITING

LONDON WITH SHEFFIELD, LEEDS,

AND THE

MANUFACTURING DISTRICTS OF YORKSHIRE.

Capital, £1,250,000, in Shares of £100 each.—Deposit, £5 per Share.

LONDON PROVISIONAL COMMITTEE.

RALPH FENWICK, ESQ.	FREDERICK HUTH, ESQ.
THOMAS FRENCH, ESQ.	WILLIAM LEAF, ESQ.
GEORGE CARR GLYN, ESQ.	WILLIAM LITTLE, ESQ.
KIRKMAN HODGSON, ESQ.	JAMES MORRISON, ESQ., M.P.
WILLIAM HOOD, ESQ.	JOHN PICKERSGILL, ESQ.

Bankers.

LONDON........ MESSRS. GLYN, HALLIFAX, MILLS AND CO.
LEEDS ....MESSRS. BECKETT, BLAYDS & CO.

Solicitors.

MESSRS. SWAIN, STEVENS, AND CO., *No. 6, Fredericks Place, Old Jewry, London.*
CHARLES PARKER, ESQ., *No. 39, Bedford Row, London.*

Engineer.

GEORGE STEPHENSON, ESQ.

SINCE the superiority of Railways over every other means of communication has been fully established, and recognized by the Legislature in the adoption of the London and Birmingham, the Grand Junction, the Great Western, and other long lines of Railway, the advisability of extending to the North of England the benefits anticipated from those undertakings has been universally felt and acknowledged.

A Company having already been established for the purpose of constructing a Railway, from the London and Birmingham Railway, at or near Rugby, to Derby, it is the object of the present Company to extend that Line from the latter place as far as Leeds, passing through a most populous and highly important manufacturing district, and either touching upon, or approaching within, an easy distance of the towns of Chesterfield, Rotherham, Sheffield, Barnsley, Wakefield, Huddersfield, Halifax, Bradford, and Leeds, comprehending a population not inferior to the manufacturing districts of Lancashire.

It will be apparent to any one who examines the Map of England, that this line, in combination with the Midland and London and Birmingham Railways, must form the main channel for the traffic of the North to London:

Left: **Prospectus for the North Midland Railway, listing the London Provisional Committee, September 1835.**

attempt to build a railway. In 1843 after the Midland Counties Railway had opened, the Erewash men issued a new prospectus for an Erewash Valley Railway to connect with the Midland Counties line at Long Eaton station. Although permission to make the junction was given, the scheme failed to proceed. It was not to be until 1847, in the early years of the Midland Railway that the line was finally built.

North Midland Railway

The North Midland Railway also had its origins in the earlier London Northern Railroad scheme and in another early project of 1824 called the Grand Junction Railroad. This latter project proposed to connect Birmingham to Derby, Sheffield and Leeds, with connections on to Hull and a branch to Nottingham – also a line from Sheffield to Manchester. The scheme had a London based board of management, with a group of country directors at Derby, among other places. Notable among the Derby directors was William Strutt of cotton mill fame, of St Helen's House, Derby together with other local worthies - the banker William Leaper Newton of The Leylands, Derby; Robert Newton of Mickleover; Bache Heathcote of Littleover Old Hall; Henry Mozley a local printer of substance of The Friary, Friar Gate, Derby; John Cox a vintner and of the Derby lead company and Francis Sandars a corn merchant of Hurt's House, Friar Gate.

The North Midland Railway was conceived soon after the Midland Counties promoted their line in 1833 and it is possible that George Stephenson was a prime initiator before becoming appointed engineer for the scheme. He had acted for the Leicester & Swannington Railway, and moved into Alton Grange, Leicestershire, following the development of his new local pits at Snibston. He had influential friends among financiers and had a sharp eye for commercial possibilities for himself from mineral workings. He was to do this along the North Midland line, with coal mining at Clay Cross after seams were found in tunnelling and, with lime quarries and works at Crich and Ambergate. He would later remove to Tapton House, Chesterfield to oversee these later enterprises and lived there until his death on 12 August 1848.

In early 1835 George Stephenson set out

Front page of the Act of Parliament 4 July 1836 for the North Midland Railway.

6 & 7 WILL. IV.——Sess. 1836.

AN

ACT

For making a Railway from *Leeds* to *Derby*, to be called "THE NORTH MIDLAND RAILWAY."

[ROYAL ASSENT, 4 *July* 1836.]

WHEREAS the making a Railway from *Leeds* to *Derby* would be productive of great public advantage by opening an additional certain and expeditious Communication between the Towns aforesaid, and the intermediate Towns and Districts, and also by facilitating the means of Intercourse between the North of *England*, the Midland Counties, the Metropolis, and the West and South West of *England*:

And whereas the KING's most Excellent MAJESTY, in right of His Crown, is entitled to certain Lands upon the Line of the proposed Railway:

And whereas the several Persons hereinafter named are willing, at their own expence, to carry into execution the before-mentioned Undertaking: BUT the same cannot be effected without the Authority of Parliament;

May it therefore please Your MAJESTY,

That it may be Enacted; And be it Enacted by The KING's most Excellent MAJESTY, by and with the advice and consent of the Lords Spiritual and Temporal, and Commons, in Parliament assembled, and by the Authority of the same, THAT *William Aldham, Edward Alexander, Richard Alison, Joseph Armstrong, John Atkinson, James Baird, Edward Baines* junior, *Edward Barlow, William Henry Barron, Benjamin Pearson Bartleet, George Bayley, Christopher Beckett, William Beckett, Burkeley Bent, William Beverley, John Birks, William Borradaile, Henry Briggs, Thomas Brook, Hannah Brotherton Barwell*

9. A *Browne,*

with his secretary from the New Inn, King Street, Derby in a bright yellow post-chaise to survey a route for the North Midland Railway. A prospectus was published in September that year, promoting the North Midland Railway as a line of 72 miles length between Derby and Leeds with a capital of £1,250,000, terminating in Derby in Darwin's Close, St Alkmund's Parish, on the north side of the Nottingham Road turnpike. This substantial capital sum would be needed as the line would involve very heavy construction works, several tunnels, river crossings and extended cuttings, such as the long one through the heart of Belper with its numerous street bridges. The Act of Parliament allowed the company to raise capital up to £1,500,000 for making the railway. But in the event this proved a gross underestimate, with the railway finally costing £3,000,000.

At the New Inn, Derby on Tuesday, 17 November 1835 the recommendation was put before a meeting that there should be a junction at Derby between the North Midland line and the Birmingham & Derby Junction Railway so as to give a through line between Birmingham and Leeds. At a further meeting held soon after in Derby Town Hall on Wednesday 2 December, a report on the proposed through route, with plans and sections prepared by their engineer George Stephenson was presented, and with "nearly every individual of any commercial importance residing in the town present, and influential deputations from other places on the line of the railway". What was not said, but eventually became apparent was that in the background were the possibilities of connecting to the London and Birmingham Railway, by then under construction, and taking passengers through to London without going via the Midland Counties projected route through Leicester. There were also to be connections to Sheffield from the NMR line via the short Sheffield and Rotherham Railway from Normanton, and a link there also with the proposed York and North Midland Railway. These proposals would create the frame of a major trunk railway system from London to York, with ultimate possibilities of future extension northward to Scotland.

The New Inn, King Street, Derby an old coaching and Post House from where Stephenson set out to survey his route for the North Midland Railway in early 1835. Built *c.*1785 by George Wallis ancestor of William Wallace Wallis of omnibus fame in the town. The Inn was demolished in 1968.

The North Midland project set up a London committee as well as ones in Derby and Leeds to further the scheme, which was then lodged for the next Parliamentary session. As has been noted there was a battle with the Midland Counties promoters over the Erewash Valley northern extension, but it seems that the financial clout and influence of the northern financiers of the NMR ensured that they ultimately had their way in the Parliamentary Committee stages. The North Midland Railway Act finally received the Royal Assent on 4 July 1836 and at the same time the small related Sheffield and Rotherham Railway link was approved.

Birmingham & Derby Junction Railway

Schemes for a railway line to link the proposed North Midland Railway onward from Derby to Birmingham were discussed in the latter city in the summer and autumn of 1834. It will be remembered that this idea had its roots in the earlier Grand Junction Railroad scheme of ten years before.

George Stephenson was eventually engaged to make an initial survey for the route. He reported back quite quickly to the founding committee that he saw no particular difficulties, the route would be of very easy grades and there would be no tunnels. He suggested a line to Stechford, Birmingham from where trains would run over London and Birmingham Railway metals in to that company's terminus at Curzon Street in the city. Plans were also afoot at that time for the proposed Birmingham & Gloucester Railway (which would eventually open in December 1840) to use the same terminus, so there were further prospects of a link for traffic down to the West Country. At the same time there would be the opportunity to make another link, with the Grand Junction Railway (which received its Act in 1833 and would open in 1837) which would run north from Birmingham, and connect with the Liverpool & Manchester Railway which had opened in 1830.

Also added into the Birmingham and Derby Junction scheme was to be a branch from the main line at Whiteacre running down to another connection on the London and Birmingham line at Hampton-in-Arden. This would provide a shorter more direct route for London traffic from Derby. It was a shrewd plan, but it immediately placed the scheme in direct competition with the Midland Counties Railway and the latter's more southerly intended connection to the London and Birmingham line at Rugby.

Public meetings to further the B&DJR were held in Birmingham, Derby, Burton upon Trent and Tamworth – all places on the intended line. After which, a provisional committee was formed to further the scheme and to make application to Parliament. The project was essentially Birmingham based and more than half of the committee, and its eventual directors, were Birmingham people and businessmen. In its passage though Parliament the Bill received very little opposition other than over the proposed Hampton branch connection. In this matter there was open conflict with the Midland Counties promoters. But, in spite of the opposition the Bill received Parliamentary Approval and the Royal Assent was granted on 19 May 1836.

The conflict between the Midland Counties and the Birmingham & Derby Junction companies would continue once the lines were opened and through the first three years of their parallel operations. There would be fierce and near ruinous competition for the London traffic. But it was a circumstance destined to be a primary reason leading to the creation of the Midland Railway by amalgamation in 1844.

Birmingham and Derby

JUNCTION RAILWAY,

UNITING

'HE NORTH MIDLAND WITH THE LONDON AND BIRMINGHAM, THE GRANI JUNCTION, AND THE BIRMINGHAM AND GLOUCESTER RAILWAYS.

CAPITAL, £500,000, in Shares of £100 each.——Deposit, £5 per Share.

Provisional Committee—Birmingham:

Joseph Walker, Esq.	James Pearson, Esq.
William Beale, Esq.	Francis Lloyd, Esq.
Daniel Ledsam, Esq.	Samuel Beale, Esq.
William Chance, Esq.	Abel Peyton, Esq.
William Francis, Esq.	Henry Smith, Esq.

Solicitors:

Messrs. Corrie and Carter, Birmingham.

Engineer:

George Stephenson, Esq.

The line of the North Midland Railway extends from Derby to Leeds, passing through the populous and important manufacturing districts of Yorkshire. The Birmingham and Gloucester Railway connects Birmingham with the Port of Gloucester and the West of England. The capital for the construction of both these Railways has been fully subscribed, and applications are intended to be made to Parliament in the ensuing session for carrying them into effect. It is the object of the present undertaking to unite these two Railways, and thus to complete the communication between the North and the West of England through Birmingham. The line is proposed to commence near Birmingham, by a Junction with the London and Birmingham Railway, and will unite with the North Midland Railway at its termination in Derby. The country through which this line will pass has been carefully surveyed by Mr. George Stephenson, and has been found to present unusual facilities as to line and construction, taking, with little variation, the natural levels of the vallies of the Tame and the Trent.

The course of this Railway will be about forty miles, and will touch upon the towns of Tamworth and Burton-upon-Trent.

From the peculiarly favourable nature of the country, it is estimated that the expence of construction will not exceed £10,000 a mile; but, in order to provide for every contingency, it is proposed to raise a capital of £500,000.

Application will be made to Parliament in the ensuing session for an act to authorise the carrying this plan into effect.

Shares to be applied for by letter, to the Provisional Committee, addressed to the Solicitors.

Prospectus for the Birmingham & Derby Junction Railway, 1835.

Building the Three Railways to Derby

"Derby, as I have had occasion to state once before, exhibits strong marks of general improvement, by an extension as well as renovation of its principal buildings. The range of edifices, consisting of the royal hotel, a new post office, and the bank in the corn-market, is a mass creditable to the town ...The junction of three railroads in this county town, bringing travellers and goods from the north and the south, and also from the west, is already sensibly changing its character, its general appearance, and its importance. I remember the time when Derby, in spite of the silk manufacturers, its lace, its hosiery, and its wrought iron and copper works, appeared to a traveller one of the dullest county towns in the heart of England. It is now full of bustle, lively, and apparently in the enjoyment of greater wealth, comforts, and even luxury, than it has ever before possessed.

Dr Augustus B.Granville, 1840

THE three companies coming to Derby all received their Acts of Parliament within two months of each other in early summer 1836.

Birmingham & Derby Junction Railway

The Birmingham & Derby Junction Railway's Act authorised a capital of £630,000 to build the main line from Derby to Stechford together with the Whiteacre to Hampton-in-Arden branch. The first meeting of the directors was held on 22 September 1836 at Dee's Royal Hotel, Birmingham when arrangements for furthering the building of the line were agreed and George Stephenson was formally appointed engineer. But soon after, due to his numerous other commitments, Stephenson suggested to the board that his son Robert should take over direction of the works. This was agreed and also the appointment of John Birkinshaw as the resident engineer for day-to-day supervision.

Since the Midland Counties Railway Act contained a provision deferring any start on their Wigston to Rugby section until August 1837, the B&DJR directors decided to take advantage of this and to gain a head start on their potential rivals. Accordingly they deferred any work on the Whiteacre to Stechford section and resolved to concentrate on the Derby to Hampton line for the London traffic.

Birmingham & Derby Junction Railway, 2-2-2 locomotive 'Derwent' built by Sharp, Roberts & Co in 1839, became Midland Railway No.36.

The main line works were divided into 18 contracts, which included 78 bridges – two of which were major structures – viaducts of stone and brick over the River Anker near Tamworth Station, and of timber over the Rivers Trent and Tame. In February 1839 it was reported that some 2,800 men were at work on the line construction. Despite two very wet winters the works progressed well so that by 29 May 1839 the directors were able to inspect the whole route by special train. On 15 July 1839 Robert Stephenson drove the engine 'Derby' a 2-2-2 type built by Taylor & Co of Newton-le-Willows, from Birmingham to Derby and back again.

The formal opening of the line was on Monday, 5 August 1839. It was a fine day when a special train of directors, shareholders and friends were hauled by the locomotive 'Tamworth' built by Mather Dixon & Co of Liverpool, from Curzon Street, Birmingham to Derby. There the passengers all had to alight at a temporary platform near the London Road before Castlefields, as work on the great joint station had not then started. The whole party were then conveyed to the 'King's Head Inn and Family Hotel' in the Cornmarket, Derby where the usual refreshments for such an occasion were laid on as a 'cold collation' for the visitors. There were congratulatory speeches, and toasts to the railway; its chairman – Henry Smith; the engineers; the towns of Birmingham and Derby; followed by replies from the two mayors – with John Sandars Esq, grocer, seed merchant,

OPENING OF THE BIRMINGHAM AND DERBY JUNCTION RAILWAY.—The Public is respectfully informed that on and after MONDAY, the 12th of AUGUST inst., the TRAINS of this Company will START from the Station of the London and Birmingham Railway, in BIRMINGHAM, and from the Company's Station in DERBY; and also that Passengers between London and Derby may be booked throughout as below mentioned:—

HOURS OF DEPARTURE.

FROM BIRMINGHAM.	FROM DERBY.
H. M.	H. M.
7 30 morning.	7 0 morning.
1 0 afternoon.	11 30 ditto.
6 30 ditto.	4 30 afternoon.

SUNDAY TRAINS.

7 30 morning.	7 0 morning.
7 0 afternoon.	7 0 afternoon.
Coaches to Nottingham, Sheffield, Leeds, York, and all parts of the North, will leave Derby immediately on the arrival of each Train.	Coaches from Nottingham, Sheffield, Leeds, York, and all parts of the North, will arrive in Derby in time for each Train.

FARES.	1st Class.	2d Class.	3d Class
Between Birmingham and Derby..	10s	7s	5s 0d
Between Hampton and Derby.....	8s	6s	4s 6d

DERBY TO LONDON.

Passengers may be booked through from Derby to London by the Trains leaving Derby, viz.:—

H. M.	H. M.
At 11 30 morning.	At 4 30 afternoon.

LONDON TO DERBY.

Passengers may be booked in London throughout to Derby, by the Trains leaving the Euston-square Station of the London and Birmingham Company, viz:—

H. M.	H. M.
At 8 45 morning	At 2 0 afternoon.

FARES.	1st Class.	2d Class
Between London and Derby......	£1 15 0	£1 4 0

By order, THOMAS KELL, Secretary.

Birmingham, Aug. 3, 1839.

Timetable and fares of the B&DJR from the public opening on Monday, 12 August 1839.

magistrate and alderman for Derby. The party left on the return journey at 4pm and arrived back in Birmingham without problems. The line opened for public use on 12 August 1839, with through carriages to Euston Square Station, London. Derby had become linked to London by rails for the first time and it was now possible to get to the capital in just five hours of railway travel (although the first journey actually took seven hours). A graphic contemporary description of this first departure to London is given by that indefatigable traveller Dr Augustus B.Granville – "I happened to be on the spot, the day on which the line to London was first opened. As a matter of study and curiosity, I determined on taking my departure by it for the capital, whither a pressing summons obliged me to go for a few hours. All Derby was in a bustle on that eventful morning. The opening of the first railway from the town to the capital was the opening of a mine of wealth. I was the first on the spot, and had ticket No.1. Every director was present. Preliminary experiments had been made daily for a week and upwards; yet everything seemed in a state of confusion, everybody spoke or commanded... when all was ready, it was found that there were but few persons who would proceed, and the train ended by being composed of three or four first-class carriages only, certainly very splendid and comfortable... We made our journey good, though not without considerable

A crowd of people pose outside the King's Head Inn, Cornmarket, Derby where the official opening of the B&DJR was celebrated on 5 August 1839, photographed R.Keene, *c.*1858.

Bridge over the River Trent at Red Hill on the Midland Counties Railway. Ironwork by the Butterley Company and erected by William MacKenzie in 1839.

anxiety, and I thanked my stars to find myself again upon my legs, passing through Hardwick's splendid arch at Euston Grove, where we arrived in seven hours from Derby."

Midland Counties Railway

The second of these railways to receive its Royal Assent was the Midland Counties Railway. Its Act authorised a capital of £1,000,000 for the 50 miles of line between Derby, Nottingham and Leicester, and onward to a junction with the London & Birmingham Railway at Rugby. The 24 temporary directors were confirmed at the first general meeting of the company on 12 August 1836 when Thomas Edward Dicey of Packworth Hall, Leicester was made chairman, with James Oakes of Riddings Hall, a coalowner and iron founder as deputy chairman. John Fox Bell was the secretary, with Charles Vignoles as engineer, assisted by Thomas Woodhouse as resident engineer.

There were several disputes with owners over the acquisition of land for the railway – notable ones being with Leicester Town Council over land in the town, and with Nottingham Council over common land in The Meadows.

The construction of the line was divided into 14 contracts – work initially being concentrated between Derby and Nottingham with a view to getting this route open as soon as possible to earn some revenue. The length of line was fairly straightforward but there would be a potential problem with a crossing over the Derby Canal near Spondon. This was fortuitously avoided when the contractor was able to take advantage of a normal repair closing of the canal. There were two major works on the length of line down from Trent Junction to Leicester – these were the river crossing over the Trent and the adjacent tunnel through Red Hill, plus a substantial cutting through Sutton Bonington. The elegant three arched, cast-iron bridge over the Trent was built by William MacKenzie with the ironwork being supplied by the Butterley Company for £9,744.12s 4d. MacKenzie also carried out the tunnel work, with its ornamental castellated portal on the north side - rather sadly lacking the refinements of the bridge design. This bridge survived until 1900 when replaced by the present structures after the quadrupling of the lines.

At the Annual General Meeting in 1837 it was resolved to push on as soon as possible with the length of line from Leicester down to Rugby. By that date the directors were empowered by the Act of Parliament to commence work on this length. By the end of that year all the

Bury type 2-2 locomotive used by the Midland Counties Railway and similar to ones on the London & Birmingham Railway – 1839.

Far left: **Beeston Station, Midland Counties Railway. Small booking office with waiting shelter alongside, typical of the small intermediate stations along the line 1839.**

Left: **Surviving stone gate pier to the original station yard Nottingham, of the Midland Counties – 1838.**

contracts had been let. Bad winters of heavy rains caused difficulties and delays in the construction. But by March 1839 most of the work on the Nottingham to Derby line was also nearing completion and it was hoped to have this section open by 1 May that year. In the event the work between Chaddesden and Derby was delayed and it was not until Thursday, 29 May that an official formal trip over the line could be arranged. This of course was the same day that the B&DJR directors made the separate inspection of their line. There was fine weather for the event and a colourful gathering of directors, shareholders and friends assembled at the new Nottingham Station on Carrington Street, with the excited atmosphere enlivened by music from the band of the Fifth Dragoon Guards. There were two trains, the first hauled by the locomotive 'Sunbeam' a Bury type 2-2-0 built by Jones, Turner and Evans of Newton, Lancashire, and the second engine no.1 called 'Ariel' - a

Nottingham Station on Carrington Street, Midland Counties Railway 1839. The first station at Nottingham, depicted on the opening day with a train to Derby.

Skew arch bridge over canal branch from Nottingham Canal into the original station yard, with canal towpath over – Midland Counties – 1838.

similar Bury type (later renamed 'Bee') built by the Butterley Company. There was only a short stop of just over an hour at Derby and the parties had to get off on to another temporary platform, since the work on building the permanent station had not then started and the five arches bridges over the River Derwent had still to be built. This second temporary platform was probably sited by the Old Meadows, north of the station area. The return journey started at 2.30pm and arrived back at Nottingham at 3.13pm without event. The reception at the Nottingham Station provided the inevitable fine 'cold collation' of food for the directors and guests, and with the band playing everyone was in celebratory mood. Train services for the general public began a few days later on Wednesday, 4 June 1839 although there was no third-class provision until the September.

Intermediate stations were first provided at Borrowash, Sawley, Long Eaton and Beeston with Spondon added later in November. These intermediate stations were of a simple 'cottage ornée' style for the ticket office with a free standing shelter for passengers. The terminal station at Nottingham had two lines with a central platform as well as side ones. These were covered with a twin pitched overall roof. The end-on accommodation block for entrance, tickets and offices was set back, fronting Carrington Street. This block had a two storey, three bay central section flanked by two bay, single storey wings. On the north side between the building and the canal was the station yard, entered between two stone gate piers. These piers can be seen on Parker's contemporary engraving. In the station yard was a small warehouse sited by a leg off the adjacent Nottingham

Midland Counties
RAILWAY.
THE PUBLIC ARE INFORMED, THAT THIS RAILWAY,
FROM
Nottingham and Derby,
TO
LOUGHBORO', LEICESTER,
AND THE INTERMEDIATE STATIONS
Will be opened for the conveyance of Passengers, Parcels, Gentlemen's Carriages, Horses, and Van Goods, on TUESDAY the 5th of May.

Far right: **Notice of the opening of the Midland Counties Railway through to Leicester, May 1840.**

Canal. This was used for transhipment between the canal boats and the railway. Rather surprisingly the original gate piers and the canal side bridge under the towpath still survive, all that is left of this first Nottingham station.

Work on the Trent to Leicester section of the line continued, with some 4,500 men and 460 horses employed on the works in the early summer of 1839. Intermediate stations on this section were built at Kegworth, Loughborough, Barrow, Sileby and Syston. Leicester Town Station was initially conceived as a terminus off the main line, but then was re-planned as a single long platform 165yds long. This was backed by the station building located in Campbell Street off the London Road. The platform was arranged on a loop off the through lines. The station building which was also the Midland Counties headquarters, was designed by the Leicester architect William Parsons. It is also very probable that he designed the Nottingham station.

The Leicester station was an elegant structure of two storeys and 11 bays in Greek Revival style, fronted by a set forward central pediment on fluted columns, and flanked with short single storey wings at each end. The company

Eleven-arch viaduct of the Midland Counties Railway over the River Avon and Oxford Canal at Rugby – opened August 1840.

offices and boardroom were upstairs, with booking office, waiting rooms and refreshment rooms on the ground floor. With some modification this station continued to be used until replaced in June 1892 by the present station and entrance fronting London Road designed by Charles Trubshaw. The Trent to Leicester section of the line was completed and brought into use on 4 May 1840, curiously without any particular ceremonies, despite the importance of this first rail link between Derby, Nottingham, Leicester. Four trains a day and two on Sundays was the advertised service running on this first section of the line.

Work on the Leicester to Rugby section was meanwhile progressing with some difficulties. Bad wet winters hampered work and there were problems with the execution of contracts by two sets of contractors. There were two short tunnels - one at Knighton, with another at Gills Corner south of Ullesthorpe, together with a series of lengthy cuttings and embank-

Typical method of tipping and building a railway embankment with horse-drawn wagons on rails.

Leicester Station, Midland Counties 1840. Original station and company headquarters at Campbell Street – designed by Williams Parsons.

Right: Robert Stephenson (1803-1859) the great engineer whose endeavours ensured his father's vision carried through to a reality. Joint engineer with his father on the North Midland, and Birmingham & Derby Junction Railways.

Far right: Castellated north portal of the Clay Cross tunnel, North Midland Railway – built 1839.

ments along this section. There was also the major engineering work on the line, the 11-arch brick viaduct over the River Avon and the Oxford Canal, just half a mile before the junction with the London and Birmingham line at Rugby. The line was eventually completed from Leicester to the Avon Viaduct by 29 June 1840 and was opened for public use the next day. Since construction of the viaduct was not yet complete, passengers had to alight at a temporary platform at the north end, before being conveyed by road into the London & Birmingham Railway station. The viaduct was not brought into use until 17 August and the delay was a further difficulty for the Midland Counties since the North Midland Railway was opened throughout on 1 July. In consequence through trains over the Midland Counties lines could not be run through for another seven weeks, so giving the Birmingham & Derby Junction Railway a continuing advantage for booking through passengers from beyond Derby on to London.

North Midland Railway

Following the Royal Assent to the Act of Parliament on 4 July 1836 the proprietors lost no time in electing directors for the new company. At their first meeting on 16 July George Carr Glyn was elected chairman, with London and Leeds committees being set up to co-ordinate the works. George and Robert Stephenson were also formally appointed joint engineers, and instructed to take all necessary steps to stake out the line, together with making early arrangements for contracts for the Clay Cross Works. At the further meeting on 29 July the Stephensons' joint salary was fixed at £2,000 per annum inclusive of travelling expenses. At this same meeting Henry Patteson was appointed secretary to the board at an annual salary of £500.

The North Midland Railway of 73 miles length was a much more heavily engineered line in contrast to the other two railways – mainly because of the more hilly nature of the country. Also there was Stephenson's insistent view of maintaining easy gradients. Along the route some 200 bridges had to be built and seven tunnels excavated, including a major tunnel of one mile length at Clay Cross and the Milford Tunnel of 800yds. At the height of the works almost 10,000 navvies and craftsmen were employed along the 73 mile length of the line. The works involved the letting of 28 contracts. Due to its scale the Clay Cross tunnel was one of the first contracts let. Preliminary anticipations of difficulties proved correct when it was found the hill was of wet coal measures and vast quantities of water had to be continually pumped away. The original contractors Harding and Cropper of Watford got into difficulties and Edward Price of London had to be brought in to share the contract. Price had recent experience of difficult tunnel construction, from overcoming the enormous problems of wet sand in Kilsby Tunnel on the London & Birmingham Railway.

In building the Clay Cross tunnel some 9,500,000 cubic yards of material was dug out by pick and shovel, aided only with gunpowder. Some 15 million bricks were laid in two concentric rings lining the tunnel. Work went on day and night. By July 1839 "one chandler alone in Chesterfield has supplied over 3,000 dozen candles" (36,000) and the works were not to be finally completed until 18 December that year.

In 1837 the North Midland Company took the unprecedented step of instructing their engineer Frederick Swanwick to build 30 houses at Clay Cross to accommodate workers building the line and tunnel. There was a scarcity of lodgings in the Clay Cross area and, "This scarcity ...has caused about 30 houses, or rather cabins to be built with sods in the neighbourhood". The contractors were concerned over losing their best men and tradesmen and this worried the NMR in turn. Swanwick was required to let a contract "for accommodation of about 100 of the superior workmen, for which rent is to be paid". The brick houses were built and completed in early 1838. They were arranged as two terraces - East and West Tunnel Rows, along either side of the main road through Clay Cross. After the opening of the line the North Midland considered using the houses for their employees, but concluded they were too much out of the way. In June 1841 they were sold to George Stephenson & Company for £2,684.3s.9d to accommo-

Frederick Swanwick (1810-1885), an articled pupil of George Stephenson, drove the locomotive 'Arrow' at the opening of the Liverpool & Manchester Railway in 1830. Resident engineer on the construction of the North Midland Railway - later, assistant engineer. On formation of Midland Railway he took charge of all new line projects under William H.Barlow.

Fine viaduct of five skew arches on the North Midland, over the River Derwent and the Derby-Matlock Turnpike at Ambergate, constructed in 1839.

Viaduct of the North Midland at Derby over the Nottingham Road Turnpike and Derby Canal – 1839 – drawn 1841.

Three ways of transport. The North Midland line at Ambergate passes beneath the aqueduct of the Cromford Canal, with the Ripley road running alongside. One of Samuel Russell's set of engravings 1840-41.

date their miners at Clay Cross and Tupton. West Tunnel Row survived until 1875, but East Tunnel Row continued in use until 1970 when it too was demolished.

Work on railway construction was dangerous – the navvies were a rough lot of men who displayed bravado and often recklessness. Serious injury was frequent, and at least 11 deaths occurred during the building of the Clay Cross tunnel. Work was also extremely hard for the men – navvies worked 12-hour shifts. The craftsmen bricklayers, after a strike, had their work stint reduced from ten hours to eight for working in the continually wet conditions.

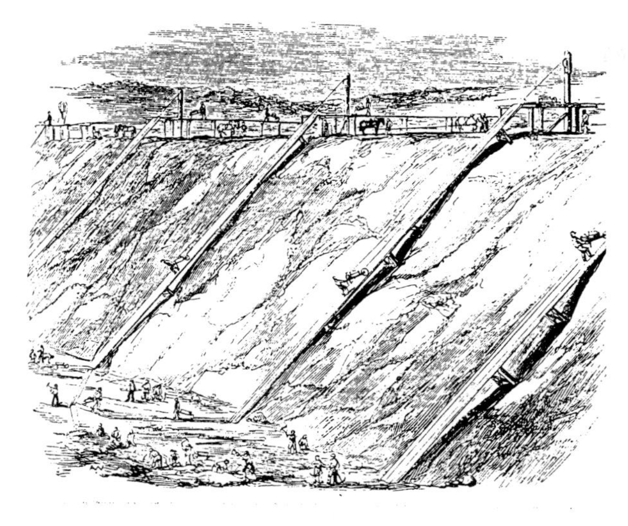

Typical hazardous method of building early railway cuttings by means of guided wheel-barrows hauled up by horse whims.

There were no special celebrations for the men following completion of this difficult tunnel, but, "A number of gentlemen afterwards partook of an excellent and elegant entertainment and passed a very pleasant evening together." In contrast, when work on the Derby-Belper stretch of line was complete, including Milford Tunnel, the contractor David McIntosh had 1,500 workers treated to dinner. They sat down in a field, near the site of the later Duffield station, on 10 June 1840 to eat hot food brought from Derby by train, and afterwards enjoyed games and wrestling.

In addition to the problems on the Clay Cross tunnel contract there were other difficulties. In July 1838 the North Midland Committee were concerned that the number of men working on the contracts were diminishing rather than increasing. Francis Swanwick the resident engineer reported that the contractors said men were getting scarce – possibly due to the pull of other railways under construction. In August the masons employed on the extensive stone works at Belper cutting and at Bullbridge went on strike. And, earlier in the January of that year, the English navvies made an attack on the Irish labourers working on the Rotherham section of the works. Lord Fitzwilliam a local landowner, applied to the Home Office for several London policemen to keep the peace. These arrived on Saturday 21 July and were lodged at the Red Lion Inn, Rotherham. Under a superintendent they patrolled the line "each man armed with loaded pistols and appears without uniform." Then in May, things were beginning to get out of hand near Chesterfield so a troop of Hussars from Nottingham was stationed in the town to keep "the excavators (who are very numerous) in order." In June there was a near riot near Barnsley when the English again attacked the Irish navvies. The magistrates called out the 7th Dragoons this time to assist the London policemen on the line to restore order.

There were extensive works to be executed at the southern end of the railway. At Derby the Nottingham Road

MIDLAND COUNTIES RAILWAY.

THE Public are informed, that this RAILWAY, from NOTTINGHAM and DERBY to LOUGHBOROUGH, LEICESTER, and the intermediate Stations, will be OPENED for the Conveyance of Passengers, Parcels, Gentlemen's Carriages, Horses, and Van Goods, on TUESDAY the 5th of May.

HOURS OF DEPARTURE.

From Nottingham & Derby to Leicester.	*From Leicester to Nottingham and Derby.*
Eight o'clock Morning.	*** Half-past 7 Morning.
Half-past 11 Morning.	** Eleven o'clock Morning.
Quarter to 5 Afternoon.	* ~~Three o'clock~~ Afternoon
Quarter to 8 Evening.	Half-past 7 Evening.
ON SUNDAYS.	ON SUNDAYS.
Eight o'clock Morning.	Half-past 7 Morning.
Half-past 7 Evening.	Seven o'clock Evening.

On the opening of the North Midland Railway, the 8 o'clock Morning and ¼ to 5 o'clock Afternoon Trains from Derby to Leicester, will be in connection with the Trains leaving Sheffield for Derby, at half-past 5 Morning and 2 o'clock Afternoon; and the half-past 7 and 11 o'clock Morning Trains from Leicester, will arrive in Derby in time for the 9 o'clock Morning, and ¼ to 1 o'clock Afternoon Trains, from Derby to Sheffield.

The Train marked *** is in connection at Derby with Coaches to Ashbourne, Leek, Macclesfield, Stockport, Manchester, and Liverpool; also to Matlock, Bakewell, and Buxton, and at Nottingham, with Coaches to Mansfield, Newark, Lincoln, Hull, &c.

The Train marked ** is in connection at Nottingham with a Coach to Southwell, Retford, and Gainsborough.

The Train marked * is in connection at Nottingham with Coaches to Mansfield, Southwell, Newark and Lincoln.

The intermediate Stations are Kegworth, Barrow, Sileby, and Syston. It is requested that Passengers will be at the intermediate Stations, and Carriages and Horses at principal Stations, a quarter of an Hour *before* the time advertised for starting. The doors of the Booking Offices at principal Stations will be closed precisely at the Hours appointed for departure; after which no one can be admitted to go by the Train.

FARES.

	First Class.	*Second Class.*
From Nottingham to Leicester.	6s. 0d.	4s. 6d.
From Derby to Leicester	6s. 0d.	5s. 0d.
From Nottingham to Loughbro'	3s. 6d.	2s. 6d.
From Derby to Loughborough.	3s. 6d.	2s. 6d.
From Leicester to Loughbro'	2s. 6d.	2s. 0d.

RATES FOR PARCELS AND VAN GOODS.

Of and under 18lbs weight, for any distance under 30 Miles	6d.
Above 18lbs. and under 28lbs.	9d.
Above 28lbs. and under 56lbs.	1s. 0d.
Above 56lbs. and under 112lbs.	1s. 6d.

Above 112lbs. 1s. 6d. per Cwt.

N.B.—The above Rates include delivery and all other charges, except the customary Twopence for Booking.

Persons desirous of having their Parcels, &c. by Railway, are requested to mark them conspicuously "Per Railway."

The Company will not be responsible for Parcels, &c. above the value of £10, unless declared as such at the time of booking, and entered and paid for accordingly.

In addition to the Offices at the Railway Stations, the following Receiving Houses have been appointed: where information relative to the Trains may be obtained:—In NOTTINGHAM, White Lion and May-pole.—DERBY, the Bell, King's Head, Tiger, and New Inn.—LOUGHBOROUGH, Red Lion.—LEICESTER, Stag and Pheasant.

By Order, J. F. BELL, Secretary.

Nottingham, 28th April, 1840.

LONDON and BIRMINGHAM

NORTH MIDLAND RAILWAY.

OPENING OF THE LINE—ARRIVAL AND DEPARTURE OF TRAINS.

THE Public is respectfully informed that the Trains of this Company, and those of the London and Birmingham, and Birmingham and Derby Junction Lines, in connection with them, will start and arrive according to the several Tables below, until further notice.

BETWEEN DERBY AND SHEFFIELD.

Departure from Sheffield.	Arrival at Derby.
H. M.	H. M.
5 30 a.m.	7 45 a.m.
9 15 „	11 30 „
•12 0 noon.	2 15 p.m.
2 0 p.m.	4 15 „
6 0 „	8 10 „
SUNDAY TRAINS.	
6 30 a.m.	8 45 a.m.
9 30 „	11 45 „
6 0 p.m.	8 15 p.m.

Departure from Derby.	Arrival at Sheffield.
5 55 a.m.	8 0 a.m.
9 15 „	11 30 „
1 0 p.m.	3 15 p.m.
3 15 „	5 30 „
8 0 „	10 15 „
SUNDAY TRAINS.	
5 55 a.m.	8 0 a.m.
9 15 a.m.	11 30 a.m.
3 15 p.m.	5 30 p.m.

The Fares between the above places will be First Class ...... 11s. | Second Class...... 7s. 0d.

BETWEEN LONDON AND SHEFFIELD.

Departure from London.	Arrival at Derby.	Arrival at Sheffield.
H. M.	H. M.	H. M.
6 0 a.m.	12 45 p.m.	3 15 p.m.
9 0 „	3 0 „	5 30 „
1 0 p.m.	7 45 „	10 15 „
8 30 „	5 40 a.m.	8 0 a.m.
SUNDAY TRAINS.		
8 0 a.m.	3 0 p.m.	5 30 p.m.
8 30 p.m.	5 40 a.m.	8 0 a.m.

Departure from Sheffield.	Departure from Derby.	Arrival in London.
5 30 a.m.	8 0 a.m.	3 30 p.m.
9 15 „	11 45 „	6 30 „
12 0 noon.	2 30 p.m.	9 30 „
2 0 p.m.	4 30 „	11 40 „
6 0 „	8 30 „	5 30 a.m.
SUNDAY TRAINS.		
9 30 a.m.	12 0 noon.	7 30 p.m.
6 0 p.m.	8 30 p.m.	5 30 a.m.

First Class £2 6 0
Second Class 1 11 0

BETWEEN BIRMINGHAM AND SHEFFIELD.

Departure from Sheffield.	Departure from Derby.	Arrival at Birmingham.
H. M.	H. M	H. M.
5 30 a.m.	8 0 a.m.	10 15 a.m.
9 15 „	11 45 „	1 45 p.m.
12 0 noon.	2 30 p.m.	4 30 „
2 0 p.m.	4 30 „	6 45 „
6 0 „	8 30 „	10 45 „
SUNDAY TRAINS.		
6 30 a.m.	9 0 a.m.	11 15 a.m.
9 30 „	12 0 noon.	2 0 p.m.
6 0 p.m.	8 30 p.m.	10 45 p.m.

Departure from Birmingham.	Arrival at Derby.	Arrival at Sheffield.
3 15 a.m.	6 40 a.m.	8 0 a.m.
6 45 „	9 0 „	11 30 „
10 45 „	12 45 p.m.	3 15 p.m.
1 0 p.m.	3 0 „	5 30 .

Announcement of openings of the Midland Counties and North Midland Railways with connections to London, Birmingham and Sheffield, 28 April 1840.

Passenger locomotive of 2-2-2 wheel arrangement supplied to North Midland Railway by Robert Stephenson & Co of Newcastle – 1839.

Turnpike had to be lowered to build a bridge over. The Act of Parliament prohibited crossing turnpike roads on the level and set out detailed dimensions for building bridges over. There was also the Milford tunnel of 800yds length through solid sandstone. Then the long cutting through built-up Belper, with its lining in masonry, and ten road bridges over to link the streets. Added to these were the five bridges to be built over the River Derwent between Milford and Ambergate, and the underpass of the Cromford Canal at Bullbridge. The NMR was liable to pay the Cromford Canal Company £100 for every 24 hours their work stopped the canal. To carry the canal over the railway an iron aqueduct 150ft long, 9ft wide and 6ft deep was made at the Butterley Company works for £800 in February 1839, and transported in sections to Bullbridge. There it was raised, assembled and rivetted with great speed to lessen the liabilities to the Canal Company.

At Rotherham there was a big 30-arch viaduct to be constructed over the River Don – and at Oakenshaw there were huge cuttings and embankments, with more at Normanton. There was much wet weather through the summer and autumn of 1839 and this seriously hampered completion of the works. In part due to this, the line was opened in two sections – the first being the 40-mile length between Derby and Rotherham, opened without any formal ceremony on Monday, 11 May 1840. This linked at Masborough Station with Sheffield trains over the associated little Sheffield and Rotherham Railway opened on 31 October 1838.

The first train started from Rotherham on that May morning. At Chesterfield, George Stephenson, with George Hudson as guest, got on the train for the rest of the run to Derby. Another train left Derby the same morning to run to Sheffield with Robert Stephenson on the pilot locomotive's footplate; this was a 2-2-2 built by Stephenson & Co of Newcastle, the second engine being a 2-2-2 by Mather, Dixon & Co of Liverpool.

The final section of the NMR from Masborough to Leeds was officially opened seven weeks later on 30 June 1840. At 8.02am a heavy train of 34 coaches carrying some 500 special guests left Hunslet Lane, Leeds for Derby. It was double headed with two engines – Stephenson & Co locomotives nos. 60 and 61. The train was so heavy that it had to be banked at the rear for part of the way by two more engines, a Laird & Kitson and the other a Charles Tayleur & Co. From Oakenshaw the North Midland train was

North end of Derby Station, North Midland Railway locomotive probably from Laird & Kitson of Leeds, note the policeman controlling train movement with flag, and single platform inside the station. At extreme left the North Midland locomotive roundhouse, works, offices, clocktower, with rural setting beyond. At extreme right the two storey joint warehouse of the North Midland and Midland Counties.

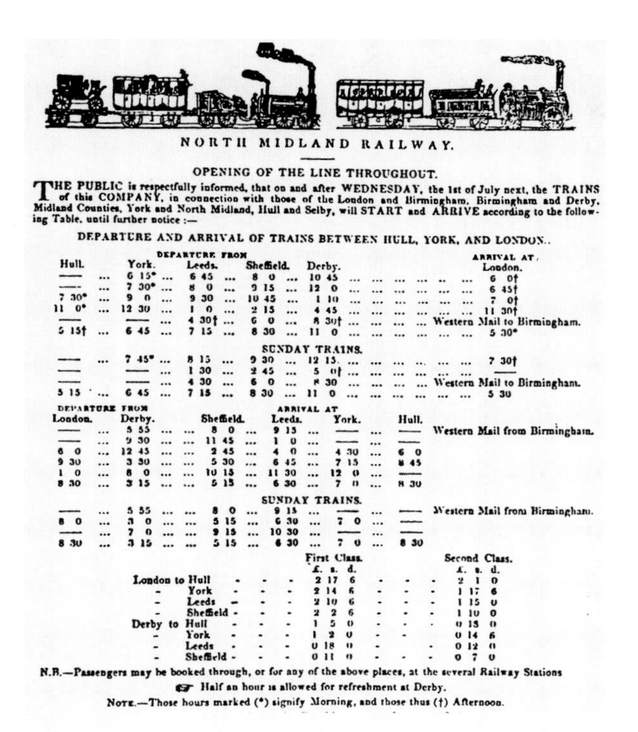

NORTH MIDLAND RAILWAY.

OPENING OF THE LINE THROUGHOUT.

THE PUBLIC is respectfully informed, that on and after WEDNESDAY, the 1st of July next, the TRAINS of this COMPANY, in connection with those of the London and Birmingham, Birmingham and Derby, Midland Counties, York and North Midland, Hull and Selby, will START and ARRIVE according to the following Table, until further notice :—

DEPARTURE AND ARRIVAL OF TRAINS BETWEEN HULL, YORK, AND LONDON.

Hull.	York.	Leeds.	Sheffield.	Derby.	Arrival at London.
—	6 15*	6 45	8 0	10 45	6 0†
—	7 30*	8 0	9 15	12 0	6 45†
7 30*	9 0	9 30	10 45	1 10	7 0†
11 0*	12 30	1 0	2 15	4 45	11 30†
—	—	4 30†	6 0	8 30†	Western Mail to Birmingham.
5 15†	6 45	7 15	8 30	11 0	5 30*
SUNDAY TRAINS.					
—	7 45*	8 15	9 30	12 15	7 30†
—	—	1 30	2 45	5 0†	—
—	—	4 30	6 0	8 30	Western Mail to Birmingham.
5 15	6 45	7 15	8 30	11 0	5 30

Departure from London.	Derby.	Arrival at Sheffield.	Leeds.	York.	Hull.	
—	5 55	8 0	9 15	—	—	Western Mail from Birmingham.
—	9 30	11 45	1 0	—	—	
6 0	12 45	2 45	4 0	4 30	6 0	
9 30	3 30	5 30	6 45	7 15	8 45	
1 0	8 0	10 15	11 30	12 0	—	
8 30	3 15	5 15	6 30	7 0	8 30	
SUNDAY TRAINS.						
—	5 55	8 0	9 15	—	—	Western Mail from Birmingham.
8 0	3 0	5 15	6 30	7 0	—	
—	7 0	9 15	10 30	—	—	
8 30	3 15	5 15	6 30	7 0	8 30	

	First Class. £. s. d.	Second Class. £. s. d.
London to Hull	2 17 6	2 1 0
- York	2 14 6	1 17 6
- Leeds	2 10 6	1 15 0
- Sheffield	2 2 6	1 10 0
Derby to Hull	1 5 0	0 18 0
- York	1 2 0	0 14 6
- Leeds	0 18 0	0 12 0
- Sheffield	0 11 0	0 7 0

N.B.—Passengers may be booked through, or for any of the above places, at the several Railway Stations

☞ Half an hour is allowed for refreshment at Derby.

NOTE.—Those hours marked (*) signify Morning, and those thus (†) Afternoon.

Announcement and timetable o opening of North Midland throughout to Leeds, with connections to York, Hull and London, 1 July 1840.

followed by the inaugural York & North Midland Railway's train of four first-class carriages pulled by their engine 'Hudson'. This train from York had run on to the North Midland line at Normanton and was carrying the York & North Midland Railway's chairman George Hudson and his wife, plus directors and guests. Stops were made at various stations on the route, where there were crowds of onlookers of the event, and with bands playing at Barnsley, Chesterfield and Belper. At last the two trains made a splendid entry into Derby Station at 1.07pm to music and great cheers from the waiting assembly.

The completed great station, initially called the Grand Central and later the Derby Tri-Junct was put into use for the first time on that June day. The station was elaborately decorated with evergreen foliage, and the great celebrations were fulsomely reported in the local press – "Two immense lines of tables stretched along the stone platform for everyone to partake of a cold collation and wine..." – there were meats, jellies, confectionery, fruits – "with wines of the very best quality".

This splendid spread was laid out at the expense of the company, by Joseph Hall the proprietor of the refreshment rooms at the station. Joseph Hall was also destined to become the first manager of the Midland Hotel when it opened in the following May of 1841. It must have been a splendid sight at the station with everyone celebrating on the long platform (essentially this was the present no.1 platform). The numbers had swollen to over 1,000 – "everyone had to stand for sitting was out of the question". The reception lasted for nearly an hour and a half before the trains set out for Leeds again. At the Music Hall, Albion Street, Leeds a "cold dinner" for 400 guests was put on that evening "with an abundance of champagne." There were "special tables for the ladies" and music was provided by the band of the Fourth Royal Irish Dragoons. The chairman George Carr Glyn was present.

Thomas Jackson the contractor for the Leeds station looked after his workmen on

Heap of stone rail sleepers found in retaining wall built adjacent to the former Derby Canal alongside Derby Railway Works. Two thirds of the North Midlands 73 route miles were originally laid with stone sleepers, and Vignoles laid 14 miles of the Midland Counties 57 route miles with sleepers of Derbyshire Gritstone. These particular stone blocks were laid in diamond alignment.

the opening of the North Midland giving "two sumptuous dinners to his workmen – at Mrs Porter's, the Railway Hotel, Kirkgate, and at Mr Priestley's the Rodney Inn, Callgate." Altogether some 600 men sat down to dinner.

It was a great time for celebrations, for on that day a trunk railway line connected for the first time – York, Leeds and Hull to London, and with connections to Birmingham and onward to Gloucester, Manchester and Liverpool.

However, the North Midland Railway had been built at a very high cost and this would soon have serious repercussions when trying to make the railway pay its way. The Birmingham & Derby Junction Railway had cost £24,683 per mile, the Midland Counties £30,019, but the North Midland Railway cost £45,871 for each mile built. Although this was substantially less than say the London & Birmingham Railway which had cost £52,882 per mile, the North Midland's traffic and other factors would prove to only produce low dividends.

A Joint Station at Derby – The Tri-Junction

A masterpiece to which all too little attention is given.

O.S.Nock, 1972.

IN THE early stages of their schemes the three companies had each been thinking of providing their own individual stations – all to be desirably close in to the town centre.

The Midland Counties with an easterly approach line from Nottingham contemplated several alternative sites for their station at Derby. The first of these in 1833 was a line across the Chequer Closes and the Old Meadows common lands to a point north of the River Derwent where Derwent Row joined Exeter Street and crossed the Derby Canal. At this point the canal had junctions with The Long Bridge, which served as a tow-path for boats crossing the river. From there the line was to pass over Exeter Place – cross the river westwards by a new bridge to be built just northside of the timber Exeter footbridge of 1810 and then terminate in a station to be built on the site of Darby's Yard which lay off the bottom end of Full Street (roughly where the police station car-park now lies). They then had further thoughts, probably because the site would have been too small for trains, and the extra cost of a river bridge unjustifiable. Instead, they proposed the line should terminate in Exeter Gardens, opposite on the east bank of the Derwent.

But then following on from this, Charles Vignoles conceived another approach line and station location. The line was to veer north from Meadow Lane at Chaddesden, then cross the Nottingham Road Turnpike adjacent to a house called Chaddesden Hill. It would then run along north of this road, through the New Pastures before terminating in a station to stand on the site of the Old Crown Derby China Works closed in 1835, and the Punch Bowl Inn, fronting Nottingham Road near St Mary's Bridge.

Indications of all these three alternatives were given when John Fox Bell the secretary of the Midland Counties wrote to Henry Patteson the secretary of the North Midland on 13 November 1835 saying – "I am directed by our board to send you, according to your request, the enclosed tracing of our proposed terminations at Derby. Which will be adopted, is not yet decided." But by the time submission was made to Parliament early in 1836 the Midland Counties had fixed on the northern route to the Old Crown Derby site, and this was the one approved by Royal Assent in the Act for the Midland Counties Railway.

The North Midland promoters, with their line coming down from the north, planned their terminal station to also be on the north side of Nottingham Road, a little to the east of the Midland Counties

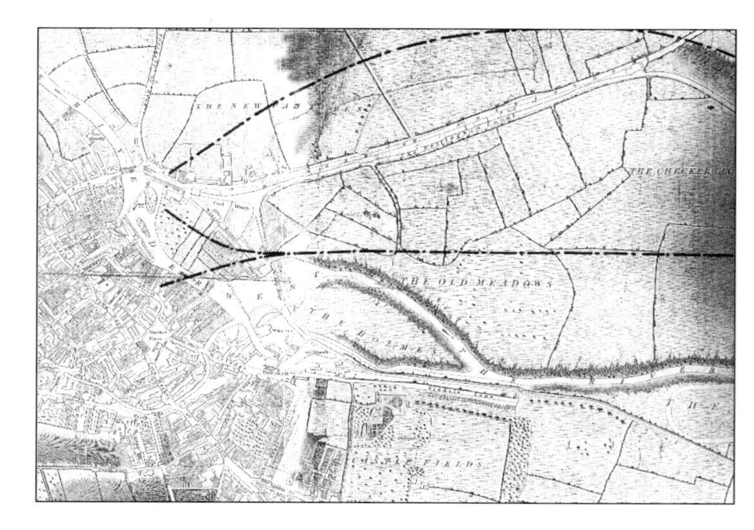

Alternative routes and terminations for the Midland Counties Railway at Derby indicated on tracing sent by John Fox Bell to Henry Patteson of the North Midland – 13 November 1835.

View of Derby from the Old Meadows looking across to The Holmes to the left. The long bridge of Derby Canal across the River Derwent is centre, with the chimney of Derwent Foundry in front of All Saints tower - Henry Burn 1846.

proposal. With this prospect in mind the promoters of the Birmingham and Derby then saw an advantage if they extended their rails northward to make an end-on junction with the North Midland line, since this would permit through running between the north, Birmingham, and London. This idea was aired at a public meeting in Derby in December 1835 and was approved in principle. From this the town council began to see that if the third railway company, the Midland Counties could be induced to connect in, then there could be all round benefits from having a joint station in the town.

At a town council meeting on 2 February 1836 with the mayor - Joseph Strutt in the chair, consent was sought by the three companies to run their lines through corporation lands on which the Freemen had commonage. The council declined to consent and instead nominated a small sub-committee of five members to negotiate with the three companies for a single joint station to be built near into the town. Two of these members - John Sandars its chairman, and John Johnson went to London and had meetings on the first two days of March with the three companies' directors. At these meetings it was agreed that there should be a single station and that it "should be fixed in a situation most convenient and advantageous to the inhabitants of the town of Derby." On the basis of this pledge the council withdrew its objections and gave every support to the Railway Bills passages through Parliament. The council relied on the pledge as a gentlemen's agreement, rather than to press for the station to be fixed by Parliament.

Other meetings followed between the council's railway committee and the companies, and where the council proposal for the station to be sited on the Holmes was discussed. There was a further meeting on 6 August 1836 between the town committee, and Henry Smith the chairman, with Sir Oswald Mosley Bt for the Birmingham & Derby; George Carr Glyn the chairman, with William Leaper Newton for the North Midland; and Charles Vignoles with John Fox Bell respectively engineer and secretary of the Midland Counties. The town representatives said that they had 'caused plans and estimates to be prepared at considerable expense' for this site, but the railway companies representatives had decided that it was too low lying and at risk of flooding - it was also felt to be too restrictive in area for requirements. Although the town was thinking in terms of one joint station the companies still seemed to have had thoughts of individual stations alongside each other. To get over the difficulties the companies then suggested that "...if the corporation would make better

A surviving part of the original North Midland Viaduct over the Nottingham Road Turnpike and Derby Canal.

approaches to the Holmes and a road across... The Railway Companies would then build a bridge over the River Derwent from this new road and fix their station(s) in the Old Meadows." These Meadows lay immediately over the river from the Holmes. (The Holmes now lies partly under new roads, with the residue being known as Bass's Recreation Ground, created by gift in 1867 from Michael Thomas Bass.) It is an interesting aside to note that William Leaper Newton the banker was representing the North Midland Company when at the same time he happened to be the Mayor of Derby – the other party. Newton also had an interest in the Midland Counties Railway since he had been on its Derbyshire Provisional Committee from when it was floated back in October 1832. His bank Crompton Newton & Co. of Irongate, had also been the MCR's Derby bank since 1832.

Agreeing this latest proposal the corporation went ahead and started depositing several thousand loads of earth over the Holmes to raise the level for the new access road to the Old Meadows. But, by early 1838 there were more difficulties. These were of an engineering nature and rose from the problem of bringing together three lines approaching from different directions, at differing levels, and with the River and the Nottingham Road to be crossed. The Nottingham Road Turnpike trustees also raised legal difficulties by resisting any change to the Parliamentary plans. To cross the road via a bridge would mean greatly raising the levels of the North Midland line, causing substantial additional expense and would preclude a site in the Old Meadows.

A search had to be made for a new site. Since the approaching railway lines of the companies were by now well under construction the matter was urgent. This resulted in the companies putting forward the new proposal to re-position the joint station in Boroughs' Fields, the Castlefields Park estate. This would be in open land where the Birmingham & Derby Junction Company had already bought land from the Borough family trustees for its line of railway into Derby. It would also be on higher ground free from flood risk, with plenty of open land available for the station and other buildings.

The railway committee of the town council were dismayed over the prospect of this new site and protested against the move from the Old Meadows in a letter from John Sandars its chairman, to George Carr Glyn, chairman of the North Midland Railway, on 7 April 1838 (no doubt he wrote in similar vein to the other two companies). Sandars protested that the move to a site a little over a mile from the town centre (and, largely over the town boundary into Litchurch) certainly did not accord with the pledge given by the companies in 1836 before their Acts were granted, namely that "the station be fixed where it will be most convenient and advantageous for the inhabitants of Derby." But, in order to achieve a single station there had to be some compromise. The protest of the town council was therefore of no avail and on 21 April 1838 it was recorded that the Midland Counties Board had "Resolved to unite in forming a joint station at Castlefields".

To facilitate the building of the station at Castlefields would mean the North Midland extending its line southward by bridging over, and lowering the Nottingham Road Turnpike; the Birmingham and Derby shortening its line; and the Midland Counties abandoning its route north of the Nottingham Road, returning

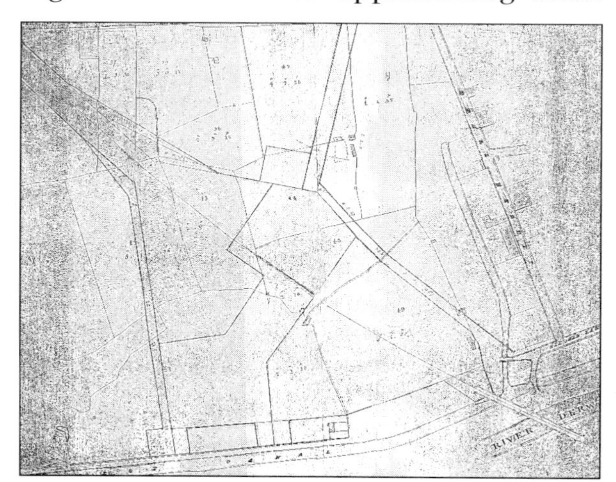

Sketch plan of land requirements for railways, station, hotel and roads in Castlefields, Derby – early 1839.

Five arches bridges at Derby Station, over the River Derwent, with bridge over the adjacent Derby Canal. Note the road coach-like carriages of the train (early 1840s) and, harvesting on the Siddals in the foreground.

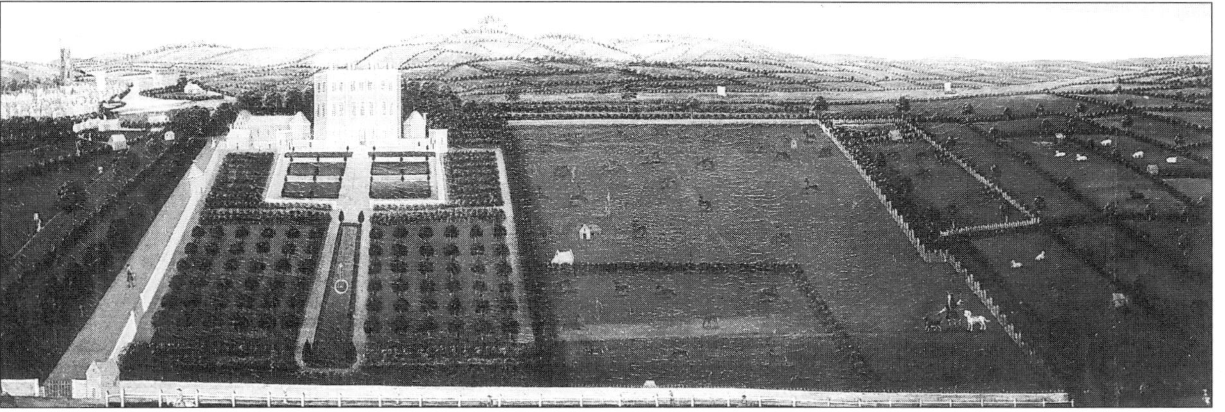

Castlefields House and formal gardens of Isaac Borrow (Borough) with Deer Park, and fields to the right which became the site of Derby Station and Works. Boats under sail on the Derwent Navigation beyond the Siddals. Horse riders on track to the front which later became the London Road Turnpike in 1758. Track alongside house became the original Traffick Street. Unknown artist, early eighteenth century, in Derby Museum Collection.

to its original concept over the Chequer Closes and the Old Meadows before curving sharply to join the North Midland rails just before the Five Arches bridge over the Derwent. It was agreed that the North Midland would build the bridge, an adjacent one over the Derby Canal and also the station. Authority for all these alterations required Parliamentary consent. This was done with a single Bill which was passed as a second North Midland Railway Act on 1 July 1839.

While the Derby Town Council had been dismayed that it had not been able to ensure the building of the station nearer to the town centre as it had wished, it had nevertheless achieved its other objective of having all three railway companies join in one station building.

The town council had other reasons for gratification. In October 1839 it was able to report that the Estates Committee had been authorised to invest £1,000 of the monies received from the Railway Company, and from John Strutt for the purchase of the Advowson of St Alkmund's Church "in Bank of England stock or Government securities ...since this sum would remain over and above after liquidating all the bonds due from the corporation." In November 1839 there was report of a proposed new water supply for the town and reference to £4,000 which had recently been received from the sale of corporation land to the Railway Companies. And, on 27 May 1840 it was reported to the town council that for the sale of its land to the North Midland Company "a much higher price had been obtained than had been got for any other similar land in the neighbourhood." The Derby Town Council had every reason to be pleased and, without any inkling then of the great expansion the subsequent Midland Railway would bring to the town.

Castlefields Estate

The Castlefields estate was created by Isaac Borrow, born at Hough Park, Hulland, Derbyshire in 1674. The family built a new hall adjacent to the old one at Hough Park in 1692 (now known as the Old Hall, to add confusion) but in 1702 Borrow bought the Castlefields land from the Mayor and Burgesses of Derby together with the third of the tithes of

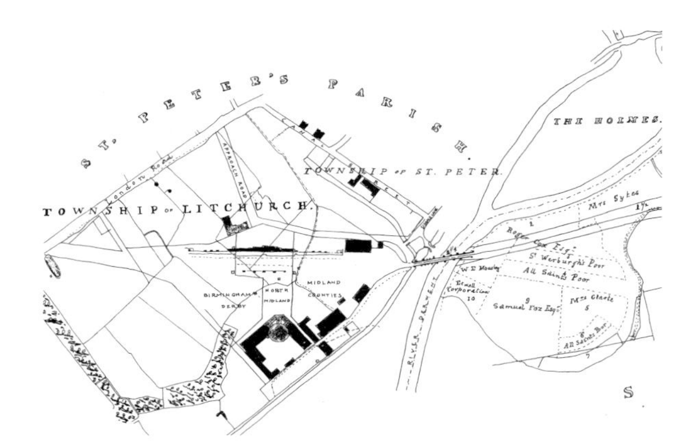

Sketch plan of land requirements in Castlefields apportioned between the three railway companies – showing station, workshops, roundhouse and hotel 1840.

Derby; and followed this in 1718 by buying more land in Castlefields and Whitecross Field. In 1712 he consolidated his estate with a purchase of more land to the south, including Gorsey Close, from Sir John Harpur of Calke and others. By 1715 Isaac Borrow had built his rather splendid new house on the land and created an estate. Little is known about the house other than its clear illustration in a painting of *c.*1730, probably executed in celebration of Isaac Borrow's term as Mayor of Derby in that same year. William Woolley the historian wrote in description "beyond is Castlefields where Mr Boroughs builds a very good house (with a curious garden and a paddock for deer) and has a very good seat" – all this can clearly be seen in the painting. By his land purchases Borrow's estate extended from Bag Lane (now East Street) Eagle Street, southward to Dead Man's Lane. On the east side was an ancient track known alternatively as Castlefields or Siddals Lane. While on the west side there was another ancient track to Litchurch hamlet, Alvaston, Shardlow and Wilden Ferry over the Trent. This track would become the London Road when it was turnpiked in 1758. The south-eastern end of the estate boundary was modified in 1795 when the Swarkestone arm of the Derby Canal was constructed.

The Borrow (later changed to Borough) family continued to live at Castlefields until 1803 when Captain Thomas Borough bought Chetwynd Park in Shropshire and moved the family there. The Castlefields estate was then gradually sold off piecemeal until the final parcel went in *c.*1870. The earliest sales of land permitted the building and development of Devonshire, Castle, Chetwynd, Rivett, Union Streets and Borough's Walk; all with small houses, and divided from the Castlefields House gardens by Traffick Street; Boden & Morley's large lace factory on Castle Street being built in 1835.

After the Borough family's departure, Castlefields House was rented out. William Leaper Newton of the Derby bankers – Crompton and Newton, lived there for a while, well before his North Midland days, and before building in *c.*1820 his own house and estate, The Leylands, off Penny Long Lane at the north of the town. Lady Grey de Ruthin was a later tenant in 1817, and there were at least two more before the house was finally vacated in 1836.

The house then lay empty for a year before being demolished in 1836-38. Even then some of the outbuildings continued in various uses, one part as late as 1895 was in use as a school. In 1822 Thomas Borough had sold the estate around the house down to near the town boundary with Litchurch Township to a Mr Copeland of Lincoln, for £22,000, who in turn sold the land off in lots for speculative building.

A wide road, Park Street was pushed through in front of the old Castlefields House, then Traffick Street and Siddals Lane were widened and made up. By 1835 more new roads – Liversage Street, Hope Street, John Street and Canal Street had all been laid out. Copeland Street followed the demolition of the house and gradually the other sub-dividing streets were put in. The whole area was almost completely covered with artisan's small houses, some soon to be occupied by railway workers when the railways opened in 1839-40.

There were also three silk mills in the area – the branch canal by Canal Street being initially cut to serve the Castlefields Mill of Simpson and Turner, and was subsequently extended when Carrington Mill was built.

The pleasing group of the Liversage Almshouses fronting London Road, were provided in 1835-36, and the elegant London Terrace houses adjacent were built in 1840 for middle-class professionals. St George's Church next door had been built as a speculative venture in 1832, eventually being replaced, by Holy Trinity on the same site in 1904.

The North Midland Act of 1839 authorised land purchase for the Castlefields Station. In addition to buying some of the land already acquired by the Birmingham & Derby Company, the North Midland and the Midland Counties also took the opportunity to buy more land from the Borough family to accommodate the large station and all the workshops and engine facilities needed. An annotated drawing of 1839

Castlefields Estate over-built with small, artisan's houses, taken in 1960 just before complete clearance. Park Street on right, running from Traffic Street past Bemrose's factory to Midland Road.

suggests that together they bought an area roughly rectangular in shape between London Road and the Derby Canal. The land areas of the individual companies were of irregular form, with the North Midland lying central and flanked by the other two companies. In the arrangement the main central buildings of the long station lay within the North Midland area – but the overall station was spread out roughly equally over each company's land. Each company also had access and frontage on to the Derby Canal.

There has to be some doubt whether the North Midland did actually buy all the land up to the London Road as depicted on the 1840 sketch, since as late as 1855 the Borough family trustees were party to a conveyance to Thomas Jackson of land in the area adjacent to The Midland Hotel.

The Railway Buildings

In the main, we require from buildings, as from men, two kinds of goodness; first, that doing of their practical duty well: then that they be grateful and pleasing in doing it; which last is itself another form of duty.

John Ruskin
'The Stones of Venice'

THE 1839 Act left it for the three companies to mutually arrange the usage and apportionment of the joint station. Since the North Midland was the largest company and the only one that intended to base its headquarters at Derby, it was accordingly agreed that it should build and own the station. Each of the other two companies would contribute towards the costs – the contract price was £39,986 of which the Birmingham & Derby agreed to pay £4,796 and the Midland Counties £4,923. The latter two companies also agreed to pay rent at 6% per annum on the proportion of the cost of their accommodation.

Francis Thompson and the North Midland Railway

Even before the Royal Assent was given to the second North Midland Railway Act the company had appointed an architect. At a board meeting in London on 7 February 1839 with George Carr Glyn in the chair, and Robert Stephenson and Frederick Swanwick in attendance, it was:-

> "Resolved that Mr Stephenson be authorised to employ Mr Thompson in preparing the plans for the stations and in executing those works at a Salary of £400 per annum during the period his services are required."

Right: **The lines of the three Railways in to Derby as built, shown annotated on Rogerson's map.**

Far right: **Portrait of Francis Thompson (1808-1895) the early railway architect as a young man.**

How Francis Thompson came to obtain the important commission of architect to the North Midland Railway is a puzzle yet

Ambergate Station. North Midland Railway, built 1839, Francis Thompson architect. Impressive design in Jacobean style. It remained in use until 1863 when it was removed and rebuilt south of Toadmoor Tunnel. Closed to passenger use and replaced by the well-known triangular layout Ambergate station in 1876, demolished by BR in 1971.

to be solved. Thompson was born on 25 July 1808 at Woodbridge, Suffolk into a family of builders in the town. His father George Thompson was not only a practical builder but was also, like others of his time, an architect/builder able to produce and execute his own designs for commissions. He worked mainly in Woodbridge itself, but later in his career he became a county surveyor for Suffolk, responsible for looking after the county's bridges and buildings, in addition to his own independent work. His son Francis was not content to stay in Woodbridge. He married Anna Maria Watson on 17 May 1830 when he was just 22, and soon after sailed from London to Canada, or British North America as it was then called. It seems a most improbable place for a young architect to go out to at that time for it was still very much a pioneer colony, and the journey on a sailing ship was not comfortable. The Thompsons settled in Montreal, still at that date a small town with a population of around 45,000 and of largely French speaking stock. From our perspective the prospects didn't look good. Nevertheless, Thompson did obtain architectural work and practised both on his own account and in partnerships. In 1831

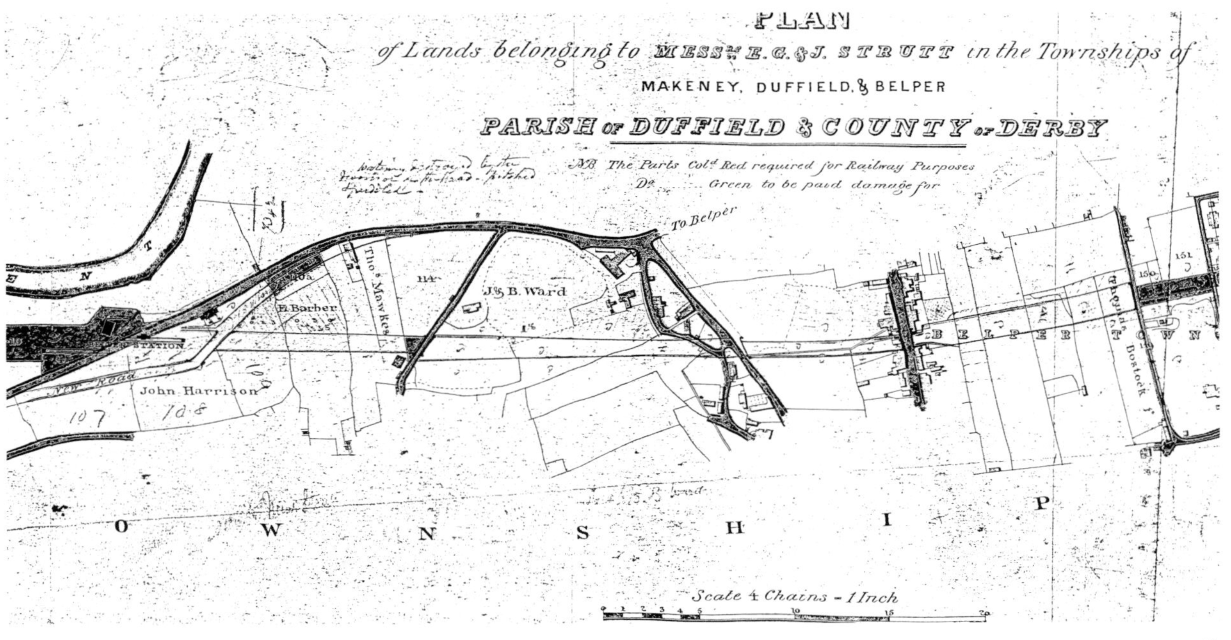

Plan of lands belonging to the Strutts at Belper with land required for the North Midland Railway and Belper station. Late 1839.

Belper Station. NMR – designed by Francis Thompson in Italianate character. It was at the south end of the town, but was demolished in 1878 and replaced by simpler buildings, just north of King Street.

a son Francis Jacob was born to Anna Maria, destined to be Francis Thompson's only child, despite three marriages. In about 1836-37 Anna Maria died in Montreal and it seems Francis returned to England in about 1838 – probably partly through his loss and partly through the state of simmering unrest in the province, that broke out into armed disturbances in 1837.

From these early years, and no obvious contacts, it is all the more mystifying that Thompson obtained the North Midland commission so soon after his return from overseas. But, he certainly repaid his employers by producing some exceptional architecture for the company – his first railway work. Christian Barman in his "Introduction to Railway Architecture" defines Thompson as only one of two railway architects in the great humanist tradition, who gave the small country station meticulous study. But Thompson also had a keen sense of grandeur as witnessed at Derby and Chester stations, and the great Menai Straits bridge with

Barnsley Station. NMR – designed by Francis Thompson in a fanciful Italianate form, with an unusual semi-circular open porch and flanking Venetian style windows. Being some 3 miles from the town it was more appropriately renamed Cudworth in 1854 – demolished shortly after this photograph was taken in 1899.

Francis Thompson's great station at Derby. Samuel Russell's engraving of 1841 shows half of the 1050 foot long façade. To the right is the side façade of the surviving Midland Hotel. Central to the station square is an elegant cast-iron fountain.

Robert Stephenson. His design work and contract administration for the North Midland Company comprised the great joint station; their railway works buildings including the workshops, locomotive round-house and offices; the large joint warehouse on Railway Terrace; the Railway 'village' together with the Brunswick Inn; all the original ten intermediate stations along the line – at Belper, Ambergate, South Wingfield, Clay Cross, Chesterfield, Eckington, Masborough, Swinton, Barnsley and Oakenshaw. There were also clerks and porters houses provided at most of these stations, together with a number of smaller warehouses; and at Leeds, there was the Hunslet station building. The joint warehouse at Derby was for the North Midland and the Midland Counties Companies.

The Midland Hotel was another fine design by Thompson, although it was for Thomas Jackson the builder/proprietor, rather than for the North Midland Company.

Following his appointment on 7 February, Thompson moved to Derby and set up his architect's office. The exact location is not certain but it is possible that it was a rented house in the Market Place, and where he set on five assistants. During that time he lodged at 163 Litchurch Terrace, Osmaston Road, Litchurch in the house of Robert Smith a clerk, with a wife and three children. The address was convenient for an easy walk down to the station site, and like the latter, about one mile distant from the Market Place.

The first design drawings produced were for the joint station building – and were followed by those for the North Midland Company's railway workshops. The station drawings were produced rapidly and approved by the three companies. As soon as 9 April 1839, the North Midland directors agreed that the drawings and specifications should be put out for tenders, to be returned by 21 May. Five tenders were received and that submitted by Thomas Jackson of Pimlico, London in the sum of £39,986 was considered the most favourable. On 30 July, Charles Parker the company's solicitor put the contract for Derby station before the board for agreement.

The station building was initially called the Great Central Station but became more usually known as Derby Tri-Junct. It had a single, extremely long platform 1,050 feet overall, 31 feet wide at the central section and 16 feet wide at the ends. The present Cambridge Station, also by Thompson, still has a single platform arrangement – a lone survivor of an early plan. The Derby platform had to be so long since it was arranged for the North Midland to use the central third, with the Midland Counties and Birmingham & Derby Companies using the north and south ends of the platform. The surviving No.1 platform is essentially that original platform.

There were seven more parallel tracks in the station but these were initially used only for goods wagons, carriage storage and transfer of goods. The small vehicles of the time could be transferred from one track to another by a large number of linked turntables. The maker of these turntables is unknown but may well have been Thomas Wright's Britannia Foundry in Duke Street; originally established by Weatherhead Glover & Co. and which would become in the later 1840s the famous firm of Andrew Handyside & Co.

The station shed was 140ft in width and

Samuel Russell excelled himself with this superbly drawn and detailed interior of Derby Station in 1841. At the north end of the long platform is a Midland Counties train, with a North Midland one approaching in the distance. Men are busily at work moving coaches and servicing the track.

400ft long. It was covered overall with a slated and glazed roof of three pitched spans, supported on light wrought-iron trusses, in a construction devised by Robert Stephenson. These trusses were supported on the perimeter walls and 60 elegant fluted cast-iron columns between, each 22ft high. A large part of the roof ironwork was fabricated by James Haywood's Phoenix Foundry of Nottingham Road, although the Butterley Company supplied the cast-iron columns.

The interior of the station was lit by 216 gas lamps on the columns and along the platform, with more outside to the forecourt. The workshops and other railway buildings were also lit by gas lamps, making a full total of 747 lamps on the site. This brilliant and innovatory installation was supplied by Thomas Crump's firm in Friar Gate. He also happened to be the manager of the Derby Gas Works in nearby Cavendish Street, an early town gas company, established in 1820. The Midland Railway Company would eventually build its own gas works by its railway workshops by the early 1850s.

Surviving stone fragments from the armorial device carved by John Thomas, which was set above the centre front of the Derby Tri-Junct Station.

The backing wall to the platform presented a pattern of arched openings and recesses to the outside. There were special openings for the entry and taking on of road carriages for conveyance with their owners by rail; and there was also provision for loading their horses. Along the top of the great wall, above the cornice, were stone shields on which were displayed the arms of Birmingham, Leicester, Nottingham and York, all relevant to the three companies. Spaced between were ornamental carved stone scrolls in the integral design.

At the centre of the screen wall was placed the two-storey, 15-bay station offices building. This, in Italianate character was the dominant element. The central bay was set forward, with the main public entrance here, below a large Venetian type window. Crowning it all was a bold stone feature, carved by John Thomas of Birmingham, with a shield, supported by two wyverns, proudly proclaiming the town arms of Derby, Sheffield and Leeds – the major towns linked by the North Midland Company. It is quite likely that Thompson derived his inspiration for the scrollwork, stone shields and the central crowning feature, from the decorations above the Derby & Derbyshire Bank, only recently built in the Cornmarket. Thompson would have passed this regularly on his way to his office in the Market Place.

Within the building was the ticket office and parcels booking to one side of the entrance hall, a ladies waiting room, two refreshment rooms and public toilets. From the hall an open staircase led up to a balustraded gallery lit by the big 'Venetian' window over the public concourse. Off this was the general office, a director's room, a commissioner's office (was this the superintendent of the line or the station master?). There was also the boardroom, a room which achieved some fame ten years later when Sir Joseph Paxton, chairing a Works and Ways Committee trying a pointsman for some minor offence, had in abstraction doodled the sketch design for the Crystal Palace building for 1851 on his blotting paper.

In the basement were the second-class refreshment room, kitchens, pantries, beer and wine cellars, together with stores for wood and coal for the fires. The arrangement of the second-class refreshment room down at this level proved a nuisance, so it was soon relocated in late 1840 at ground floor level in an addition to the building.

On 6 November 1839 the directors of the North Midland advertised in the *Derby Mercury* and elsewhere that they invited tenders for building the 'offices and other buildings and works connected with the intended stations... at Belper, South Wingfield, Chesterfield and Eckington'. The plans and specifications could be inspected at The Bell Inn, Derby, and the contract at the North Midland Office. Little time was given for preparing tenders as the directors announced they would meet to consider them at The Bell Inn on Tuesday, 19 November. Contracts were subsequently let to George Radford of Alfreton for South Wingfield; to John Waring and Co for Chesterfield; and to Smith and Brown of Sheffield, for the elegant little Eckington Station to serve the Sitwells of Renishaw Hall nearby.

By 25 December that year contracts had also been let, for Rotherham Station to Joel Buxton of Sheffield; and for Barnsley and Wakefield station to Leach and Co of Bradford. By February 1840 a further contract was let to Crawshaw and Rush to build a station at Sheffield alongside the one already there of the little Sheffield &

Stone scroll-work supporting shields of the town and county's arms, set as symbolical ornament above the Derby & Derbyshire Banking Company's premises of 1839 in the Cornmarket, Derby, and which may have inspired the carvings on the Derby station façade.

Rotherham Railway, which had opened in 1838. An agreement between the two related companies in March 1840 would permit through working by North Midland trains over the Sheffield & Rotherham line.

Early in March 1840 the foundations were laid at Hunslet Lane for the Leeds terminus station. Thomas Jackson was awarded this further contract, which in addition to the station building, included offices and a warehouse – all at a cost of £14,000. Like Derby the train shed had an overall roof across the two platforms and six in-between storage lines. Outside – "at the grand entrance, in the centre, the

Originally chimney-piece in the North Midland Railway boardroom by Francis Thompson – shortly before demolition in 1985.

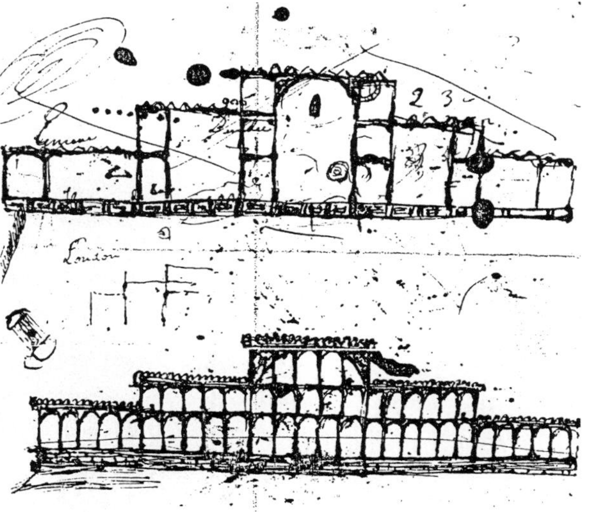

Sketch doodle for the Crystal Palace design of 1851, done by Joseph Paxton on his blotting paper at a meeting in the old North Midland boardroom.

Derby Tri-Junct Station drawn by J.F.Burrell in about 1842. Note the cows being driven in for loading a goods train – also the additional rooms added in front for second class Refreshment Rooms.

Chesterfield Station – NMR by Francis Thompson. In Jacobean style like Ambergate, it was the largest intermediate station on the line. Beyond can be seen an equally elegant building, the steam pump house with columnar chimney and related water supply tank for the locomotives.

arcade is ascended by flights of stone steps, with a row of four highly ornamented centre pilasters, terminating in an arch at the apex." It was a classical portico, with the arms of Leeds, Sheffield and Derby again displayed on a sculpted stone shield as at Derby, and similarly carved by John Thomas. The two-storey office building had a booking office, ladies and gentlemen's waiting rooms, and rooms for guards, police and porters. Upstairs were rooms for the directors, and a clerks office.

Thompson commissioned the artist/engraver Samuel Russell of Camberwell, London to record the stations of the North Midland for publication. From the opening of the Liverpool & Manchester Railway in 1830, scarcely any new line of

Eckington Station. A special small station of the NMR to serve the Sitwells of nearby Renishaw Hall. Designed by Francis Thompson, with baluster shaped chimneys and, a cylindrical entrance porch like a classical Greek monument.

North portal of Milford Tunnel nearing completion 1840 – North Midland Railway. A detailed drawing of construction, by Samuel Russell. Note the Chevin Signal Tower on the ridge above.

note was opened without illustrations being issued in the form of engravings. Railway directors recognised the publicity value of such illustrations and generally encouraged their production. Thompson was no doubt influenced by the works of the better known railway artists like T.T.Bury and J.C.Bourne, but instead he commissioned the lesser known Russell. Nevertheless, his choice was rewarded with a splendid set of engravings. Russell was exceptional in some respects in that he not only made the original drawings but he then himself transferred these on to the lithograph stones – ensuring accuracy. Russell had a good eye for detail and his drawings convey the quality of the buildings and other works – they are much less romantic than some other railway artists. Russell also illustrated many of the bridges and tunnel mouths – the north portal of Milford Tunnel is shown being worked on

Wingfield Station, NMR and designed by Francis Thompson. Has been authoritively described as "the most perfect of all station houses". Its late Georgian character relieved by a sculpted surround of swags and tassels to the clock and, paired ornamental chimneys. Closed as a station in 1967, the building still survives although in desperately decaying condition.

at near completion. Some of the engravings are special, being zincographs, a then only recently invented experimental process for printing in colour, rather than hand colouring. The great front of the Derby Station is one fine example of this work.

The influential writer John Claudius Loudon who had only just finished his creation of the Derby Arboretum, the first public park in England which opened in 1840, the same year as the station, wrote:-

"Those who wish to see the beautiful engravings of the railway stations... should have recourse to Mr Thompson's splendid work entitled Railway Stations, folio, 1842, price 25 shillings. This work contains engravings of the other beautiful station houses on the same line of railroad, besides the splendid terminus at Derby." Unfortunately, no complete folios seem to have survived.

Loudon went further since he was so impressed by the North Midland buildings and eulogised them in rather flowery words:-

"We cannot sufficiently express our admiration of the public spirit of the directors of the North Midland Railway in causing the erection of such architectural gems along their line of works. They are great ornaments of themselves, and, as they will be seen by many thousands of all ranks, and remain it is to be hoped for several generations standard models of cultivated design, they can hardly fail greatly to improve the general taste of the country. We wish we could see the same spirit actuating the directors of all railroads, so that the rail-

Swinton Station – NMR – Francis Thompson. Like the larger Masborough station it had a classical Greek simplicity. An extremely refined and dignified design. Swinton was the North Midland's station for Doncaster some seven miles away by omnibus.

The historic North Midland Railway Roundhouse designed by Francis Thompson and built in 1839 to house 30 locomotives. Shown in use for repairing Midland Railway locomotives in 1905, and last used for repairing breakdown cranes of British Rail in the 1980s.

The oldest known photograph of Derby Works and Station *c.*1860. In the foreground is the roof of the North Midland Roundhouse behind the clocktower. Flanking are the old North Midland locomotive and carriage workshops. Stephenson's roof cover to Platform 1 is seen beyond, with the rear of the original joint North Midland and Midland Counties Railways Goods Warehouse, another Thompson building.

ways of England might become the most interesting public ways in the world." However, there was another more cautious view point. Francis Wishaw in a book published in 1842, described the various railways that had been opened up to that time. He then went on to set out his own ideas on planning railway works from an evaluation of the pioneer railways. While clearly admiring the architecture on the

View within Derby Works *c.*1890. A number of Kirtley class locomotives alongside the erecting shops. The building with roof ventilators is the original North Midland Railway locomotive shop wing of 1839, since demolished. The taller section to the left survives, part of the clock-tower office building. the Roundhouse lies behind, with one of three original engine entrances seen left, filled in with a window.

North Midland Railway he had reservations over the expenditure:-

"But although highly estimating the elegantly chaste designs which characterise the architecture of the North Midland Stations, we cannot but deplore the growing evil of expending large sums of money on railway appendages. Instead of cottage buildings which, for the traffic of most of the intermediate stopping places on this line, would have been amply sufficient, we find the railway literally ornamented with so many beautiful villas, any one of which would grace the sloping lawn of some domain by nature highly favoured."

He was correct in some respects, since the North Midland soon ran into difficulties after its opening, through over-expenditure in a severely depressed economic period.

After leaving the North Midland, Francis Thompson tried to recover some of the costs of producing Russell's lithographs. The board had originally indicated to him that they would contribute, but in June 1842 the board responded to his request with – "That they do not consider their finances in a state to enable them with justice, to contribute towards the expenses of the drawings." They liked the drawings for their publicity value, but times were hard!

The North Midland had established its headquarters at Derby, and so it built its Railway Works adjacent to the station at a cost of £62,000. The buildings were arranged in a vee layout, about the central engine house which was of a polygon shape of 16 sides, with a conical slated roof crowned by a lantern top for smoke ventilation. The roof was supported on an inner ring of cast-iron columns within the outer brick walls. Inside was a central turntable around which were radiating lines to accommodate some thirty of the small engines of the time.

At right angles about the North Midland roundhouse were two buildings – one wing was the engine workshop, 184 feet long by 70 feet, its roof also supported on cast-iron columns. Attached to this were more, smaller workshops for forges and furnaces. These workshops were solely for repair, no locomotives being built at Derby until September 1851 when Matthew Kirtley's first Midland Railway engine rolled out.

The other wing was the workshop for the carriages, of some 190 feet by 70 feet. Linking these workshops, and in front of the roundhouse were the works offices, topped with a short stone tower, and works clock by the younger Whitehurst, respected clockmakers of Derby. The North Midland workshops had been completed as early as the middle of October 1839, and building railway carriages began soon after.

The North Midland Railway works offices and clocktower today. The original ground floor storey and lower clock-tower designed by Francis Thompson. The large door in the leftward wing is the sole remaining entrance to the Roundhouse, and beyond is the surviving NMR's carriage work-shops.

At the north end of the station building on Railway Terrace, the North Midland and Midland Counties jointly built a substantial two-storey goods warehouse – 165 feet by 90 feet, costing £11,000. There were five openings for wagons with short lines in, off turntables on the railway line. Inside was a raised platform for loading and off-loading goods. In the street wall were more openings for loading goods on to carts.

All these buildings were designed by Francis Thompson, and the contracts were supervised by him under his employment by the North Midland. They were all built by Thomas Jackson of Pimlico the main contractor for the station and the North Midland Railway Works. To build the full extent of the station and works over a level area, the land had to be raised some eight feet at the north end, necessitating the carting in of many loads of fill material. This raised level can be seen from the steep slope of the old works approach road opposite the Brunswick Inn. Raising the land here also resulted in the Inn being provided with an upper and lower cellar at its north end.

There was argument with Thomas Jackson over his claim for the final costs of the extensive earthworks, and this was reported to a board meeting on 7 August 1841. Robert Stephenson advised the board that "no further progress can be made in settlement of these accounts until Mr Jackson shall have furnished... a more explicit statement according to the request repeatedly made by Mr Thompson." Despite this, it did not stop the board soon after on 25 August from letting further contracts to Jackson for clerks and porters houses at a number of the intermediate stations.

Back in September 1840 Thomas Jackson had also contracted to build small goods warehouses designed by Thompson, each 42 feet square, for the company at Mexborough, Barnsley and Wakefield. There may have been others. The surviving warehouse by the line at Ambergate was

Station clerks and porters' houses at Ambergate. North Midland Railway 1841, designed by Francis Thompson, built by Thomas Jackson.

Goods shed at Ambergate. North Midland Railway 1841 – designed by Francis Thompson, built by Thomas Jackson.

End view of the Midland Counties repair workshops of 1839.

Right: **Midland Counties Railway workshops at Derby 1839. Engine repair workshops in single storey section – carriage workshops in two-storey section.**

Far right: **Interior view of the Midland Counties repair workshops of 1839.**

one of those built by Jackson.

All in all Jackson undertook a considerable amount of contract work for the North Midland Company. In addition to all these buildings he also built the Derby railway houses and the Brunswick Inn for the company. For the construction of the line he undertook two major contracts – the Belper North contract of £60,500 and the Bullbridge, Ambergate contract of £63,000 which included the Cromford Canal aqueduct. Added to which he built the Derby Midland Hotel at his own expense.

Midland Counties Railway Workshops

The Midland Counties also built its main workshops at Derby. For the maintenance of its engines, carriages and wagons. These were substantial, and were located immediately adjacent to the North

Midland Counties Railway.

CONTRACT FOR WORKS AT DERBY STATION.

THE Directors of the Company meet at the KING'S HEAD, in Loughborough, on Thursday, the 14th day of March, when they will be prepared to receive TENDERS for the under-mentioned portion of the Works, viz.,—for building and completing an Engine Shed, 130 feet long by 47 feet wide; also, a Coke Store, adjoining the same, with a Water Tank of Cast Metal fixed upon it, 40 feet by 20 feet, and 4 feet 6 inches deep; also about 600 lineal feet of Iron Roof for the Passenger Station, with Platforms, &c. complete; but the Ironwork and Masonry may be tendered for separately.

Plans and Specifications of the Works may be seen at the Office of Mr. WOODHOUSE, Engineer, Leicester, on or after the 1st day of March.

As soon as the Plans of the Offices, repairing Establishment, &c., are prepared for inspection, notice will be given, fixing a time to receive Tenders for executing the same.

By order,

J. F. BELL, Secretary.

High-street, Leicester, 20th February, 1839.

Advertisement for contract for building engine shed, coke store and water tank for Midland Counties Railway at Derby, 20 February 1839.

Midland's carriage workshop. One building was for repairing and building carriages, with a paint shop adjacent. Next

Midland Counties Railway engine shed, Derby, 1839.

again was another workshop for engine repair and maintenance. The larger workshop was 200 feet by 93 feet and, the other 93 feet by 88 feet. Immediately beyond was the Midland Counties engine shed 134 feet by 52 feet. These buildings were built of brick with stone dressings, and slated roofs. The roof structures were of timber trusses, with spans supported on intermediate cast-iron columns.

Included in the buildings were a copper smith's workshop, brass furnaces, turning, and pattern makers workshops, offices, and a boiler house. The specification detailing the scope of the works was dated 13 April 1839 and was issued from the Midland Counties' engineer's office at Leicester. It specified that tenders had to be delivered to J.F.Bell, the secretary, at the railway office, Nottingham by 22 April. It also required that the whole works were to be fully completed by 1 September that year. The designer of this impressive range of buildings is unrecorded. But it is quite possible that it was William Parsons a well known Leicester architect, since he was engaged by the Midland Counties to produce the designs and drawings for their Leicester station – their headquarters offices.

Prior to this, on 20 February 1839 the MCR invited tenders for their engine shed, together with a coke store, and water tank, at Derby which they considered at the board meeting on 14 March at the King's Head in Loughborough. Also to be included in that tender was a requirement for "about 600 feet of iron roof for the passenger station, with platforms etc. complete". This was before the final agreement that the North Midland Company should undertake the whole of the Derby Station building to Francis Thompson's design.

It wasn't until after the Derby station contract had been let to Thomas Jackson on 11 June 1839, that the Midland Counties Company advertised invitation to tender on 19 June for their Leicester Station and for these tenders to be sent in by 17 July. The plans and specifications were only available for viewing from 1 July, at the office of T.J.Woodhouse the resident engineer, at Humberstone Cottage near Leicester.

The first general meeting of shareholders of the new Midland Company was held on Tuesday 16 July 1844 in the Old

Hampton-in-Arden Station 1839 – Birmingham & Derby Junction Railway – small engine workshop building beyond.

Midland Counties engine shed. This continued to be used for many years for Midland Railway shareholders' meetings, (presumably well cleaned up beforehand) until one unfortunate attender was knocked down and killed by a train while crossing the lines. The meetings were then transferred to the floor of the large warehouse on Railway Terrace, until in 1857 the Midland Railway built the splendid new shareholder's room alongside the station entrance.

Birmingham & Derby Junction Railway buildings.

A smaller concern than the other two railways, it originally had its headquarters' offices at Waterloo Street, Birmingham, until the company extended its line into central Birmingham. For that it built a new terminus station at Lawley Street, with accompanying headquarters offices, opened in February 1842. The company had initially built a modest sized locomotive repair workshop at Hampton-in-Arden. This was used until replaced with the new expanded locomotive workshops at Lawley Street in June 1842, after which the Hampton workshop was closed. The company's only building at Derby was a "handsome engine shed of brick" 150 feet by 48 feet, with a smith's workshop and some office accommodation adjacent, all sited adjacent to its line into the station, near the London Road bridge. It was built for around £4,000 by Messrs Thomas and William Cooper of Derby, who had just completed the Royal Hotel, Athenaeum, and the adjacent Derby & Derbyshire Bank in the Cornmarket.

The North Midland Railway Village

Happy are those who see beauty in modest spots where others see nothing. Everything is beautiful, the whole secret lies in knowing how to interpret it.

Camille Pissarro (1830-1903)

IN EARLY February 1841 the North Midland Company let a contract to Thomas Jackson to build a group of houses close to Derby Station to accommodate a major number of its employees. The houses were to be built in a triangular layout, as a small railway village – the form of the layout being dictated by the shape of the available site. It was fronted by Railway Terrace, the extension of the old Siddals Lane up to the station, and the branch off the Derby Canal to the north. The new streets in the layout in addition to Railway Terrace, were called North Street (changed to Calvert Street in *c.*1870) and Midland Terrace (soon changed to Midland Place) – the names thus spelling out the name of the North Midland Company. Two more integral short streets were named Leeds Place and Sheffield Place.

Houses, Shops and Railway Staff

This group of houses was one of the earliest railway villages to be built. Not quite the first, since that distinction belonged to Wolverton where the London & Birmingham Railway built its railway works, with streets of houses adjacent, soon after its opening in September 1838. By 1840 that railway had built some 80 houses at Wolverton. Other railways had hitherto built single houses at crossings, and for a ticket clerk at intermediate stations. Earlier, the Liverpool & Manchester Railway had built small groups of cottages

North Midland Railway houses in triangle fronting Railway Terrace built 1841-42 by Thomas Jackson and designed by Francis Thompson.

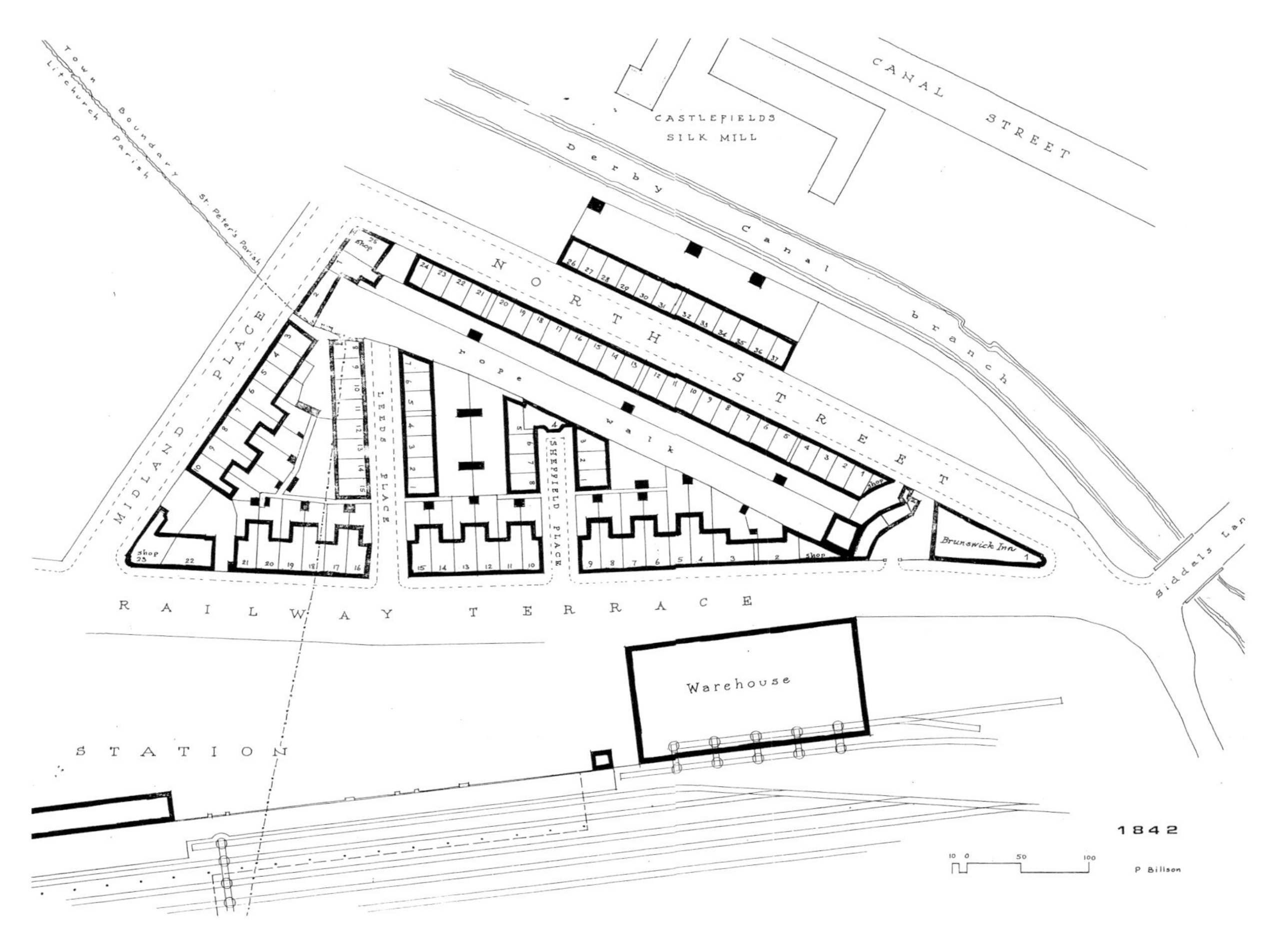

Layout of the North Midland Railway houses at Derby. 1842.

for employees – six houses at Chat Moss in 1830, then similar groups at Edge Hill and Sutton. But after Wolverton, Derby would be the next place to have a railway village.

Building railway houses in those early days of railway developments, ensured that the company's employees were adequately housed and in locations where they were needed for work. They were also a sound investment for the companies, providing a good return on capital invested while still only charging a reasonable rent to the tenant. No record of early rent charges for the Derby houses has survived, but by way of some comparison, railway houses built soon after at Crewe were being let at rents varying from 2s (10p) to 4s 3d (21p) per week according to size and amenity. Since this represented a return of only four to five per cent on capital, it did indicate a degree of benevolent philanthropy towards the employees.

The North Midland Company built a total of 92 houses in the group at Derby of which 80 were within the triangle, the other 12 were over on the canal branch side of North Street, approximately midway along the road. Also incorporated within the triangle were four shops to serve the needs of the inhabitants – a butcher on North Street, a grocer/baker on the corner with Midland Place, a bookseller/stationer on the corner of Railway Terrace, and a general provision shop along the Terrace next to the Brunswick Inn, the latter providing the other essential component of any community – a public house. The boundary between Derby and the Litchurch Township ran across the site, with 13 houses built wholly on the Litchurch side, together with parts of another five dwellings. There was a sizeable community in the railway houses when completed. Some 586 men, women and children are listed in the 1851 Census Return, plus others residing and staying

Parish boundary marker denoting line between (St) Peter's Parish and Litchurch, on plinth of No.2 Midland Place.

North Midland Railway houses on Midland Place, with former shop on corner – looking towards station front of 1892.

over at the Brunswick Inn.

All the houses were soundly constructed and for urban industrial housing all were surprisingly roomy for the time, particularly the houses fronting Midland Place and Railway Terrace. In many respects they anticipated a standard of housing that did not generally begin to appear until much later, well after the Public Health Act of 1875 compelled the making of by-laws for better urban standards.

The houses fronting Railway Terrace and Midland Place are larger and more distinctive. They are well proportioned in

Only known view of the North Midland Railway houses on corner of Midland Place before demolition to make way for the Midland Railway Institute. View taken in 1891 through 'green' decorations for the state visit to Derby of Queen Victoria.

appearance, with a plain late Georgian character. Those houses now gone, which formed the corner of Railway Terrace and Midland Place were larger than any of the others and were three storeys high above ground, plus cellars below. The probable reason for their extra height was to complete the visual composition of the square around the front of the station building. It has to be remembered that all the buildings at and around the new station were built on open land, so that at the time there was a clear unobstructed view of the station to the public and prospective passengers on the main approach down Station (Midland) Road from the London Road. It was all calculated to impress.

The houses along North Street and in Sheffield and Leeds Places were of a smaller, simpler character, more akin to other early industrial housing, with two rooms up, two down, and a basement kitchen and stores.

A superficial look gives the impression that there are just two individual plan types; and possibly another two or three originally if we include the lost houses on the corner where the Institute now stands. In actuality there were over 14 plan variants to fit the houses into the site limitations.

One of these constraints was the fact there was originally a rope-walk running across the back of the Railway Terrace houses and occupying the near half of the subsequent North Street house gardens. This can be seen on the 1852 Local Board of Health map. There is no sign of it in the 1835 New Map of Derby by I.T.Swanwick, so it is more than probable that it was set up for the production of ropes in connection with the railways. It also must have been laid out only shortly before the houses were planned in late 1840, so that the houses then had to be fitted around the rope-walk.

At the North Midland board meeting on 13 February 1841 'The agreement with Mr Jackson for the cottages at Derby was put before the directors for sealing.' Then at the board meeting of 28 October 1841 the directors discussed proposals "respecting the occupation of some of the houses of the company lately executed at Derby..." and went on to establish an Estates Committee to deal with this matter, as well as the lands and buildings of the company generally.

It is probable that the North Midland intended to build more houses at Derby – at least to have completed the row on the north side of North Street, but there is no information on this.

In the early summer of 1841 the board found it necessary to appoint a committee to look into economies on their railway – abandonment of building more houses may well have been one of the resultant cuts.

In 1892 the Midland Railway built a new Staff Institute on the corner of Railway Terrace and Midland Place. To accommodate this new building the company had to demolish 15 of the original North Midland houses. Others were necessarily lost in enabling the Derbyshire Historic Building Trust to carry out the conservation scheme completed in 1982, for the 55 houses now surviving.

Unfortunately none of the houses were occupied when the National Census was taken in June 1841. But, we do have a list of 85 householder employees, giving names and occupations in Glover's *Directory of Derby 1843*. This list had been taken in 1842. Many people listed had moved on by the time of the census of 1851 but others remained in the houses and had become employees of the Midland Railway. Some who started with the North Midland as plain tradesmen or minor employees eventually ascended to more senior positions. For example James Melrose started as a smith with the North Midland and eventually rose to be in charge of the Smiths and Wheel workshops for the Midland Railway. Robert Harland who joined the North Midland as a joiner, by 1851 had become a rail carriage builder and followed this by becoming chief foreman of carriage and wagon production for the Midland. William Athey started as an engine driver and later became the first regular locomotive inspector at Derby – he would eventually become the Midland's locomotive running foreman. Reuben Chambers who started work as a fitter for the North Midland, by 1871 was yard foreman for the Midland Railway. Some of the original occupants stayed in this group of houses for many years – some in the same house – others moved into different houses, and then others left and moved elsewhere. Sons followed their fathers into railway service. Joseph Mycock a railway porter was an original occupant of a North Midland house, but he had died by 1851. His widow still lived there and by that

North Midland Railway houses of 1841-42 on North Street, now renamed Calvert Street. original butcher's shop at the near end.

time his two young sons, Henry only 13 years old, and Thomas a mere 11, were employed by the Midland as "crane boys at the station."

Some houses had just man and wife in occupancy. But several houses in 1851 were extremely crowded with nine or ten people in a two bedroomed cottage. There were 11 occupants at the cottage of Thomas Edwards, an engine driver at no.8 (now 29) North Street. Even this was eclipsed by an astonishing 12 at no.13 (now 39) North Street, where Joseph Nadin a rail porter and his wife Catherine lived with their ten children, the eldest aged 19, the youngest just one year old.

At no.11 Railway Terrace in 1851 there lived Sarah Smith with her two unmarried sons Frederick and William, aged 25 and 22 years respectively – both were engine drivers. Sarah's granddaughter Sophia Smith aged 18, from Liverpool lived with them as a servant. Sarah was a widow aged 68, so she might have had older family who had gone away, and the sons were late arrivals in her married life.

In the late 1850s the Midland Railway carried out experiments to substitute coal, for the more expensive coke which had hitherto been used as locomotive fuel. Experiments at Derby works had produced a potential solution, and in 1859 a new engine was turned out incorporating these modifications. The locomotive was driven for the trials by Frederick Smith, attended by William Athey the locomotive inspector, who as a plain engine driver had been living at no.22 (now 57) North Street in 1851. Frederick Smith would eventually succeed Athey as locomotive inspector when he was later promoted to the post of running foreman.

There is evidence that ordinary people did move about the country quite a bit in those days. Robert Harland, mentioned already, and his wife were born in County Durham, the eldest son was born in Dorking, Surrey, the second son born in Liverpool. Robert Harland would be about 35 years old when he joined the North Midland Railway.

The range of occupations of the early householders is extremely varied – engine drivers, firemen, engine cleaners, guards, porters, switchmen/pointsmen, smiths, fitters, coppersmiths, sawyers, painters, joiners, engine and coach inspectors, warehousemen, book-keepers, station master, locomotive superintendent, labourers. What also emerges from the list is that both in the North Midland time, and during the first few decades of the Midland Railway era, employees were allocated houses without discrimination over their occupations. There is a school of opinion that the Railway Terrace houses were always reserved for employees of higher status. If this was so then it was not until the end of the nineteenth century. In 1851 Edward Walker a labourer at the cheese warehouse lived at no.21 Railway Terrace, between Joseph Sunter at no.20 a foreman in the loco department, and Matthew Kirtley the locomotive engineer superintendent living at no.22. Elsewhere in that year along Railway Terrace were ticket collectors, fitters, a goods manager, engine drivers, porters.

On a December night in 1850 a small group of Midland Railway employees met in one of the rooms of the Brunswick Inn and agreed to form a Reading Society. A letter had appeared in the *Derby Mercury* in February 1848 signed by a Mr Newton and a Mr Lewis criticising the absence of a library for the use of the Midland Company's railway servants. It referred to the provisions that had been made by the Grand Junction Railway at Crewe, and the Great Western at Swindon – which included a lecture hall, baths and a mechanics institute. The letter continued,

North Midland Railway houses of 1841-42 in Sheffield Place, after restoration by the Derbyshire Historic Buildings Trust in 1981.

saying that although between 4,000 and 5,000 were employed by the Midland at Derby "not one single farthing has yet been appointed toward the intellectual culture of the moral training of the men and boys in their employ."

After their meeting at the Brunswick Inn the railwaymen approached the directors for accommodation and support for their Reading Society. The directors in turn granted the men the use of the end houses nos.8 and 9 Leeds Place, which were conveniently vacant, to use as rooms for a reading room and a subscription library. There also, evening classes were soon set up to teach reading, writing, grammar and arithmetic to the railwaymen. This small beginning was soon to be improved by a larger space on the ground floor beneath the new shareholders' room in the block added to the station building in 1857, and would finally culminate in the splendid Midland Institute of 1892 on Railway Terrace – with its extensive library, concert hall, meeting and games rooms, dining room and café. There the members of the Midland Natural History Society, the Horticultural Society and other such groups were able to meet to further their interests.

The Midland Company additionally provided sports facilities for its staff, with a cricket ground being laid out as early as 1852 on the Old Meadows by the railway line. This was later followed on adjacent land with an athletic ground complete with pavilion.

There was also a Midland Railway Friendly Society for the support of staff. This followed on from the earlier North Midland Railway Friendly Society which that company required "all porters and other subordinate servants of the company" to join.

North Midland Railway houses nos. 1 to 4 Leeds Place as later converted to the Midland Railway ticket printing office, pictured in 1977, demolished in 1980.

In the late 1870s four cottages nos.1 to 4 Leeds Place were taken over and converted for use as the Midland Railway's ticket printing office. Where the tickets had been printed before this date is uncertain. There was a distinct change in the design of the tickets around this time, and the earliest known of this new form is dated June 1878. The familiar small pasteboard railway ticket was the invention of Thomas Edmonson (1792-1851) in 1839 when employed as station master at an intermediate station on the Newcastle & Carlisle Railway. He also invented the first ticket-printing machine, and the well-known date press in about 1848. As early as 1841 the North Midland Railway and the other two companies joining at Derby were all using the Edmonson system. Where their tickets were printed is unknown, but it seems the Midland Railway after its creation in 1844 centralised all ticket printing at Derby. These former houses continued in ticket printing use right through to the end of the Midland Railway in 1923, then on in the LMS era until May 1934 when ticket printing was transferred to Euston. The original printing machines were made by Waterlow and Co and continued in use until the office closed at Derby. These premises never reverted to houses but were in various uses, finally by a long established firm of local printers J.H.Hall and Sons, before final vacation and sale by British Rail with the rest of the houses. They were necessarily demolished in 1980 as part of the conservation scheme.

Other houses were used temporarily for Midland Railway offices. In 1852 no.14 on Railway Terrace was used as the telegraph office under its manager J.A.Warwick – also, nos.19 and 20 were at a time used for the Midland's goods superintendent. These all eventually returned to domestic use.

George Henry Rickman, the first station master at Derby from 1840, was born at Shotton near Deal, Kent. In earlier employment he was a stage-coach driver on the London-Dover Road. He moved to London, and eventually came to Derby after obtaining the post with the North Midland Railway. When the houses were completed he moved into no.22 Railway Terrace, one of the larger houses on the corner with Midland Place. Rickman

The Royal Hotel on corner of the Cornmarket in Derby, built 1839, with the Athenaeum of the same group fronting Victoria Street.

continued on into Midland Railway employment. By 1850 he had become so highly esteemed in his job that a special subscription was raised by his friends and regular railway travellers who knew him. The splendid sum of £588 was collected, and it was presented to Rickman by the Mayor of Derby, in a fine velvet purse embroidered in gold thread, at a special assembly at the Royal Hotel, Derby on 1 November 1850, with many toasts and congratulations.

George Rickman and his family moved over to live at the Station building when Matthew Kirtley came to Derby to take up the post of first superintendent of the locomotive and carriage department of the newly formed Midland in 1844. Kirtley moved into no.22 Railway Terrace and lived there until the 1850s when he went to live at The Mount on Burton Road. George Rickman then moved back into no.22 until his death. Rickman was accidentally killed on 1 November 1866 on the railway that he had long served. For some inexplicable reason he was walking within the railway lines after supervising a leaving train to King's Cross, London, when shortly after he was run down by a train from Nottingham. Some 800 Midland Railway employees followed the funeral procession to the Uttoxeter Road cemetery, and an estimated near 15,000 people turned out to watch it pass. George Rickman was followed into Midland service by his son Frederick Gladwin Rickman who started as a railway clerk. George's brother Thomas also joined the Midland in July 1845 as a passenger train guard.

Another person who lived in one of the houses was Edward Clulow the progenitor of the book shop in Irongate, Derby, that still bears his name. Clulow was born in 1813 at Hathern, Leicestershire and came to Derby to work as a book-keeper for the North Midland. With his wife and family he moved into no.8 Midland Place when it was finished in 1842. Sometime about 1849 he had become head clerk in the Midland's booking office, and had moved into no.23 Railway Terrace, the house and shop on the corner of Midland Place. From the shop Clulow was running a business as a bookseller, stationer and newsagent, in addition to his railway employment. He had also secured the right to trade on the station itself, and continued to do so until W.H.Smith took over the rights in *c.*1859. On 31 December 1850 Clulow bought a substantial plot of land from the Castlefields Estate trustees on the corner of Midland Road and Park Street. On half this site he built a new shop and house for himself. Within a few years he was running a business there under the style E.Clulow & Son 'Printers, bookseller, binders, subscription library, and agents to the Railway Passengers Assurance Co', together with another shop in the centre of Derby. Clulow also obtained the concession to open a branch post office in the Midland Road shop in 1865 and from there he supplied all the Midland Railway Company's postal needs at Derby.

One of the most exciting and frightening events in the history of the railway houses and the station was probably on the night of 18 June 1868. Just before 9.00pm a pointsman named Blackwell was on duty at the north end of the station platform, when he saw fire suddenly break out of the windows of the top floor of the big goods warehouse next to him. After the amalgamation in 1844 the building had passed into Midland Railway ownership and use, but after the transfer of the Goods Depot to St Mary's Wharf, Little Chester in the late 1850s, the building became mainly used as a cheese warehouse let to the Derby firm of Cox, Smith & Co and two other smaller cheese factors. The top floor had been retained by the Midland for the storage of unclaimed goods from the railway – a lost property store for which a sale was held each July. Back in August 1843 it was reported that among the "surplus stores" to be sold by the North Midland were – "144 umbrellas, 19 parasols, 16 mackintosh coats and 10 top coats". The store in 1868 was pretty well full and the fire probably started after men had been in sorting goods for the next sale. A smaller warehouse also for cheese had been built adjacent on the south side in the late 1840s and was used by Edward Etches another firm of Derby cheese factors.

Blackwell immediately gave the alarm and the Midland Company's fire engine quickly came to tackle the blaze from the station side. Mounted messengers were hurriedly sent for the town fire brigade, while the company, alarmed by the size of the fire, also sent telegrams to Trent, Burton, Nottingham and Leicester for their station fire engines. The fire became so intense that the Nottingham town brigade was also sent for. With great despatch the Nottingham brigade, with its steam fire-engine under the direction of its superintendent, plus their chief constable left by rail for Derby at 10.15pm and joined the other fire fighters at the warehouse. At about 4.30am the roof had fallen in and flames were shooting out of the lower windows on the Railway Terrace side. The heat was so intense that the windows and doors of the houses opposite began to char and there was risk of the fire spreading not only to the station but also across to the houses. The occupants had all been got out safely with as much of their possessions as was practicable. To protect themselves and to save the houses the firemen wrapped themselves in wet blankets and played their jets on the houses. The houses were saved but the warehouse was left a gutted shell. The total loss of cheese was valued at £20,000 of which Cox, Smith and Co lost £8,000 worth. The Etches warehouse next door suffered some damage, but the fire was prevented from entering. Some 40 tons of Etches cheese was brought out into the street for safety, but it was found to have been "pretty well toasted".

The Midland Company was sufficiently frightened by this serious fire on their property that it quickly decided to set up a proper fire brigade of its own. Frederick William Medcalf was taken on from the London Metropolitan Fire Brigade in later 1868 to organise this and become its superintendent. The company also bought a superior new Shand-Mason fire engine for the brigade, replacing this with an even better one by Merryweathers in 1873. Soon after his arrival in Derby, Medcalf moved into no.7 Railway Terrace, curiously immediately opposite the scene of the severe fire and the cause of his employment.

Mention has been made of John Alfred Warwick who became manager of the Midland Railway Telegraph Office, which for a while around 1852 was temporarily located in no.14 Railway Terrace. Warwick had another significance. After he came to Derby to take up a post in the signals and telegraph department in around 1851, he became friendly with another young man who had recently opened premises in Irongate, Derby as a printer, publisher and bookseller. This was Richard Keene who was later to achieve particular significance as a pioneer topographical photographer. In the early days of their friendship they became interested in the then quite new art of photography, through contacts with the Revd Edward Abney another enthusiast in the town, who enjoyed a somewhat tenuous connection

The Brunswick Railway and Commercial Inn, Railway Terrace, Derby of 1841. Built as part of the railway houses group by the North Midland Railway - builder Thomas Jackson - architect Francis Thompson.

with the pioneer of photography, William H.Fox-Talbot of Lacock Abbey. Keene and Warwick became keen amateur photographers and made joint expeditions into Derbyshire recording the county in some of the earliest photographs. Warwick himself took early official photographs for the Midland Railway, but after his promotion to superintendent he recommended that his friend Keene, who by then had become a professional, be employed as freelance official photographer. Keene was employed in this way through the 1860s and 1870s until he found other work too pressing. In 1882 Warwick persuaded the board to appoint Keene's assistant Thomas Scotton (1844-1894) in his place, and the company responded by making Scotton its first full-time staff photographer. He was joined the following year by his own son as assistant, and together the Scottons built up a substantial archive of Midland Railway locomotives, carriages, railway stock pictures and general scenes.

The Brunswick Railway and Commercial Inn

The Brunswick Inn was built by the North Midland Railway as an integral part of the railway village. It provided both for the refreshment of the railway employees and for accommodation for commercial and other travellers. The Brunswick appears to have been the first ever specifically built railway inn, its intended trade clearly indicated in its first title 'The Brunswick Railway and Commercial Inn'. The inn was designed to be in character with the rest of the houses along Railway Terrace. In the Brunswick Inn we have a remarkably interesting example of a period of transition in the history of the English pub. Although built as late as 1842 it still retains the characteristics of an earlier nineteenth-century urban public house, where in all essentials it was still a private house with parts open for the public to enter. As Mark Girouard says in his book 'Victorian Pubs' - "Above all, a public house from the outside looked exactly like a private house, except for the signboard hanging over the door." The Brunswick Inn had the classic range of rooms of the more substantial public house of the time. Each room providing for the distinct stratification of society in the Victorian age - a tap room (bar), a smoke room (saloon) and a parlour (best room). It also had a small private bar or snug for private groups and sometimes used for women only. The rooms would have had no service bars. The curved internal sash window off the hall is a remarkable survivor of "the bar or office, to which all enquiries are addressed and all orders given... so that the bar mistress may observe all comers and goers as they pass." Service would have been by pot-boys

Advertisement of the opening of The Brunswick Railway & Commercial Inn by its first proprietor Harvey Lane in late June 1842.

THE BRUNSWICK Railway and Commercial INN, Railway Terrace, adjoining the Station, Derby.
H. LANE begs to inform the Travelling Community, that this House is now open for the reception of Families and Commercial Gentlemen. The Charges are framed with a view to the strictest economy consistent with the best quality of articles.
H. L. begs to assure all those who may favour him with their patronage, that the Wines and Spirits have been selected with the greatest care, and that no expense has been spared to render every appointment in this Establishment both comfortable and convenient to its Visitors.

TERMS:

Breakfast, plain, ...	1s. 6d.
Ditto, with Meat, &c., ...	2s. 0d.
Dinner, ...	2s. 0d.
Tea, ...	1s. 6d.
Supper, ...	1s. 6d.
Beds, ...	2s. 0d.
Wine, ...	5s. per Bottle.

No fees are allowed to be taken by any servant in the Establishment. Horses and Carriages let to Hire.—H. LANE, Proprietor.

bringing each customer his drink. Ale was produced in the brew-house in the yard. Upstairs there was a large room which still survives, where the landlord and his overnight guests sat down for dinner and a convivial evening, with 'mine host' sitting at the head of the large table.

The Inn opened to trade on or about 27 June 1842 with Mr Harvey Lane the proprietor. Harvey Lane later advertised in the local press that his opening dinner would take place on 20 September that year and announced that he would be most happy to meet his friends at 'the festive board'. He was not actually the lessee of the premises, that was a Mr Singleton who had taken a lease from the North Midland Company for seven years at £230 per annum from 1 May 1842; and it was he who had borne the cost of £392 for "finishing and fitting up the inn."

Almost all older inn names have an historical significance – in this case it was in honour of the young Queen Victoria, who at that time was known as of the Royal House of Brunswick, before this was later changed so that she became in continuation, the last monarch of the House of Hanover. The Brunswick Inn brewed its own ale in a brewhouse in the yard and continued to do so well into the twentieth century. The main yard was divided into three parts by low walls, with the brewhouse sitting in the middle section.

In the adjacent small yard next to Railway Terrace was a stable, with a pig-sty adjacent next to the brewhouse. Alvaston centenarian Mrs Gertrude Dakin, who died in 1990 in her 104th year, lived as a young girl at no.10 Railway Terrace from 1899 to 1911 recalled – "Going to the Brunswick Inn was fun. My mother used to send us there to fetch a ha'porth of balm to make ginger beer – that trip was best on Thursday, pay day (for the Midland men), when the landlady would have piles of change laid out on the bar ready to break up the men's sovereigns."

During its long life in railway ownership the inn passed through many tenants. It was purchased from the LMS Railway in May 1947 by Hardy and Hanson – brewers of Kimberley, Nottinghamshire, just prior to the nationalisation of British Railways. Hardy and Hanson ran the house with tenants until the doors closed in 1974. The old pub remained vacant, deteriorating until decay reached a very advanced state, before being rescued and rehabilitated by the Derbyshire Historic Buildings Trust as part of their Railway Houses Conservation Scheme. It was sold privately in May 1987, and the new owners sympathetically completed the fitting out as a pub once again. The Brunswick Inn reopened its doors to trade on 3 October 1987. In June 1990 the owners went further and built a new brewhouse on the premises, so that the Brunswick Inn once again proudly serves its own beers.

The Creation of the Midland Railway

Railway travelling is a delightful improvement of human life... Everything is near, everything is immediate - time, distance and delay are abolished.

Sydney Smith (1771-1845)

THE opening of the railways brought profound changes in this country. Before this happened life moved slowly; in many senses hardly at all. The railways greatly accelerated the rate and change of life in Britain into a modern industrial nation. Towns, trade and industry all developed faster. The mass conveyance of goods around the country was facilitated and, over greater extent than on the earlier canals. For example, with the greater speed in the delivery of goods, William Jackson - fishmonger of Full Street, Derby was able to advertise in 1843 that he could "supply fish - cod, skate, haddock and salmon, fresh from London every morning." Of special effect was the revolutionary opportunity for everyone, including quite ordinary people to travel for the first time quickly and easily. The numbers of railway passengers travelling nationally increased dramatically over the 14-year period from 1838 to 1851. In 1838 there were 5.4 million travellers, rising rapidly to 21.7 million in 1843. This had continued to rise with 54.4 million in 1848 and by 1851 there were 79.7 million.

Another significant change brought about by the railways was the abandonment of local time and its replacement by standard, London 'Railway time' in around 1840 to enable trains to run and keep to timetables. The introduction of the electric telegraph brought complete synchronisation.

Prior to the coming of the railways the stagecoach system had developed to a high degree with a network over the whole country. In 1820 there were some 1,500 coach departures from London every 24 hours - nearly 300 going northward. But by 1842, one proprietor's 73 former departures had dropped to a mere three. By 1844 the last Royal Mail coach had driven out of London, its successors transferred to the railway lines.

In 1839 some 30 coaches, including the Royal Mail were running daily through Derby - linking the town with London, Birmingham, Nottingham, Manchester, Sheffield and Leeds. By mid-1840 all these towns were linked to Derby by railway lines. The Royal Mail had been transferred to the Birmingham & Derby Junction Railway soon after it opened in 1839, and it followed on to the Midland Counties and the North Midland after they opened: running through from London to Sheffield via Derby from 16 July 1840, then on to York from 19 August that year. The Royal Mail's Travelling Post Office followed, eventually running right through to Newcastle via Derby in June 1845. The coaching routes were soon closing, with only four coaching services leaving Derby in 1842. While there were many benefits on the opening of the railways, and new employment to be had on their construction and service, the consequences were disastrous for the coach operators, the old established coaching inns and, the many people in related employment.

But there was opportunity for other enterprises and when the station opened in 1840 a certain William Wallace Wallis, a coach operator living in Friar Gate, with offices in King Street and Sadler Gate,

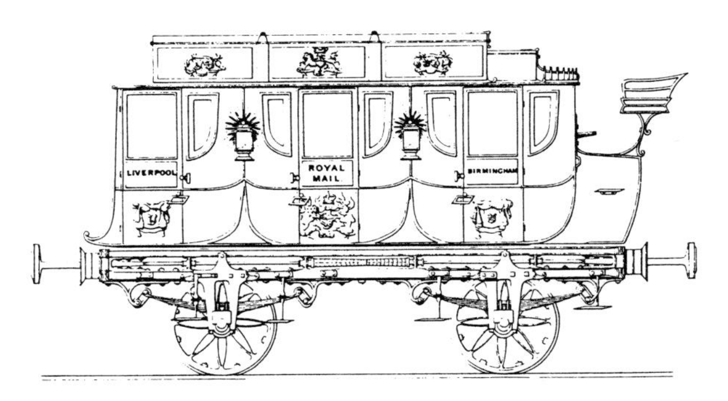

Type of early Royal Mail carriage as used on the Grand Junction Railway 1840 and similarly over the North Midland, Midland Counties, and Birmingham & Derby Junction Railway lines from 1839.

Advertisement by William Wallace Wallis of his venture into conveying goods and merchandise by railways. *Derby Mercury*, October 1840.

GOODS BY RAILWAYS.

W. W. WALLIS begs most respectfully to inform his Friends and the Public, that finding his business of Mail and Coach Proprietor, in which he has been so long engaged, gradually declining in consequence of the opening of Railways, and feeling highly gratified for the support and patronage which he has so many years received, is induced still to devote himself to the promotion of public accommodation, and has directed his attention to the establishing of an Improved System of Carriage for GOODS and MERCHANDIZE of all description, to every part of the Kingdom. This System he has at length matured by making the necessary arrangements with influential Railway Companies, and is enabled to offer to the Public all the advantages of Expedition and Economy, which this new mode of conveyance alone possesses. With confidence in the great improvements which he contemplates in the conveyance of Goods, he ventures to found his claim for support on the following ground, that the charge for Carriage will include every item, viz., delivery, porterage, cartage, &c.

W. W. W. also begs to state that he is not in any way connected with Canals; full reliance may be placed on all Goods entrusted to his charge being forwarded by Railway only.

Goods taken in, Orders received, and every information given relative to the above business, at his OFFICE and WAREHOUSE, opposite the BELL INN, SADLER GATE, DERBY, where all communications on the subject of the Merchandize business will be promptly attended to.

Goods intended to be forwarded by his conveyance will be received by the undermentioned Agents, to whose care W. W. W. respectfully requests they may be consigned.

London, ...Chaplin and Horne, Hambro' Wharf, Thames-street.
—— Swan-with-two-Necks, Lad-lane.
—— Spread Eagle, Gracechurch-street.
—— Universal Office, Regent-circus.
—— Cross Keys, Wood-street.
—— George and Blue Boar, Holborn.
—— Griffins, Green Man, Oxford-street.
—— Golden Cross, Charing Cross.
—— And at their Office, Camden Station.
Birmingham, ...Hardy, Lawton and Co., St. Martin's-lane.
Bristol and Bath,...Haines, Bland and Co.
Liverpool, ...Junction Railway Office.
Manchester, ...Ditto Ditto.
Nottingham, ...Hardy, Lawton and Co., Hounds-gate.
Lincoln, ...Black Goat's Inn.
Newark, ...Hardy, Lawton and Co.
Grantham, ...Mr. Burbridge, George Hotel.
Hull, ...J. Nevinson, Wellington-street.
Leicester, ...Chaplin, Horne and Co.
Leeds, ...M. Outhwaite, Royal Hotel.

W. W WALLIS begs to solicit a share of public patronage, to deserve a continuance of which no exertions shall be wanting on his part to ensure the punctual and early delivery of all Goods entrusted to his care.

Advertisement by Hannah Spencer of the New Inn, Derby dating from 1842 informing the public that the new omnibus runs from the inn to meet each train.

HANNAH SPENCER, NEW INN, King Street, Derby, FAMILY and COMMERCIAL INN, and Posting House, begs to inform the Public, that her house affords superior accommodation to Families, and Commercial Gentlemen, whether travelling by Railway, Coach, or in their own Carriages. Neat Post Chaises, good horses, and steady drivers are in constant readiness to forward Families. Coaches to Manchester, Nottingham, Newcastle, &c., every day. The Omnibus runs from her house to meet every train. Good Stabling, Lock-up Coach-houses, and every convenience attached to her establishment.

started the first horse-drawn omnibus service in the town. This ran from the New Inn, King Street, the Old Bell Hotel in Sadler Gate and then via the Corn Market, connecting up at various inns and posting houses *en route* to the station. The Samuel Russell 1841 engraving of the station clearly depicts the Wallis omnibus picking up passengers outside. A similar omnibus operated from Ambergate station to Matlock Bath twice a day to convey visitors to the spa hotels. The fare was 1s 6d (7½p) including luggage.

In 1841 railway employment was still in a fairly rudimentary state. The first real railwayman only came into existence in 1825 with the opening of the Stockton & Darlington Railway. The Liverpool & Manchester Railway in its first ten years of operation from 1830 was the company that essentially established the basic methods and rules for running a public railway.

Right: A William Wallace Wallis omnibus for connecting the station with the town (see page 43 with omnibus outside the station).

In mid-1840 the L&M drew up a new set of rules for the operations of locomotives over their lines, and, in 1841 issued comprehensive "Rules and regulations to be observed by enginemen, guards, policemen and others" to their employees. Under their existing regulations of 1839 the directors ordered "Every overlooker, engine man employed in the Liverpool and Manchester Railway shall keep a copy of these rules constantly on his person under penalty of five shillings". Respect for the L&M regulations led to a general railway conference being held in late 1840. The conference was organised by the Birmingham & Gloucester, the Chester & Birkenhead, London & Croydon, London & Birmingham, Newcastle & Carlisle, Great Western, Manchester & Leeds, Grand Junction, and the Birmingham and Derby Junction Railway, with the purpose of drawing up general safety regulations. The L&M representatives were asked to prepare a draft set for the other companies. This was done and presented at a second conference, with

AMBER GATE STATION FOR MATLOCK.

The Public are respectfully informed that the OMNIBUS will run on Week-days for the ensuing Season between Matlock Bath and the Amber Gate Station TWICE A DAY, viz. :—

In the Morning to meet the UP Train which leaves Leeds at 6h. 45m. a.m.,* and also the DOWN Train which leaves Derby at 9h. 30m. a.m., and which arrive at Amber Gate about 10h. 0m. a.m.

And in the Afternoon to meet the UP Train from Hull, York, and Leeds, which leaves Leeds at 1h. 0m. p.m.,* and also the DOWN Train which leaves Derby at 3h. 30m. p.m.,* and which arrive at Amber Gate about 4h. 0m. p.m.

On SUNDAYS, the Omnibus in the Evening will meet the DOWN Train which leaves Derby at 7h. 0m., and also the Western Mail to Birmingham, which leaves Leeds at 4h. 30m. p.m.,* and which arrive at Amber Gate about 7h. 30m. p.m.

☞ Trains marked thus (*) are direct to or from London.

Passengers accommodated by being taken up or set down at any place which time will permit to come within range of the Omnibus.

No gratuities allowed to be received by Servants.

The Omnibus Fare (including luggage), between Matlock Bath and the Amber Gate Station, One Shilling and Sixpence.

Parcels under 14lbs., 3d.—28lbs., 6d.—beyond, ¼d. per lb.

N.B.—Post Horses are kept at the Station. Orders for Flys, Phaetons, &c., punctually attended to.

Cumming's Old Bath Hotel, Matlock Bath,
October 5th, 1840.

Advertisement of omnibus connecting with North Midland Railway trains at Ambergate for conveying visitors to the Spa at Matlock Bath: October 1840.

most of these regulations then being universally adopted by the other companies. These concepts became the basis for all subsequent British railway operation.

A wide range of skills was needed to run a railway and at first learning was mainly by doing what was needed. By the time that the North Midland, the Midland Counties, and Birmingham & Derby Junction Railways started operations they were able to attract a core of experienced men. In turn these passed on their experience to raw recruits in all departments. We know from surviving records that the North Midland initially set high standards in its recruitment of railway men. An applicant for employment was required to be under 35 years of age, able to read and write, and had to be generally intelligent and active. He had to be in good health with a strong constitution. He was examined by a surgeon who had to issue a certificate that the applicant was suitable for the situation applied for. (See Appendix D.) The North Midland also ran a Friendly Society for the benefit of its employees and all lower ranks of staff were required to join on entering the company's service.

The earliest engine drivers and firemen came from the seedbed of railway operation, the colliery railways of Durham and Northumberland. These men moved from one railway to another as new ones were opened, so as to improve their positions. Workshop operatives were drawn from mill engineers, and blacksmiths came in from town and rural smithies.

Former soldiers and sailors were recruits for a system which needed to establish strict disciplined loyalty, instinctive readiness for the needs of safety and emergencies from train operation, and for experienced smartness in dress and person.

But, all train and permanent way staff had to accept and surmount tough working conditions. Early railwaymen worked long and arduous hours. A 14 or even 15-hour working day was not uncommon. Footplate and trackmen could in reality be at the call of the company day and night, seven days a week. Together with the policemen, who carried out primitive signalling systems and train control generally, they had to work out in all weathers with negligible protection against the elements. Early locomotives had open footplates, cabs of the most rudimentary sorts were a much later luxury.

Nevertheless, there was no shortage of recruits for the work. Discipline could be harsh, and disobedience of orders, misconduct or intoxication were liable to immediate dismissal. But, in return for good service most companies generally paid relatively high and regular wages and looked after their employees well for those times. There is little information on pay for either the North Midland or the Midland Counties but we do know that in 1842 the Birmingham and Derby Junction was paying the following rates of wages and salaries:-Engine drivers were of five grades. Two drivers were on the highest, the 'night mails' receiving 7s (35p) and the lowest 4s (20p) per worker shift. Guards were paid 26s (£1.30) per week and an errand boy 5s (25p). The general manager (James Allport) was paid £500 per annum. The locomotive superintendent (Matthew Kirtley) received £200 pa, superintendent of the audit department £150 pa, and an office boy earned £15.13s (15.65p) pa.

Midland Counties Railway train approaching Nottingham through Lenton Meadows *c.*1841. Note the people watching the new trains going by, and the Castle and St Mary's Church on the high ground.

In June 1842 the North Midland Railway works department (see Appendix E) numbered 197 employees. These included 20 enginemen, 20 firemen, and 20 cleaners, as well as all the craftsmen and labourers. The overall total also included 11 boys "paid at 2s (10p) per day and under." Drivers were paid 7s (35p) per day and firemen 4s (20p). The total weekly wage bill of the Locomotive Department was then £261 13s 10d (£261.69p). There had been a drastic reduction in manning from the previous year when severe economies had had to be made and where on 5 June 1841 the board had first made recommendations to reduce the loco works staff from 374 down to 267.

In October 1841 there were 40 locomotives owned by the North Midland and generally 16 of these in steam daily. All were of the 2-2-2 wheel arrangement with central driving wheels. There were four types of engine, all standard patterns from eight makers. All the engines bore numbers and none were named. By the time of the amalgamation into the Midland Railway in 1844 the locomotive stock had risen to 49, with 34 passenger engines, and 15 goods engines made up of ten 0-4-2s, four 2-4-0 types and one long boiler 0-6-0 type.

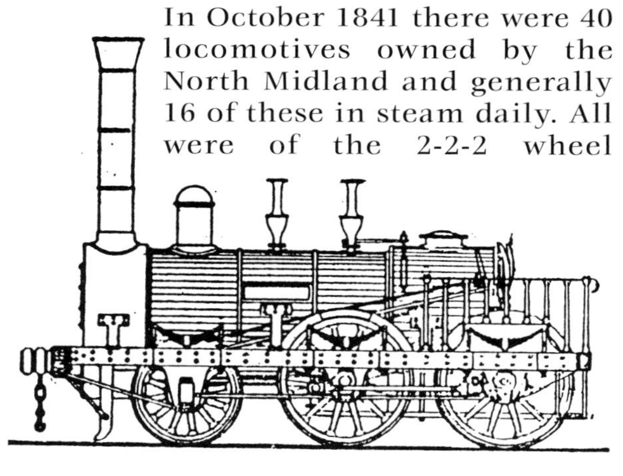

Typical 2-4-0 locomotive for the North Midland Railway as supplied by Stephenson & Co's works at Newcastle upon Tyne.

The Birmingham & Derby Railway bought 12 engines of the 2-2-2 type, three each from four different makers. These were for passenger trains. In 1841 the company bought two goods engines of 0-4-2 wheel arrangement from another company. All the engines were named – bearing either station names or the names of rivers along the company route.

The Midland Counties had acquired a fleet of 47 locomotives by 1844. Almost all of these were of the Edward Bury four-wheeled design, the same type used on the London & Birmingham Railway and, most were built by Bury. Two of the first ordered engines had outside cylinders, in contrast to Bury's inside ones, and were built by the Butterley Company. But it is recorded that these two did not perform well and there was a dispute over payment. The Bury engines had their own problems with a fairly common breakage in the forged inside cranked axles. All the Midland Counties locomotives bore names – a variety of names of animals, winds, mythical beasts (including no.29 'Wivern') oriental lords (Sultan and Vizier), natural phenomenon, plus random names such as Mammoth, Rob Roy and Bee. The company ordered two long boilered 0-6-0 type engines in December 1843 but these were not delivered until after the amalgamation in 1844.

Coaching stock, goods wagons and brake vehicles of all the three companies were of a four wheel pattern, and the coaches were described as being "similar in most respects to those already in use on the London and Birmingham and Grand

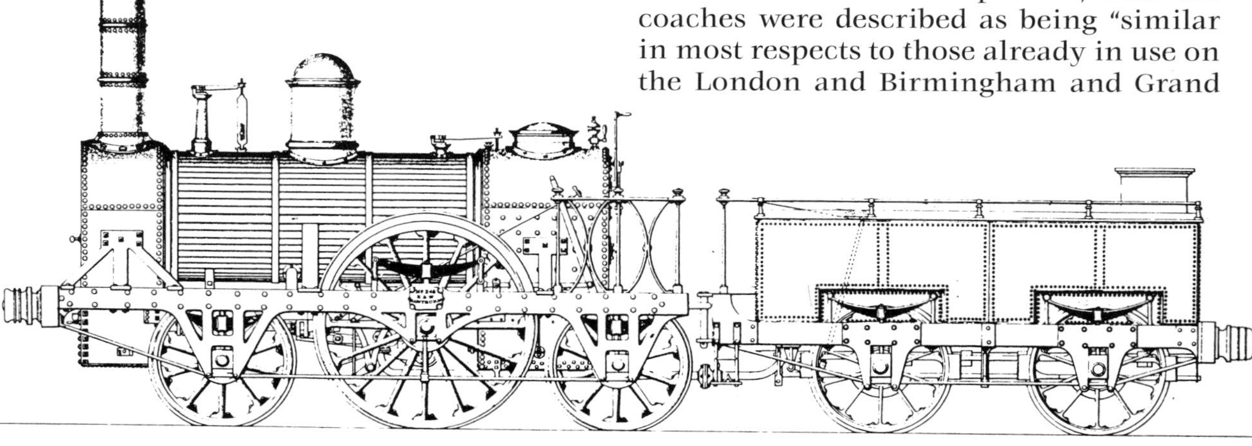

Typical 2-2-0 passenger train locomotive for the Birmingham & Derby Junction Railway as supplied by R. & W.Hawthorn of Newcastle upon Tyne.

Junction lines" The Birmingham & Derby Junction Railway coaches were painted a different colour for each class – First class, bright yellow; Second class, blue; Third class, dark brown. Each coach had a number and bore the arms of the company on the centre door panel.

The first-class carriages of all three companies were like three conventional road coach bodies joined together and mounted on a flat base. Upholstery and finishings inside were like road coaches. Second class was similarly of three enclosed compartments, but of simpler form and much more basic furnishing inside. Some of the Midland Counties early second class had been covered, but were open at the sides – by the end of 1842 these had been glazed in. On all three lines, the third class was very basic – with no roofs, low sides and, not even seats on the Midland Counties until some third-class carriages were fitted with benches in 1842. Whishaw said that "Stanhopes were used on this line when first opened to the public, but have very properly been discontinued". The name Stanhopes was actually a punning nickname for 'stand-ups', boxed areas with no seats in some third class wagons – sometimes made into a fourth class on a few lines. Although

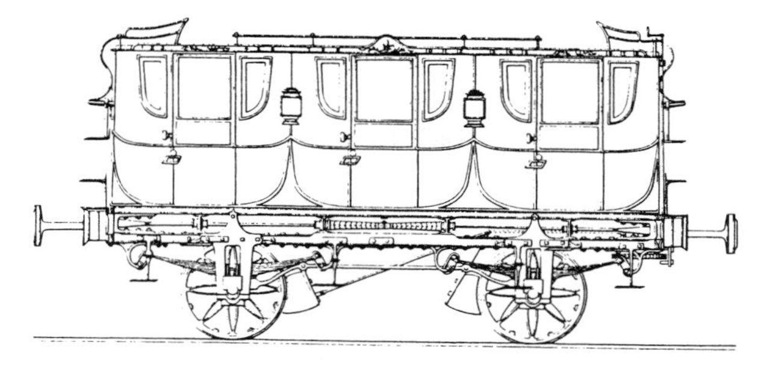

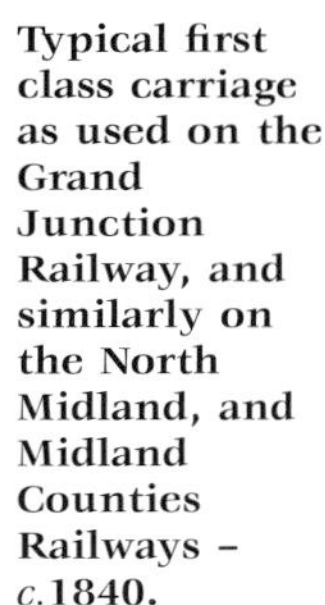

Typical first class carriage as used on the Grand Junction Railway, and similarly on the North Midland, and Midland Counties Railways – *c.*1840.

Left: Armorial badge of the Birmingham & Derby Junction Railway, 1840.

obviously a dangerous way of conveyance for railway passengers a few railways continued to run them until 1844, when the Railway Act of that year (sometimes known as the Gladstone Act) ended the practice. The primary provisions of the Act were -

- One train with provision for carrying third-class passengers, should run on every line, every day, in each direction, stopping at every station.
- The fare should be 1d (½p) per mile.
- Its speed should not be less than 12 mph.
- Third-class passengers should be protected from the weather and be provided with seats.

The North Midland carriages were described by Francis Whishaw as "similar to those of the London & Birmingham" and with the bodies painted "Spanish

The travails of third class 'Parliamentary Train' passengers – *c.*1844.

brown-picked out with black". On the door panels was a cast-iron plaque bearing the arms and name of the company.

The North Midland first-class coaches were upholstered inside with light drab cloth and lace trimmings. Their second class were not upholstered. Third class had plain benches for seats.

The North Midland on its opening in 1840 was running six trains on weekdays from Leeds to Derby and with five trains then going through to London. On Sunday there were four trains with two through to London. Derby to London was scheduled on the timetable on average to take 6¾ hours. The fare from Derby to Leeds was 18s (90p) first class and 12s (60p) second class. The fare from Derby to London was respectively £1.15s (£1.75p) and £1 4s ((£1.20p).

Armorial badge of the North Midland Railway in cast iron as fixed to the railway coach doors 1840.

Some of the North Midland's carriages were built in their works at Derby but the company also had coaches built by outside contractors. The *Derby Mercury* reported in February 1840 that "Mr Bradley - coach proprietor of Sheffield has built 40 neat 2nd class carriages for the North Midland Railway... another 60 are contracted elsewhere... (plus) 50 decidedly superior 1st class ones."

In March 1841 it was reported that the North Midland directors had decided to open a number of additional stations on their line. Then one month later it was reported that 11 new intermediate stations had been opened including Duffield, Smithy Moor, Staveley, Killamarsh, Woodhouse Mill, Treeton, Kilnhurst, Wath, and Royston. Nothing is known of their station buildings, and it is assumed that these were very simple halts.

On the Midland Counties there were initially four trains in each direction on weekdays between Derby and Nottingham and two on Sundays. All Sunday trains on each of the three railways were resisted at first but then objection was over-ruled for commercial considerations. Fares between the two towns were first class 4s (20p) and second class 2s 6d (12½p). These were soon reduced to first class 3s 6d (18p) and second class 2s (10p). Third-class accommodation was not available until early September 1839, and then only on early and late trains. At first this fare was 1s (5p) but it went up to 1s 6d (7½p) from 5 June 1840. The second-class fare also went back up to 2s 6d (12½p). When the rest of the Midland Counties opened on 30 June 1940 down to Rugby, third-class passengers would travel that far, but then could not travel in that class further as the London & Birmingham Railway did not have a third class until October 1840.

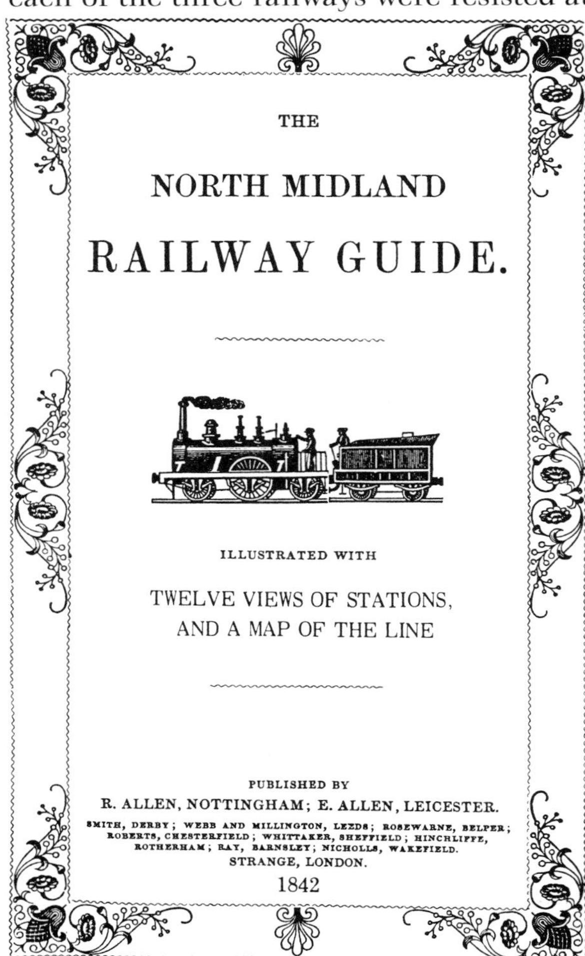

THE

NORTH MIDLAND

RAILWAY GUIDE.

ILLUSTRATED WITH

TWELVE VIEWS OF STATIONS,
AND A MAP OF THE LINE

PUBLISHED BY
R. ALLEN, NOTTINGHAM; E. ALLEN, LEICESTER.
SMITH, DERBY; WEBB AND MILLINGTON, LEEDS; ROSEWARNE, BELPER; ROBERTS, CHESTERFIELD; WHITTAKER, SHEFFIELD; HINCHLIFFE, ROTHERHAM; RAY, BARNSLEY; NICHOLLS, WAKEFIELD.
STRANGE, LONDON.
1842

Far right: Cover of R.Allen's North Midland Railway Guide 1842 - for the enlightenment of the railway traveller.

Present day railway travel is luxurious beyond all conception of the early rail passenger. There was no heating at all, but then first class was still reasonably

The more spacious upholstered comforts of first class railway travel – *c.*1843.

comfortable provided you had good warm clothing and a thick rug. Second class passengers were less fortunate. A passenger on the Manchester & Leeds Railway complained of holes in the floor of carriages which let in cold currents of air about one's legs; he asked if there was any object in these holes, other than to drive passenger's into the first-class. Third class was cheapest but much more rough, a traveller on a long distance route could remain exposed for eight or nine hours, sometimes longer, and a great part of which would be at night time – "tightly compressed between two rough specimens of humanity ... doomed to semi-suffocation, partial extinction of vision ... and deprivation of movement by large bundles, boxes or baskets..."

Smoking was not permitted in the carriages of any of the three railways, nor in any of their stations. If you wished to take your dog with you it could not go in a carriage, but had to travel separately at a charge of 1s (5p).

Your own road carriage could be conveyed for you on a flat wagon and horse boxes were available for your animals. Cheap fares on certain trains on the Midland Counties lines were introduced in late May 1843 and day return tickets at a reduced fare were available from 1 January 1844.

The Birmingham & Derby Junction Railway initially operated three trains each way each week day between Birmingham and Derby.

On Sundays there were two trains. There were three classes on this route from at least 3 August 1839. The fares were first class 10s (50p), second class 7s (35p) and third class 5s (25p). Passengers could be booked through from Derby to Euston Station, London on one train each way each day for fares of £1 15s 0d (£1.75) first class, and £1 4s 0d (£1.20p) second class.

At first the London & Birmingham Railway allowed the Birmingham & Derby

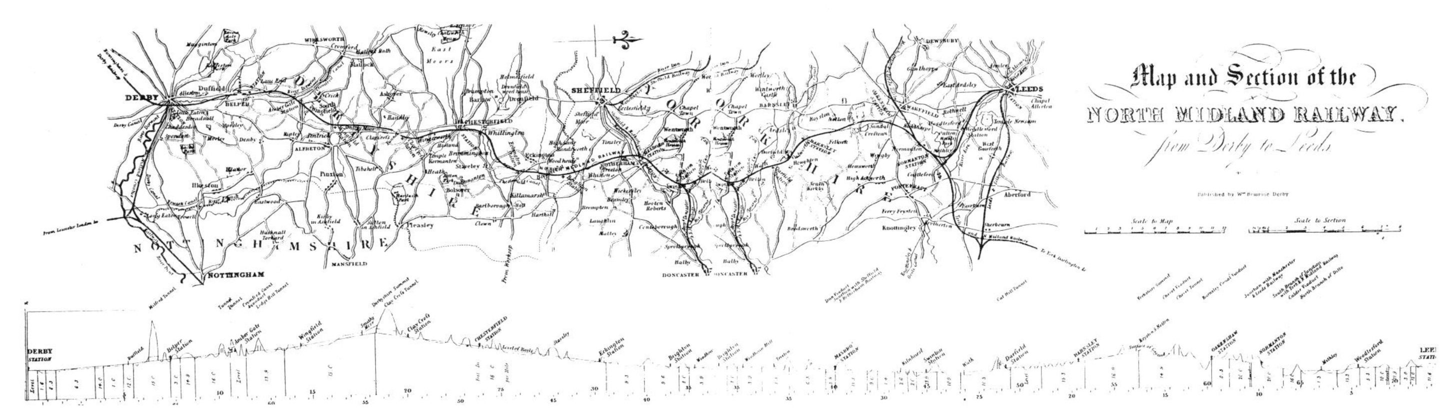

Map of the North Midland Railway route from Allen's Railway Guide. 1842.

Public notice published by the North Midland Railway April 1840 setting out regulations for their passengers and notably prohibiting smoking and dogs in the carriages. Note this early notice was printed by Wm. Bemrose of Derby.

NORTH MIDLAND RAILWAY.

By virtue of the Powers and Provisions contained in an Act of Parliament passed in the sixth and seventh years of the reign of his late Majesty King William the Fourth, entituled "An Act for making a Railway from Leeds to Derby, to be called the North Midland Railway." **We the North Midland Railway Company** established and incorporated by the abovementioned Act—Do hereby make the following

ORDERS AND REGULATIONS

relating to Travellers passing upon the said Railway, and for preventing the Smoking of Tobacco and the commission of any other nuisance in or upon any of the Carriages or in or upon any of the Stations or Premises occupied by or belonging to the said Company, **OF WHICH** all Persons whom it may concern are hereby required to take notice.

1. **ALL PASSENGERS** are required upon booking their places to take a Ticket and to produce the same (if required) previously to taking their Seats in or upon any of the Company's Carriages, and to deliver up the same previously to quitting the Company's premises. And any Person refusing to produce or deliver up such Ticket when required by the Company's Officer, is hereby made subject to a Penalty not exceeding Twenty Shillings.

2. **PASSENGERS** at the Road Stations will only be booked conditionally (that is to say) in case there shall be room in the Train for which they are booked; in case there shall not be room for all the Passengers booked, those booked for the longest distance shall have the preference, and those booked for the same distance shall have priority according to the order in which they are booked.

3. **ANY PASSENGER** riding in a First Class Carriage having paid his Fare for a Second Class Carriage only, shall pay the difference in the Fare, and is also made liable to a Penalty not exceeding Twenty Shillings.

4. **DOGS** will not be suffered to accompany Passengers in the Company's Carriages.

5. **SMOKING** is strictly prohibited both in the Carriages and in the Company's Stations; any Passenger persisting in Smoking after being warned not to do so, is hereby subjected to a Penalty not exceeding Forty Shillings, and in case of his persisting after a second warning, he will immediately or if travelling, at the first stopping place be removed from the Company's premises and forfeit his Fare.

6. **ANY PASSENGER** in a state of intoxication committing any nuisance, or wilfully interfering with the comfort of other Passengers, obstructing any of the Company's Officers in the discharge of their duty, or not attending to the directions of such Officers where the personal safety of himself or any of the Passengers is concerned, will be immediately removed from the Company's premises, or in case the Train shall at the time be moving, then at the next Station, or as soon after the offence as may be, and shall forfeit his Fare, and is also made liable to a Penalty not exceeding Forty Shillings.

7. **ANY PASSENGER** wilfully cutting the linings, removing or defacing the number plates, breaking the windows or otherwise damaging or injuring any of the Company's Carriages, shall forfeit and pay a sum not exceeding Five Pounds, in addition to the amount of damage done.

Given under our Common Seal, this fourth day of April, One Thousand Eight Hundred and Forty.

THE foregoing Orders and Regulations were pursuant to the Provisions contained in an Act of Parliament passed in the second and third year of the reign of Her present Majesty Queen Victoria, intituled "An Act to alter the Line of the North Midland Railway, and to amend the Acts relating thereto,"—submitted to the Justices assembled at the Quarter Sessions of the Peace, for the West Riding of the County of York, held at Pontefract, in the same County, on Monday the Sixth day of April, One Thousand Eight Hundred and Forty, and duly allowed by them.

WHARNCLIFFE,
Chairman.

PRINTED BY WM. BEMROSE, DERBY.

Junction Company to hook their carriages on to any London and Birmingham train calling at Hampton-in-Arden, for onward conveyance to Birmingham Curzon Street Station or, they were permitted to run their own trains over the London and Birmingham rails. But, both alternatives entailed the paying of a heavy toll of 1s 6d (7½p) per passenger to the London & Birmingham Company. This arrangement was short lived, as by late September 1839 the London & Birmingham decided to no longer permit Birmingham & Derby locomotives over their lines – but the toll remained for the journey. The Birmingham & Derby were not happy with these limitations on their traffic to Birmingham and decided to revive their original plans, and construct their own independent route into Birmingham. So, in February 1840 they promoted a bill through Parliament to enable them to build a new line branching off from Whiteacre, to run through Castle Bromwich to a new terminus in Lawley Street, Birmingham – between the Grand Junction Railway and London and Birmingham Railway junctions. There were no difficulties with this additional bill and it received Royal Assent on 4 June 1840. A contract was let on 28 October for £14,250 to John Waltham to build the new Lawley Street Station, with offices, engine workshops and carriage shed – then on 23 December the contract for the line was let to Jackson and Bean for £44,993. The route was an easy one, with no natural difficulties. It was completed by 9 February 1842 and passenger traffic began running over it the next day. There was an immediate relief in toll payments – dropping from £117 in the first week in February 1842 down to as little as £12 in the last week of May and to nothing in July.

Lawley Street Station became the headquarters of the Birmingham & Derby Junction Railway, and the earlier Waterloo Street offices were closed.

Early Royal Travellers and Distinguished Visitors

During this period of operations prior to the formation of the Midland Railway, Derby station had royal visitors on two occasions. The first was the Dowager Queen Adelaide who came just three weeks after the station first opened. On Saturday 18 July 1840 the Dowager Queen had travelled from the capital, over the London & Birmingham Railway before changing to the Midland Counties line from Rugby to Leicester, where she then went by road to Belton House, Grantham. On the following Wednesday 22 July she came to Nottingham station early in the morning and, after having breakfast there she got on to a special three-coach train for Derby. The train also had four trucks to carry road carriages for the royal party plus a luggage van. "On arrival of the train (at Derby) at 10 o'clock her Majesty, attended by her sister, the Lord Chamberlain Earl Howe, Lady Sheffield and the rest of her suite alighted upon the platform, which was superbly carpeted from the carriage to the door of the refreshment rooms, which they entered and partook of refreshments provided by Mr and Mrs Hall, in their usual style of

The Dowager Queen Adelaide's railway coach, built by Hooper's of London for the London & Birmingham Railway, and loaned for her journey from Nottingham into Derby on 22 July 1840.

elegance and excellence. During this time, the train was preparing for her Majesty's departure to Leeds, and one of the North Midland carriages elegantly fitted up, was substituted for that in which she arrived. Many of the North Midland directors were present on this occasion, and several of them accompanied the train to Leeds... The train was attached to Engine no.10 of the North Midland Company, and attended by another in case of accident."

The railway coach in which the Dowager Queen arrived at Derby had been borrowed from the London & Birmingham Railway. It was that company's royal coach built purposely for the Royal Family. (This coach survives, known as Queen Adelaide's coach and can be seen at the National Railway Museum, York.) Although Queen Adelaide rented Sudbury Hall from Lord Vernon from late 1840 to 1842, there seems no other record of her travelling on the three railways connecting at Derby. The Dowager Queen Adelaide was one of the first royal travellers by train in England. Her early passage over the North Midland and Midland Counties lines may be the reason why her initials, with royal crown, appear solely on those company's adopted armorial devices, and not on that of the Birmingham & Derby Junction Company.

Queen Victoria leaving the Midland Counties Station at Nottingham 9 December 1843 to travel on by road coach to Belvoir Castle after travelling from a visit to Chatsworth House.

Armorial Badge of the Midland Counties Railway as painted on their railway coach doors – 1840.

Queen Victoria passed through Derby station on 1 December 1843 and again three days later, but only made brief stops on her way to and from a stay with the Duke of Devonshire at Chatsworth. The Queen came again to Derby station on 28 September 1849, in the early Midland Railway era, *en route* to Balmoral, with Prince Albert, the young Prince of Wales and the Princess Royal, Victoria Adelaide. They stayed overnight at the Midland Hotel. Queen Victoria made one more overnight stop at Derby and the Midland Hotel in 1852, but thereafter her long distance rail travel to Scotland went via the east or west coast routes.

In July 1850 the Queen and Prince Albert had to pass through Derby but on that occasion the royal train stopped only to change engines, near the Nottingham Road bridge. The Midland Company provided a special train of open carriages to convey the gentry of Derby and around, to where the royal train stood, and during the wait, the Mayor of Derby conversed with Prince Albert.

Through 1840 and 1841 the famous virtuoso pianist and composer Franz Liszt travelled extensively around Britain by horse and carriage, and by rail. With four companion artists – three singers and a flautist, and his Erard grand piano they gave concerts in 65 towns over the period. They came to Derby by rail from Leicester on 10 September 1840, shortly after the opening of the Midland Counties line, to give a concert in the hall of the Mechanics Institute in the Wardwick. Liszt as the star attraction gave his usual stunning performance to a large audience. However, Liszt was less than impressed by Derby Station, or rather the staff, since the diary record of the tour records that he thought the staff "were not well behaved" and that "he was diddled out of 12 shillings". The party stayed at the King's Head Inn in the Corn Market, and then went on to Nottingham by carriage, with four horses brought from The Bell Inn; presumably rather than go back to Derby Station!

Early Excursions

The coming of the railways, providing easier and quicker travel led to the promotion of the railway excursion. It is generally accepted that the famous excursion arranged and promoted by Thomas Cook (1808-92), born at Melbourne, for a special train to run on the Midland Counties line between Leicester and Loughborough on 5 July 1841, was the first publicly run excursion by someone outside the railway companies. This 'first' excursion was for 'the friends of temperance' to attend a special festival in the South Fields park of W.Paget Esq., at Loughborough. There were 485 excursionists on the train, and these were squeezed into open third-class carriages, at a return fare of 1s (5p), something less than half the normal fare. Many others travelled to Loughborough later, by regular train.

But, the first actual record of an excursion train was on 20 July 1840 when members of the Nottingham Mechanic's Institute went to visit a Leicester Exhibition. After receiving the names of the intending passengers the Midland Counties arranged for them to travel together at half fares. This was so successful that one week later the Leicester Mechanic's Institute was granted a similar facility by the MCR for a run to Nottingham.

In August that year the Midland Counties ran its own excursions in both directions between the two towns. It was reported that 2,400 passengers were booked on one train from Nottingham, which stopped at intermediate stations. Sixty-five coaches were needed to accommodate the number and the train was hauled by "numerous engines"!

Curiously the Midland Counties did not seize or follow on this potential for excursions, and it was left to Thomas Cook to become the acknowledged pioneer and developer of the concept.

But was Thomas Cook's the first publicly arranged excursion by an outsider, in view of the Nottingham and Leicester Mechanics Institutes' outings.

DERBY MECHANICS' INSTITUTION.

THE COMMITTEE and FRIENDS of the above INSTITUTION having made arrangements for a visit to the NOTTINGHAM EXHIBITION, a SPECIAL TRAIN will leave Derby at 10 o'clock on MONDAY next, the 19th inst.

THE FARES FOR THE EXCURSION WILL BE AS FOLLOWS:

1st Class - - - - -	3s.
2nd ditto - - - - -	2s.
3rd ditto - - - - -	1s.

No charge will be made by the return train, which will leave Nottingham at Six o'clock in the evening.

Tickets may be had at the Institution, Wardwick, or at my residence, No. 1, Curzon-street.

RICHARD STONE,
Oct. 13th, 1840. Secretary.

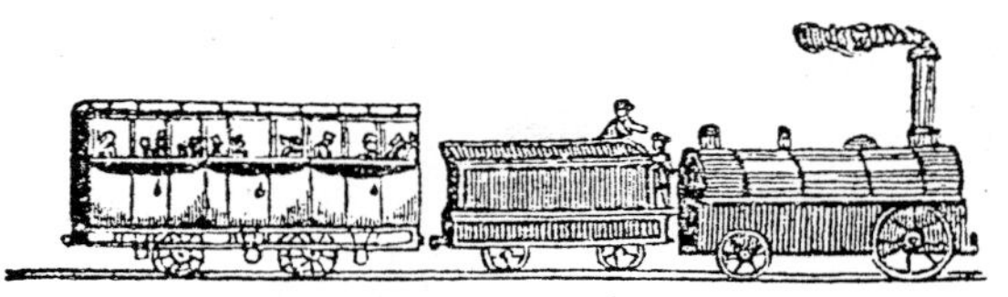

MIDLAND RAILWAY.

CHEAP PLEASURE TRIP TO LONDON, AND BACK.

THE Public are respectfully informed, that a Train of First and Second Class Carriages for London, from the undermentioned places, will join a Train from Newcastle and the North for London, on MONDAY, the 22nd inst., with the choice of returning either on Saturday, the 27th, or Monday, the 29th inst.

ONE FARE, THERE AND BACK.

		First Class.	Second Class.
From Leeds - -	at 9.30 a.m.	50s. 0d.	35s. 0d.
„ Normanton -	10. 0 a.m.	50s. 0d.	35s. 0d.
„ Sheffield -	10.30 a.m.	45s. 0d.	30s. 0d.
„ Masbro' -	11. 0 a.m.	45s. 0d.	30s. 0d.
„ Derby -	1.30 p.m.	35s. 0d.	23s. 6d.
„ Nottingham -	1.30 p.m.	35s. 0d.	23s. 6d.
„ Loughborough	2.15 p.m.	30s. 0d.	20s. 6d.
„ Leicester -	2.45 p.m.	27s. 0d.	18s. 6d.

Further information may be obtained at the Stations.

By order,
Derby, June 8, 1844. J. F. BELL, Secretary.

Left: **First advertisement by the Midland Railway of a Railway Excursion from Leeds to London calling at Derby, 8 June 1844.** *Derby Mercury.*

Far left: **Advertisement by the Derby Mechanics Institution of a Special Train Excursion to the Nottingham Exhibition, 13 October 1840 –** *Derby Mercury.*

And again, there was the Derby Excursion. On 13 October 1840 Richard Stone the secretary of the Derby Mechanics Institute advertised in the Derby Mercury that the Committee and Friends of the Institution had made arrangements for a visit to the Nottingham Exhibition by Special Train on Monday 19 October for 3s (15p) first class; 2s (10p) for second Class; and 1s (5p) for third Class. Barely 200 tickets had been sold by late Saturday evening, but Monday morning's weather was bright and clear, so that from 6am onwards Mr Stone's house was besieged by would-be excursionists for tickets. Just after 10 am an "immense train drawn by two engines left the station", shortly followed by "another still greater, containing altogether little short of two thousand persons". At Nottingham a procession was formed headed by a band. The visitors and trains left for Derby again between 6 pm and 7 pm and arrived without incident, other than a number who lost their hats through putting their heads out of the windows.

In the summer of 1842 there were several excursions to Matlock from Leicester. On one occasion some 700 people travelled in a 23-carriage train via the Midland Counties and then over the North Midlands line to Ambergate station, then by boat along the nearby canal to Cromford wharf, before walking the rest of the way into Matlock. There were subsequent similar excursions to Matlock from Derby and then from Nottingham.

In May 1842 the Birmingham & Derby Railway organised a holiday trip to the Birmingham Whitsun Fair, with cheap fares for the three days of the fair, at the rate of 'a fare and a half only' for the return trip.

In 1843 the Royal Horticultural Society held its first show at Derby, the first of many through the rest of that century and up until the 1939-45 war. The Midland Counties Company advertised special rates through to Derby, and the London & Birmingham Railway agreed to co-operate with through bookings and extra trains from London, and from Birmingham.

The earliest outing of all on the North Midland Railway had been on 23 June 1840, when one week prior to the official opening of the line, members of the West Riding Geological and Polytechnic Society had an engine and carriages provided for them, so that they could make an interesting examination of the geological features of the railway cuttings between Leeds and Derby.

These early excursions were the beginnings of a substantial business in holiday Special and Excursion trains promoted by and throughout the Midland Railway era. Shortly after the creation of the Midland in May 1844 the company advertised its first Excursion to London on Monday 22 June. This precursor would lead to cheap outings for the masses as never before and, would be good revenue for the company.

Difficulties and Amalgamation

The successful opening of the three railways was soon clouded by financial problems. The Birmingham & Derby Junction Railway, through the energies of its board and, with its shorter and more easily constructed route had opened almost a whole year before the other two Derby-

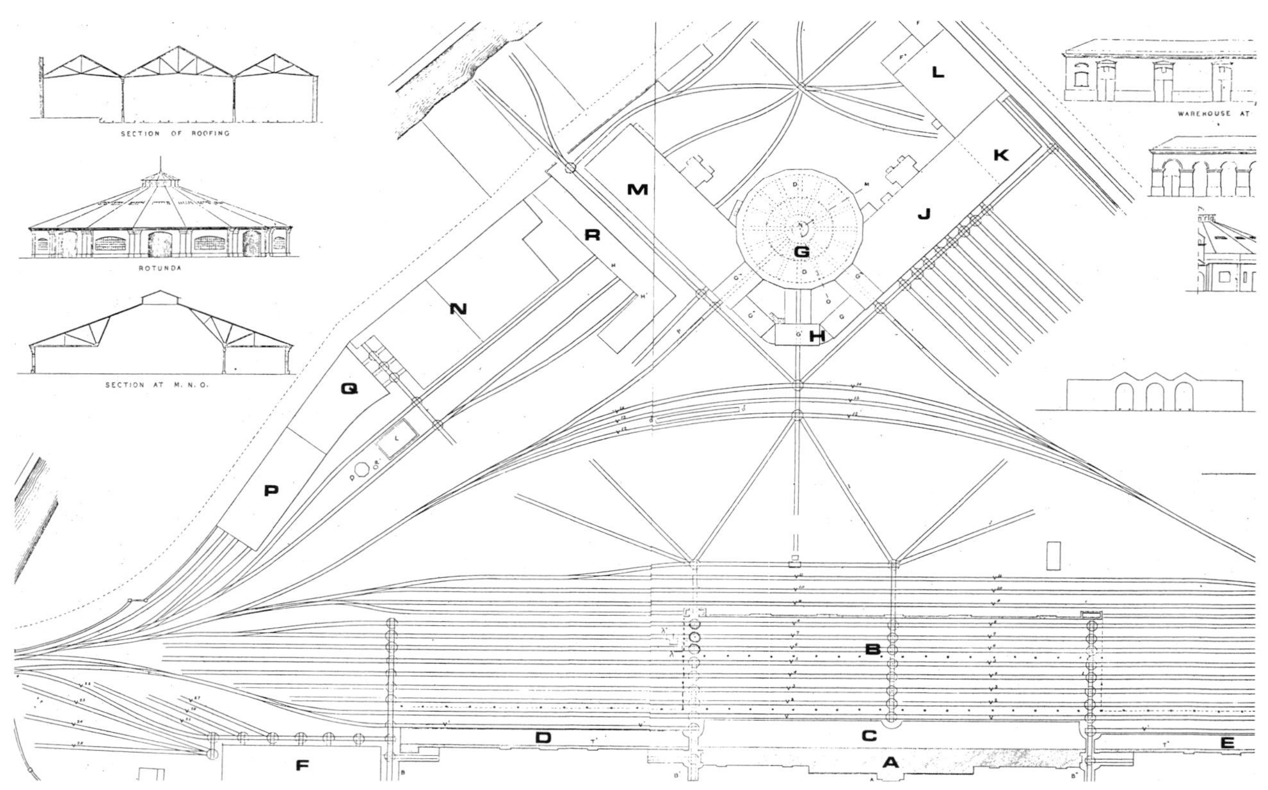

Layout of Derby Station with North Midland, and Midland Counties Works from "Railway Practice" by S.C.Brees and C.E.Direx *c.*1842.

Key.
A. Station building B. Station train shed C. North Midland platform. D. Midland Counties platform. E. Birmingham & Derby platform. F. Joint North Midland/Midland Counties goods warehouse. G. North Midland engine round-house. H. NMR works offices. J. NMR engine work-shops. K. NMR engine smithy. L. NMR forges M. NMR carriage workshops. N. Midland Counties carriage work-shops and paint shops. P. MCR engine shed. Q. MCR carriage shed R. MCR smithy and forges.

joined railways. But opening ten months before the North Midland Railway was completed meant that the Birmingham & Derby was without through traffic from the north for that period. Its takings were low, and having to bear the heavy toll charges of the London & Birmingham Railway for traffic from Hampton to Birmingham left the Birmingham & Derby with barely sufficient revenue to cover working costs.

When the North Midland finally opened in July 1840 the Birmingham & Derby were then faced with direct competition from the Midland Counties Railway for the through traffic for London. The mere seven week advantage before the Midland Counties opened right into its Rugby junction with the London & Birmingham was of little avail. After 17 August the Midland Counties had not only the benefits of the Nottingham and Leicester traffic for London, but could also offer a 17 mile shorter and therefore cheaper fare for through traffic from Derby and the north. The Birmingham & Derby had not been blind to this potential competition, but had hoped to effect an accommodation with the Midland Counties. But, their approaches to that company met with a straight rebuff. The Birmingham & Derby directors then responded with the only means open to them which was to drastically cut their through fares from Derby to London. They therefore cut both the first-class fare from 8s (40p) and the second-class fare from 6s (30p) down to 1s 6d (7p) for the element of the fare from Derby to Hampton and vice versa. Although this act was challenged by the Midland Counties in the Court of Chancery in August 1840, they lost their case for an injunction against the Birmingham & Derby on the ruling that cheap travel was in the public interest.

Following this failure the Midland Counties board in turn tried to open negotiations with the Birmingham & Derby to evenly share the through traffic. But in September the Midland Counties not scenting any success, reduced its own fares so that their Derby-London charges should equal those of the other company.

Nothing developed in these negotiations and throughout 1841 and 1842 the traffic war continued. In mid-1842 the two companies made separate approaches to the London & Birmingham Railway with proposals for the latter to take over the running of their lines. They were well aware that the L&BR had paid a dividend of 10% in 1841, whereas the Midland Counties had only managed 4½% and the Birmingham & Derby a poor 2¼%. In 1842 the London & Birmingham did well and increased its overall dividend to 11 1/10%, whereas the Midland Counties fell to 3% and the Birmingham & Derby slumped to a miserable 1⅗% (In these years the North Midland did little better, paying only 3½%

REDUCED FARES

FROM

COVENTRY TO DERBY

AND THE NORTH,

BY THE

MIDLAND COUNTIES RAILWAY.

Passengers may be Booked through from COVENTRY to DERBY, by the following Trains:—

Leaving Coventry at		Arriving in Derby at
9. 12 a. m.	First Class, - - -	12. 0 Noon.
2. 4 p. m.	First and Second Class,	5. 30 p. m.
4. 47 -	First Class, - - -	7. 15 -

FARES.

FIRST CLASS 5s.

SECOND - 3s.

Being 5s. 6d. First Class and 4s. 6d. Second Class LESS than by the Birmingham and Derby Railway (via Hampton).

HORSES.

One Horse, - - - - - -	£1. 5s. 0d.
Two ditto, - - - - - -	2 7 6
Three ditto, - - - - - -	3 10 0
Carriages, - - - - - -	1 10 0

BY ORDER,

J. F. BELL,

SECRETARY.

Leicester, 8th April, 1843.

Advertisement of a reduction in the railway fares between Coventry and Derby over the Midland Counties Railway, in their price war with the Birmingham & Derby Junction Railway - 8 April 1843.

and 2⅝%). But, the London & Birmingham did its best to stay outside the two companies' quarrels. Richard Creed the secretary wrote - "although this company is interested in promoting the traffic over the longest portion of their line ...they feel it is their duty... to act towards all with the strictest impartiality." Nothing came from these negotiations with the London & Birmingham, but if they had, then subsequent history would have been very different - there would certainly not have been a Midland Railway Company. In January 1843 Henry Smith the chairman of the Birmingham & Derby approached the Midland Counties directors to suggest an immediate amalgamation between the two companies. The initial terms proposed were not acceptable to the Midland Counties, but it was mutually agreed to pursue negotiations for rapprochement and possible amalgamation. By April 1843 negotiations had got nowhere and the MCR had reduced its fares. So, the Birmingham & Derby again drastically reduced its fares through to London from Derby and vice versa, effectively including a cost of only 1s (5p) for the 38 miles from Derby to Hampton and the London & Birmingham. These were measures of desperation. The *Yorkshire Gazette* sarcastically remarked "there remains only one step to finish the contest and that is to pay passengers for the trouble for travelling!" A special General Meeting of the Proprietors of the Midland Counties Railway was held at The Athenaeum Rooms, Derby on Tuesday 14 February 1843. With Thomas Dicey the chairman in the chair, it was to consider a report by a sub-committee on possible financial savings to cope with the serious financial problems. The Meeting agreed the proposed reductions in expenses and the pursuing of a course of rigid economies.

Following this act the Midland Counties again took legal advice over its rival's action. This time the Court of Queen's Bench accepted the Midland Counties case and issued a judicial writ against the Birmingham & Derby Company, enforceable from November 1843. But, by that date other events had overtaken the decision.

During this ongoing conflict between the Midland Counties and the Birmingham & Derby Junction Railways, the North Midland had been struggling with its own problems. The construction of its line had been enormously expensive, partly due to the greater and more extensive works of bridges, cuttings and tunnels and, because it had paid high prices for the necessary land. The North Midland had high debt costs; these with its running costs were too great to be adequately covered by revenue, leaving the company unable to pay adequate dividends to the shareholders. An additional aspect that affected all three railways was that they had been authorised in good economic years, but they didn't start running until the country was in the depths of a severe depression.

The six years from 1837 to 1842 were probably the severest period of depression over the whole course of the nineteenth century. In 1841 several established banks failed and there were many bankruptcies of shopkeepers and tradespeople. Food prices were high and there was unprecedented industrial unemployment with consequent hardships. It was not until 1843 that the national economy began to revive, with a steady progression upward into the 1850s. Even then there was a further, smaller, depression in 1847-48. Generally, the second railway building boom of the mid-1840s did much to stimulate economic recovery.

But these problems were not what the North Midland Company shareholders wanted to hear; their interest was in good dividends so they pressed for economies in the running of the company to improve returns. Having observed the returns achieved by George Hudson's adjacent, but much smaller York & North Midland Railway, which produced a dividend of 6½% in 1840 and 9½% in 1841, against the North Midland's 3½%, a body of shareholders proposed Hudson's election to the board at the meeting on 26 February 1841. However, Hudson declined being fully busy at that time with his other railway empire building schemes and, astute as he was, possibly because he thought he might yet gain an even more advantageous time.

George Hudson was born the son of a farmer in 1800 – he became apprenticed to a York draper, after which he became a partner. After receipt of a substantial legacy of £30,000 at the age of 27 he ventured into finance and set up a joint-stock bank in York. From this base and with shrewdness he acquired connections which eventually enabled him to climb to the respected position of Lord Mayor of York. His financial position and his interest in railways led to him being a promoter, and then chairman of the York & North Midland Railway. He thus soon acquired a grasp of the practicalities of railway construction and operation which led him to real achievements – but ultimately arrogance and greed would destroy him.

In efforts to improve the financial situation the NM's directors were looking for economies, and at their board meeting on 5 June 1841 a number of recommendations were put forward for consideration. These included reducing the Locomotive Works staff down from 374 to 267, together with general reductions of staff in all other departments of the company. They also proposed terminating the employment of their architect Francis Thompson and his staff of five assistants to save £1,090 12s p.a., including the rent of a house; and to remodel their assistant engineer – Frederick Swanwick's office at Chesterfield, which with three assistants and a house was costing £1,572 16s p.a. In the event both Thompson and Swanwick continued in service until their contracts were finally ended on 25 March 1842. Soon after this date Francis Thompson left Derby for London.

George Carr Glyn (1797-1873) – banker, and second chairman of the London & Birmingham Railway, first chairman of the North Midland Railway, the Railway Clearing House, and of the London & North Western Railway. Created 1st Baron Wolverton in December 1869.

On 9 October 1841 the North Midland chairman George Carr Glyn resigned, but remained on the board as a director. His resignation was probably because he felt his position was conflicting with his other railway interests, since he was at the same time the chairman of the London & Birmingham Railway. Glyn was an able man and a shrewd banker. The fourth son of Sir Richard Carr Glyn, banker and one time Lord Mayor of London, his mother Mary was the daughter of John Plumptre gentleman, of Nottingham giving George Carr Glyn local midland connections. The family banking company of Glyn Mills, Currie & Co., had the reputation of having a then larger business than any other private banking house in the City of London. Glyn had been an able chairman of the North Midland since its authorisation in July 1836, and had seen it into operation. He had been elected as the second chairman of the London & Birmingham Railway in 1837, the year of the opening of its first section from London to Tring. He would continue to serve as its chairman until 1846, guiding through the second great amalgamation of railways in Britain, after the inspiration of the Midland Company – of the London & Birmingham, the Grand Junction, the Liverpool & Manchester, the Manchester & Birmingham railways to create the London & North Western

William Leaper Newton (1779-1851) – Derby banker, Crompton, Newton & Co., Iron Gate, JP, alderman, Mayor of Derby 1836, director of the North Midland Railway, chairman 1842-44, of The Leyland's, Derby.

Railway on 16 July 1846. George Carr Glyn became the first chairman of the new LNWR and served until 1852. By that time the LNWR had become one of the Midland Railways' main rivals.

Following Glyn's resignation J.W.Childers MP replaced him as chairman. Then in December 1841 William Hanson was appointed chief superintendent of the line, relieving Robert Stephenson who had been temporarily acting in this capacity following the death of Mr Bagster. Around this time the company also discharged the five London policemen who had been appointed as recently as November 1840 as superintendents of the railway policemen.

Early in 1842 another long-serving director, William Leaper Newton, the Derby banker, took over as chairman of the North Midland. There was more mounting dissatisfaction with the company's financial performance, this time led by two wealthy shareholders of the Liverpool faction. These were held off until the declaration of the half-yearly dividend, but when these proved to have fallen to a mere 1% the discontent increased again. A new alliance was formed between the strong Lancashire interest and Yorkshire shareholders, who together forced the setting up of a Committee of Inquiry. This consisted of the two Liverpool financiers and five Yorkshiremen, including George Hudson. The astute Hudson now saw his opportunity to intervene with strong backing, to achieve power and his own way in running the North Midland.

The committee was appointed in September 1842. Within a little over a week under Hudson's drive they had examined all the departments at Derby, visited all the intermediate stations, the terminus at Leeds, and Sheffield station. They then produced their detailed report within the month. The report proposed swingeing economies in all departments and on the maintenance of the line. The overall savings to be achieved were estimated to reduce annual costs by £17,788 5s 9d. This great saving was to be made up from the following:- secretary's office, auditor and accounts from £2,547 to £1,200; engineering dept from £2,397 14s to £800 00; stores from £919 16s to £619 16s; coaching and carrying incl. porters from £15,306 16s to £10,608; loco and carriage dept. from £19,438 13s 9d to £9,913 18s.

George Hudson (1800-1891) son of a farmer, apprenticed to a York linen draper. A substantial legacy enabled him to set up a joint stock-bank. He became Lord Mayor of York, MP for Sunderland, first chairman for the Midland Railway: The so called 'Railway King' was an inspired railway promoter but an unprincipled financial manipulator.

The cuts in the engineering dept. for the permanent way were the most severe – but the locomotive and carriage department costs were to be halved, with reductions in staff, wages and privileges.

The directors were shocked by the detailed proposals. The cuts meant many employees would be thrown out of work in a time of general hardship and unemployment. Many of the directors were local residents and had no wish to incur obloquy by making such large numbers of their employees redundant in the 'Hungry Forties'. They felt there was enough unrest and risk of riot in most industrial towns at that time without themselves inflaming the general situation. The directors consequently countered with a statement that the Committee of Inquiry's proposals, and in particular the drastic reduction in locomotive staff and line control, would put the travelling public at risk. Even so, they managed to further weaken their own position by putting forward an alternative proposition to make £11,000 savings a year.

At a Special General Meeting on 16 November 1842 at Leeds, the directors faced a packed and hostile room of shareholders. Hudson rose to cheers and sensing the moment, he forcibly attacked the directors' proposals as totally inadequate. He'd gauged the emotions of the shareholders, who had convinced themselves that Hudson could achieve splendid dividends for them. With aggressive rhetoric he carried the majority with him and forced the election of six members of the committee, including himself, on to the board of directors in place of six existing. William Leaper Newton remained chairman for the time being, but effectively initiative and control of the North Midland Company passed into the hands of the unscrupulous George Hudson. One of his first actions was to force the resignation of Henry Patteson, the respected secretary since 1836, and to bring in Peter Clarke one of his own placemen. This would ensure that the future accounts of the company could be presented as Hudson might think fit. Clarke was the general superintendent of the Leeds & Selby Railway which had been taken over on lease by Hudson's, York & North Midland Railway in 1843.

On 6 December 1842 a new sub-committee of the board resolved to implement extensive cuts immediately. Beighton, Killamarsh and Kilnhurst stations were to be closed; a number of trains to be discontinued; five engine drivers and five firemen (a quarter of the strength) were to be sacked; sixty carriages were to be sold; the fares between Derby and Leeds to be increased by 2s (10p); the wages of the rest of the Loco Department and of all other employees of the company would be cut; and boys were to be employed instead of men to work points at junctions on the line (a favoured idea of Hudson for cheaper labour).

The engine men protested at the intended reductions in their pay and privileges, to which Hudson high-handedly replied by dismissing every one of the company's drivers and firemen. This was a particularly harsh action as it came on Christmas Eve 1842 and the men were not given their legitimate week's notice or pay. In their place Hudson brought in a so-called "number of skilled and practised drivers from other lines."

In reality these new engine drivers were hopeless replacements; they included a plate-layer, a fireman, a stonemason, two unemployed drivers discharged from another company for drunkenness, and another who had been sacked for carelessly overturning 30 wagons from a train. The consequence for the North Midland was a state of chaos. The first train from Leeds on Christmas Day was two and a half hours late.

There were breakdowns and repeated engine troubles through using such unskilled men. At a stroke Hudson managed to antagonise all the surviving staff, raising complete hostility to the direction of the company and undermining the essential loyalty of experienced workers.

There were strong complaints in the press which condemned the North Midland directors of being oblivious of the risks to "property and life". A culmination of this situation was when a luggage train on the foggy night of 12 January 1843 crashed into the rear of a stationary train at Cudworth near Barnsley, killing one passenger. The inquest aired the risks of the cutbacks, particularly when it was revealed that the luggage train driver, one Edward Jenkins, had only three weeks driving experience on an engine. There was wide publicity of the accident and the subsequent trial of the driver for manslaughter. The outcome was that the jury acquitted the driver but instead censured the directors of the North Midland.

The matter sufficiently alarmed the directors that they agreed to bring in Thomas Cabrey, the engineer of Hudson's York & North Midland Railway, to reorganise the Locomotive Departments at Derby and Leeds and replace any employee he might think unsuitable. The Railway Department of the Board of Trade was also aroused by these events and wrote to the company on 7 February. The board inspector's investigation had followed with a report which severely criticised the directors' sweeping changes, that had "compromised the safety of the Public travelling on the line." The Board of Trade letter required the overworking of the enginemen to stop and for there to be a return to former working practice. In a reply the directors brazenly blamed the former enginemen for bringing about the problems, and gave assurances that the present enginemen were quite satisfied with the work timetables! But, in a mollifying tone they added that they would take immediate steps to allow additional rest intervals for the men so as to allay the anxieties of the Railway Inspectorate. The Inspectorate appears to have accepted these assurances and the matter rested.

Meanwhile the war between the Midland Counties and the Birmingham & Derby for passengers, made for continuing damaging losses to those two companies. The value of their shares had fallen by over a quarter during 1842 and the dividends to their shareholders had dwindled. Their respective shareholders looked with envy at the York & North Midland and the London & Birmingham Railways' dividends.

By 1843 Matthew Dicey, the chairman of the Midland Counties, was being challenged over the directors' policies, and his own position was threatened.George Hudson first intervened in the affairs of the Midland Counties on 4 February 1843 and pressed for amalgamation with the Birmingham & Derby. The idea for amalgamation had been first envisaged by Robert Stephenson, but it was Hudson who pursued it and forged the alliance. Indeed in reality, Hudson's vision went much further with a concept of railways under his control, all the way from London north via Derby, York and then on to Newcastle and so to Scotland.

George Hudson in pursuit of his grand ambition perceived that if the Birmingham and Derby, as the weaker element, could be persuaded to co-operate with the North Midland against the Midland Counties they could between them squeeze the latter into negotiations for a triple amalgamation. On 1 August the directors of the North Midland presented the Midland Counties with an ultimatum to amalgamate, or, face a juncture of the other two companies. There followed more haggling, until eventually at a heated meeting of irate and restless Midland Counties shareholders on 21 September, the meeting went against their chairman and carried Hudson's concrete scheme for the triple amalgamation. The North Midland shareholders had approved the proposal previously on 18 September and the Birmingham & Derby Junction's on 20 September.

A Joint Management Committee was then formed to agree the terms of amalgamation and to work the three companies until a Parliamentary Act could be obtained. It was agreed that there should be a new directorate of 15, made up of six from the North Midland, five from the Midland Counties and four from the Birmingham & Derby.

The Midland Railway Consolidation Bill was admitted to Parliament and went into the committee stage at the end of February 1844. The Bill was engrossed on 29 March and passed with all amendments on 6 May. It received the Royal Assent on 10 May 1844 and from that point the original three companies ceased to exist. From 1 July 1844 there was full unified working of all the three lines. The creation of the Midland Railway on 10 May was the first great railway amalgamation.

All these negotiations had been additionally fortunate for George Hudson. They had served to divert attention from the failure of his reckless claims in 1842 when he had rashly promised savings of over £17,000 a year on the North Midland. At the board meeting in August 1843 the financial report could only show a saving of £11,500 – little more than had been promised by William Leaper Newton and his much-abused fellow directors.

The Midland Hotel, Derby

"the Proprietor of the Midland Hotel . . .and the Lessees of the Brunswick Inn . . .shall have the exclusive privilege of sending porters on the Station Platform to solicit the custom of passengers to their respective premises . . .the parties to conduct themselves with civility and propriety in all respects . . .

NMR Minutes, July 1843

THE Midland Hotel at Derby was only the second purpose-built railway hotel, and it is unique in having been in continuous use from the day it opened in late May 1841.

In the early Victorian era purpose -built hotels were a fairly new innovation. The traveller had hitherto gone by road and stayed at inns. A few hotels had been newly built but these were mainly in spa towns for visitors taking the waters, such as the Grand and St Ann's Hotels at The Crescent, Buxton and the New Bath Hotel at Matlock Bath. It also happened that the centre of Derby had only recently been provided with a new hotel in 1839. The imposing Royal Hotel on the corner of Victoria Street and the Cornmarket. This building was promoted by the company which had created Victoria Street from Brookside, by culverting the Markeaton Brook in 1837. It was designed by the London architect Robert Wallace who was also involved in the new premises of the Derby and Derbyshire Bank next door. It is likely that the promoters of this new hotel anticipated prospects of greater trade in the town with three railways already under construction to Derby.

The distinction of being the first ever railway hotel built belongs to the twin Victoria and Euston hotels in London, which were arranged on either side of the railway approach in front of the great Doric Arch. Like the arch the hotels were designed by the architect Philip Hardwick. The prospectus for raising capital for these hotels was published in April 1838 and entitled the *London and Birmingham Railway Hotel and Dormitories*. Railways could only be built through an Act of Parliament and the share capital could only be spent on the railway itself. When the directors wished to provide something additional such as an hotel, then it needed either an additional Act or, the money could be raised through the promotion of a separate company with trustees.

At Derby, Thomas Jackson the London contractor working on the North Midland's railway contracts, offered to build an hotel adjoining the station at his own

The Midland Hotel, Derby *c.*1849. Built by Thomas Jackson at his own expense, opened May 1841, designed by Francis Thompson. Acquired by the Midland Railway in March 1862.

expense. The board of the North Midland were pleased to accept this offer at their meeting on 17 December 1839. The land required for the hotel was bought by the North Midland Railway from the Castlefields Estate trustees and leased to Jackson.

A sketch drawing from 1840 shows the Castlefields area with the original field boundaries, and with the outlines of the land apportionments for the three railways, the buildings of the station and the North Midland and Midland Counties works buildings annotated. Also shown on the drawing is an outline of the hotel, but only the section nearest to the station is drawn together with a wing at the rear extending in a westerly direction. These parts were as built. There is no sign on the drawings of the parallel west wing of the hotel as we know it. This second wing must have been added soon after, since *Glover's Directory* compiled in 1842 mentions "upwards of fifty superior bedrooms, and numerous dining and sitting rooms." It would have needed both wings to accommodate all these rooms.

It is more than possible that the double wing plan of the Midland Hotel derived to an extent from the arrangements of the twin hotels recently opened at Euston. The Euston Hotel opened in December 1839, was described at the time as being "arranged for the purposes of an hotel, with a spacious coffee room, for the accommodation of (visitors), and of the persons in the dormitories (The Victoria) who may wish to use the Hotel coffee room." The other twin hotel the Victoria had opened beforehand in September 1839. It was divided into "as many rooms of convenient dimensions as the allotted space will admit . . . a proportion of the number to have small sitting or dressing room attached . . . so that passengers may be accommodated on their arrival with a sleeping room, and if required, a sitting room; each apartment to be charged at a price varying according to the floor and scale of accommodation. A coffee room was established in the same building for breakfast and refreshments. . . but not licensed for wine and spirits." Baths in "convenient situations" were provided in both buildings. It was also made clear that the "dormitories" were an altogether separate establishment from the hotel. The expression coffee room was commonly used at that time to denote a room for meals which was also open to the general public, whereas an hotel dining room usually would only be open to hotel guests. In reality these twin hotels were modest in scale and character rather like large terraces of Regency houses. They were eventually linked as one by a bridging block in 1881 but were swept away by British Rail in 1962 along with the old station, and the wanton destruction of Hardwick's great Doric arch.

The description of the Euston hotels gives us some insight into a concept for early railway hotels.

The second, western wing of the Midland Hotel whilst matching the other on the Midland Road frontage is different along the west side where it has a bare rather unfinished appearance. This may be because Jackson envisaged a further future extension out from that side – but, it was never built. At the date of building, the present day garden area on the west side was not part of the curtilage. It was not acquired until 1855, with land going through to Nelson Street. Thomas Jackson of Pimlico, Middlesex and a William Meyrick, of 16 Parliament Street, London bought the land that year from the Borough family estate for £1,029 10s 6d.

The Midland Hotel was designed for Jackson by Francis Thompson and it is integrated into the overall layout of the station, the large warehouse and the railway houses, as part of a grand scheme around an open square. Engravings of the time depict a central fountain featuring in the square – this may just have been artistic license, although not so likely with the artist Samuel Russell. Although within the scheme, the hotel design is for a building in its own right, and in respects it has the character and refinement of an elegant country house with classical Italianate proportions.

Originally the entrance to the hotel was via a formal entrance in the single storey link between the wings fronting Midland Road, with an open court and, another ornamental central fountain. The portico was surmounted by the Royal Arms with lion and unicorn supporters, added probably after Queen Victoria stayed with her family overnight in 1849 on her way north to Balmoral. The menu for "Her Majestys' Dinner" survives at the hotel and is still proudly displayed. The Queen came again in 1852 and stayed overnight.

The hotel was first opened on an unknown day in the last week of May 1841 with the name – "The Midland Hotel and

Menu for Queen Victoria's dinner during her stay over at the Midland Hotel, Derby on 28 September 1849, and, to its right: advertisement of the opening of the Midland Hotel and Posting House, Derby in May 1841 under the management of Joseph Hall.

HER MAJESTY'S DINNER.

MIDLAND HOTEL, DERBY,
September 28th, 1849.

POTAGES.
Crême de riz
A la Julienne.

POISSONS.
Le turbot sauce homard
Les rougets al Italienne
Les soles frites.

RELEVES.
Le janbon
Les poulets au riz.

ENTREES.
Les pigeons aux pois
Des riz de veau panés
Des cotelettes de mouton
Vol'au vent de ragoûs.

ROTS.
Poularde Perdreaux
Les sarcelles.

ENTREMETS.
La tartelettes de comfitures
La gelú de fruits
La charlotte depommes
Le pudding de biscuits.

SIDE TABLE.
Roast beef
Roast mutton.

Bouillie gratiner.

NORTH MIDLAND RAILWAY.

MIDLAND HOTEL
and
POSTING HOUSE,
RAILWAY STATION,
DERBY.

J. HALL, begs to announce to the Nobility and Gentry, that this Hotel under his management is open for their accommodation; and where, he trusts, those who honor him with their patronage, will find the style and comfort of the Establishment equal to that of any in the Country.

Porters are in constant attendance on the arrival of the several Trains at Derby for the removal of Luggage, &c., to the Hotel.

Posting House", under the management of Joseph Hall, who was already the proprietor of the refreshment rooms at the station since its opening on 1 July 1840.

On 24 November 1842 Thomas Jackson entered into a new legal agreement with the North Midland board which permitted him to underlet the hotel and the station refreshment rooms to a John Cuff. In *Glover's Directory of 1843* there is, an advertisement for "Cuff's Midland Hotel, Railway Station, Derby", which has led to it repeatedly being stated that it was called "Cuff's Hotel" from the beginning. It has also been erroneously stated in print that it was originally called the "Station Hotel" and that the name Midland did not appear in the title until after the Midland Railway Company took over from 1862. How long John Cuff continued as the lessee is unclear but he was certainly there into the 1850s. A Mrs Susan Chatfield was the housekeeper in 1851, and in 1861 she was the hotel manager.

In Glover's 1843 Directory, beds were advertised at the hotel for four shillings (20p) a night for a single one, or 5s (25p) for a double. A sitting room cost an extra 5s (25p) – with a fire costing 2s (10p). A fire in your bedroom was less at 1s (5p). A fine breakfast with chops and eggs could be had for 3s (15p). Tea with meat and eggs, or just a plain one cost 3s (15p). Dinners and wines were set out in the full bill of fare. Wax candles were charged at a rather expensive 2s (10p). There is no mention of oil lamps. There may well have been gas lighting in the public rooms since there was already gas lighting at the station.

In late 1859 Thomas Jackson got into financial difficulties through his contract on the construction of the Riga and Dunaberg Railway in Latvia, when that company refused to pay certain large sums of money due to him. On 26 October that year there was a meeting of his creditors and it was subsequently reported in the press that the Midland Hotel owned by him was subject to a mortgage. The hotel was put up for sale and was bought by a Mrs Julia Ann Blunt and others. In August 1860 the Midland Railway directors discussed the desirability of having good hotels adjacent to their main stations. It was following this that the hotel was acquired from Mrs Blunt for £10,050 by the trustees, with its ownership being eventually transferred by indenture to the railway company on 1 March 1862. This followed the grant of power to purchase in the Midland Railway Additional Powers Act of 1861. There were major extensions to the Midland Hotel in 1874 when the near end of the right hand wing was added, and more building at the rear in 1884. Then in the early 1930s the new dining room was added between the wings and the main entrance moved round to the station side.

When transferred to Midland Railway ownership from 1862, the catering and management was let by contract to Spiers and Pond, who after success in Australia, were newly establishing themselves in catering ventures in London and taking on railway hotels. But by the year 1871 the Midland Railway Company, with imminent prospect of its great St Pancras Hotel opening, changed its policy and in that year appointed the very young William Towle to manage the Midland Hotel. From this point onwards the Midland Company's Hotel and catering enterprises would expand and prosper into a large enterprise entirely under its own management.

The Midland Hotel passed into LMS Railway ownership in 1923 when the Midland Railway ceased to exist, and then to British Railways after nationalisation of the railways in 1948. The Midland Hotel then came under the control of British Transport Hotels Ltd. In 1982 BTH put its hotels on the open market for sale. The Midland was then sold to a local private firm as part of Midland Hotels Limited but still retaining its long-surviving name 'The Midland Hotel'. In recent years the old hotel has been extensively refurbished inside, and the exterior cleaned up together with the provision of a new entrance portico on the east side - a sensitive rehabilitation to give this historically and commercially important hotel, many more years of useful life.

William Towle (1849-1929) - born son of Edward Towle blacksmith/ farmer of Twyford, Derbyshire. Manager of Midland Hotel, Derby 1871, subsequently general manager Hotels & Catering Service, Midland Railway from 1884 until retirement in 1914. He was knighted in 1920.

Midland Railway Hotels and Catering Services

After the Midland Railways acquisition of the Midland Hotel, it became a cornerstone of a growing hotel enterprise. This almost entirely owed its credit to the Towle family. William Towle was born at the village of Twyford near Derby in 1849 and started work as a junior assistant at the Midland Hotel at the age of 15. He must have showed exceptional ability and promise for at the very early age of 22 in 1871 he was appointed manager of the hotel and the refreshment rooms at the station. In 1884 he was asked to reorganise the Midland Grand Hotel at St Pancras, London, opened in 1873. Under his direction the hotel business of the Midland Railway expanded greatly. The Midland Hotel, Bradford was opened in 1890; the Adelphi, Liverpool, bought in 1892, Heysham Towers Hotel bought in 1896; the Queens Hotel, Keighley bought in 1902, the vast Midland, Manchester, designed by Charles Trubshaw the Midland Company architect, opened in 1903 with 500 bedrooms, five restaurants, banqueting hall, winter garden, concert hall. The Midland had also bought the small station hotel at Normanton on the original North Midland line, in 1861; this was eventually to close in 1902.

The Adelphi, Liverpool proved inadequate for the business it attracted, so in 1912 it was demolished and completely

MIDLAND HOTEL
AND
REFRESHMENT ROOMS.

DERBY.

NOTICE.

On and after MARCH 1st, 1875,

LUNCHEON BASKETS

Will be provided at the DERBY STATION, at the following charges:--

No. 1, containing Half-a-Chicken, with Ham or Tongue, Salad, Bread, Cheese, Butter, &c., and a Half-Bottle of Claret or Burgundy. - - - - 3s.

No. 2, containing Veal and Ham Pie, with Salad, Bread, Cheese, Butter, &c., and a Bottle of Stout. - - - 2s.

The Baskets will be fitted with the necessary appointments, which it is earnestly requested may be replaced in their proper position, and the Baskets handed to one of the Company's Servants that they may be returned to DERBY.

WILLIAM TOWLE,
Midland Hotel, Derby

Advertisement for the Midland Railway Hotels *c.*1900, and Notice of provision of luncheon baskets for train journeys from Derby Midland Station – 1 March 1875.

rebuilt to the designs of the architect R.Frank Atkinson. The new Adelphi opened in March 1914 with 600 rooms, the ultimate in the fine range of Midland Hotels. Altogether the Midland Railway owned 10 hotels at its greatest extent – as many as its rival the London & North Western Railway, both of which owned more than any other railway of the time. The Midland Railway's capital expenditure on its hotels prior to the 1914-18 war had also been greater than the other railways, and its nett receipts in 1913 of around £122,450 were also much more.

For the travelling passenger railway travel was particularly tiring in the earlier days, and there was the problem of food. The railways had installed refreshment rooms at their principal stations from fairly early days, Derby station having one from its opening. But, as the *Railway Traveller's Handbook* of 1862 commented on refreshment rooms – "As there are usually some two or three hundred persons requiring refreshments, and only about a dozen hands to supply them . . .we shall advise the railway traveller to take his refreshment with him." Railway refreshments came under criticism from the earliest days. A ten minute stop was far too short for a large number of each trains' passengers to obtain and consume the food. Quality also left much to be desired. Charles Dickens wrote of "brown hot water stiffened with flour" for soup, and "glutinous lumps of gristle and grease called pork pie" and, "brown patties composed of unknown animals within".

Spiers and Pond the catering entrepreneurs had noted the problem that many travellers were left without food in the scramble, and of course others couldn't face the crush. Their idea, first put into operation in the summer of 1871 was to make food baskets available from their managed refreshments rooms on the Midland Railway. The passenger consumed the food on the train and left the basket with its used crockery to be collected by station staff at a station halt further along the journey. It was following William Towle's appointment as hotel and catering manager that he took over the idea and began the Midland's own basket service organised from Derby station from 1875. The baskets were like small cane hampers similar to family picnic baskets – they came in two sizes 3s 0d (15p) and 2s 0d (10p), the superior one containing –

Buffet trolley on platform 1, Derby Station, 22 February 1908 manned by Frank Torrington outside the refreshment room. He earned "3s 6d (17½p) a week, uniform provided, and one week's holiday a year."

"Half a chicken, with Ham and Tongue Salad, Bread, Cheese, Butter, and Half Bottle of Claret or Burgundy." The 'lower class one ' containing – "a Veal and Ham Pie, with Salad, Cheese, Butter, and a bottle of Stout," the company did very good business with this offering. Other companies quickly followed this practice and the basket lunch soon became an established feature on all the major lines. Passengers' orders for midday lunch baskets could soon be ordered and telegraphed ahead for collection on route. In 1887 William Towle's catering service even introduced a "hot basket meal" with a chop, vegetables and wine or stout – how it was kept hot is now unclear.

William Towle retired in 1914, but in his long and dedicated service to the MR he showed that railway hotels could be profitable and excellent. He had radically improved the fare offered at the station refreshment rooms over the Midland system, and ensured good catering on train restaurant cars introduced from 1882. Towle set up an efficient management organisation for all this, based on Derby, and later, St Pancras. Although most of the hotels bought their produce locally, they were supplied centrally for wines and spirits from the extensive cellars established beneath and adjacent to the Midland Hotel, Derby.

William Towle's long and especial service to the hotel industry was finally fully honoured when he was awarded a knighthood in 1920. He lived on in retirement until 1929.

In 1896 Towle's sons Francis and Arthur joined him in the service of the Midland. Two years later they were appointed joint assistant managers of the hotels, under their father. Following his retirement in 1914 they were appointed joint managers. In 1916 Francis left for wartime government service, but Arthur continued as manager until the end of the Midland Railway in 1922.

Midland Hotel, Derby in 1983.

The Early Years: Consolidation and Growth

Rumbling under blackened girders, Midland, bound for Cricklewood,
Puffed its sulphur to the sunset where that land of laundries stood.
Rumble under, thunder over, train and tram alternate go,
Shake the floor and smudge the ledger, Charrington, Sells, Dale and Co,
Nuts and nuggets in the window, trucks along the lines below.

from *Parliament Hill Fields*
John Betjeman, 1945

THE directors of the newly-created Midland Railway held their first meeting in the boardroom at Derby station on 24 May 1844. It was unanimously agreed there that George Hudson should become chairman of the new company, with John Ellis from the Midland Counties as vice-chairman. The First General Meeting of shareholders of the new company then followed on Tuesday 16 July, and was held at the Railway Station.

The new board had immediate, pressing demands, to standardise and rationalise into a single cohesive system, the mixed collection of locomotives, rolling stock, stations and buildings, workshops and the previously differing methods of the three former companies. One of the first decisions had been to agree that Derby should be the centre of this enterprise since it was already set at the juncture of the three railways. Derby also had the works of two of the companies handily adjacent to each other, together with space for foreseeable expansion.

Matthew Kirtley (1813-1873) born at Tanfield, Co.Durham. Started work at 13. Worked on a number of early railways. Credited with driving the first train into Euston in 1838. Joined the Birmingham & Derby Junction Railway in 1839 rising to locomotive superintendent. Appointed to same post on new Midland Railway in 1844. Served the company splendidly until his early death in 1873.

The first need was to keep the trains running and this required the appointment of a Locomotive and Carriage & Wagon superintendent. The three obvious candidates were the men who had been serving the former companies – Josiah Kearsley of the Midland Counties, Matthew Kirtley from the Birmingham & Derby, and Thomas Kirtley from the North Midland, the elder brother of Matthew. Rather surprisingly, since he was the least experienced, and only 31 years old, the board chose Matthew Kirtley. But, it was an imaginative and prescient choice since Matthew would serve the company well and set a good tradition of motive power. Although he was relatively young for this important post he did have the experience of having worked on the three formative companies of British railways – from joining the Stockton & Darlington at the age of 13 years, then on to the Liverpool & Manchester, before eventually joining the London & Birmingham Railway on its opening. He had then maintained the Birmingham & Derby Junction Railway's stock from its opening in 1839 – first as locomotive foreman at Hampton, then with promotion to locomotive superinten-

'Class 60' 2-2-2 locomotive of 1847 by Sharp Brothers & Co of Manchester for the Midland Railway.

dent from the opening of Lawley Street workshops in 1842.

Kirtley brought order to the new Midland Company works. He disposed of the less satisfactory locomotives. Eventually all the small Bury type four wheeled engines went and he made six-wheeled locomotives the basis for the stock. He saw the need to depend less on spares being obtained from the makers of the locomotives, and aimed to make the company much more self-sufficient and the Derby workshops gradually developed on this basis. In the first years of the new company the Derby works continued to only repair and maintain locomotives. A few of the former companies' locomotives were rebuilt to improved patterns as they aged. New engines were bought from outside contractors. In the early years these were still built to the outside engine contractors patterns. During the periods of office of both Kirtley and his successor Samuel Johnson, a high proportion of the Midland Company's locomotives were built by outside contractors, simply because of the quantity required. But from the time Kirtley began to produce the Midland Company's own designs, the contractors manufactured the orders to the Midland's own specifications.

It was in September 1851 that Kirtley's first locomotive design, no.147 a six coupled wheeled goods engine came out of the Derby workshops. This was soon followed by three more engines, before in December that year the first new passenger engine came out – no.96 with a 2-2-2- wheel arrangement. Three more of these single driver engines then came out in the following six months. A steady stream of new engines followed, with the beginnings of some standardisation of types. By the end of 1855 a total of 33 new locomotives had been built in the Midland workshops since 1851; with a further 16 coming from outside contractors. Another 14 engines were completed in the works in 1856, and eight more in 1857.

As the extent of the Midland Company's lines extended through development and absorption of other companies, so the traffic and trains increased, keeping up an increasing workload and momentum for the works. By 1862 the workshops for locomotives, carriages and wagons had increased to four times its area in 1844 and now employed a total works staff of some 2,000 men. Much new machinery had been installed, including travelling overhead cranes in some of the fitting shops, steam hammers, hydraulic presses, tyre cutting machines, tyre hooping furnaces, wheel slotting machines and others, together with the installation of a brass foundry.

Matthew Kirtley was at the same time overseeing the Carriage and Wagon Departments in his capacity as overall superintendent. As with the locomotives, outside contractors built most of the coaches and wagons for the pre-1844 companies and early Midland years, but gradually the Midland began to build these itself and produce its own designs and specifications. Carriages remained relatively small on the Midland Railway up until the 1870s, with four wheels and usually only three compartments. But there was a range of types – individual first, second and third class carriages, some composites, family saloons, post office carriages, guards and luggage vans.

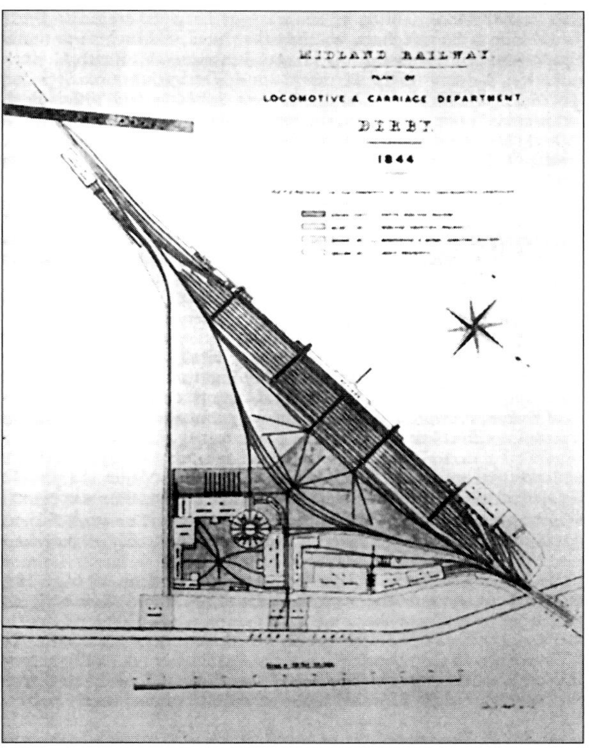

Midland Railway – plan of the Locomotive and Carriage Departments. 1844.

Early Midland Railway passenger coach *c*.1845, probably taken over from one of the earlier constituent companies of the Midland.

William Gladstone's Railway Act of 1844 had, among other measures, improved provisions to be made for third-class passengers. Some railways had hitherto provided little more than open carriages like cattle trucks for this class. Now third-class passengers were guaranteed at least one train a day, running at not less than 12mph, at a rate of no more than 1d (½p) per mile. Their carriages now had to be provided with seats and enclosed from the elements. Some railways paid only lip service to these rules – making special third-class trains run at inconvenient times, starting in the early hours, providing bare bench seats, and covering in the upper sides of the carriages with leather curtains or sliding shutters. The Midland thought better of its third-class passengers from its earliest days, providing three compartments, glazed windows to the sides, and an oil lamp in the roof – fitting out to only a slightly lesser standard than its second class. At the beginning of 1875 the Midland Company took the revolutionary step of abolishing second class for passengers over its whole system. All the second class carriages became third class and the old third-class carriages were withdrawn and broken up as soon as they were replaced. The other railway companies were shocked and disapproved of this breaking of the strict social class distinctions of the Victorian era – it was viewed as "pampering to the working class."

From the early days of carriage and wagon building at Derby, there was increasing variety in the types of vehicles as traffic grew – low sided wagons, timber trucks, milk vans, poultry and cattle vehicles, horse vans, brake wagons, boiler trucks, coal wagons, and vans for many specialised uses – for meat, fish and manufactured materials. For building the locomotives, carriages and wagons there needed to be men employed with an ever widening range of skills – smiths, for iron, brass and copper, foundry-men, mill-wrights, boilermakers, erectors, wheel-wrights, joiners, upholsters and many others.

From the amalgamation in 1844, rapid expansion was a clear factor in George Hudson's mind, to hold back encroachment by the numerous other railway proponents. On 21 July 1845 the little Sheffield & Rotherham Railway with its six locomotives was absorbed into the Midland Railway. The shareholders were given the special privilege of preferential dividends of 6% over other shareholders until the stock was converted in 1897. Its collection of rather inadequate engines were soon condemned by Kirtley and replaced with Midland types.

Also in July 1845 George Hudson sent a proposition to the comparatively veteran Leicester & Swannington Railway for acquisition by the Midland Company. The offer was a good one and the Swannington board recommended acceptance to its shareholders. At a special meeting on 15 June 1846 the Bill for absorption was passed with almost unanimous agreement. After a separate existence of 16 years the historic Swannington line became a small, but nevertheless still important element of the Midland Railway from 1 January 1847, and the oldest part of its system. Its eight locomotives were small machines for main line working and had already become inadequate for the rapidly expanding coal traffic they were built to serve, so they were soon replaced by the Midland. The Swannington Railway helped bring increasing prosperity to the North Leicestershire coalfield but being an isolated line it needed further outlets. Approaches had previously been made by the Midland Counties Railway and there had also been consideration of extensions from Desford on the line, to run and connect to Rugby and the London & Birmingham Railway. After the Midland Railway acquisition the Leicester & Swannington was extended to connect with the Midland main line at Knighton Junction. At the same time a connecting line was extended to Ashby-de-la-Zouch and run to Burton upon Trent. These two connecting lines were put into traffic from 1 August 1849 when a through passenger and goods service between Leicester and Burton was begun.

The Leicester & Swannington is also regarded as memorable for bequeathing to the Midland railway its notable device the 'Wyvern', a mythical legless dragon (although a legged variety did appear in the awning brackets at Keighley Station). This heraldic beast had been the crest of Thomas of Lancaster, Earl of Leicester, so with this strong local connection it was adopted by the Leicester & Swannington as its badge, although curiously it did not appear on the company's seal. However, what does not seem to have been noticed hitherto, is that the Wyvern device at Derby pre-dated the Leicester & Swannington Railway joining the Midland Railway Company. There had been a pair of Wyverns (with legs!) at Derby Station from early 1840. They are depicted by Samuel Russell in his engraving, supporting the shield of the armorial device above the centre point of Thompson's Tri-Junct Station. Russell was finely accurate in his drawings so there is little reason to doubt the fidelity of the picture. It is notable that the Midland Counties Railway were also using the Wyvern device before 1844, on the reverse side of the special tickets for the use of their directors.

The Midland Company eventually used the Wyvern device as its own Company badge, extensively and in an infinite number of ways and places – incorporated into station seats, etched into glass in windows – including coach toilets, in luggage support brackets in coaches, in station awning brackets, as uniform cap badges, on uniform buttons, on horse brasses, bridge structures – the range is a subject in itself. Surprisingly the Wyvern did not appear in the Midland Company's armorial device until the final design, used from 1906. The Wyvern disappeared from the front of Derby Station when Thompson's office section was increased in height to three storeys in 1853. But three new Wyverns reappeared central and dominant on Charles Trubshaw's 1893 final frontage to the Midland's Derby Station. Since the misconceived demolition of the station this central pediment, clock and surmounting Wyvern has been conserved and incongruously re-erected against the wall at the north end of the station car-park.

The next acquisition by the Midland Company was of a much more substantial line, and was accomplished by John Ellis, formerly of the Leicester & Swannington and first Vice-Chairman of the Midland, while travelling by train. The Great Western Railway had been in negotiations to acquire the Bristol & Gloucester Railway, and the Gloucester & Birmingham Railway, to give it access to the Midlands. The Bristol & Gloucester, and the Gloucester & Birmingham Companies were also concurrently involved in joining their two railways into one, as the Bristol & Birmingham Railway. For this

A pair of supportive Wyverns on the crowning centre-piece above the Derby Tri-Junct Station of 1840 sculpted by John Thomas. The first Wyverns at Derby.

A Wyvern appearing on an ivory director's ticket of the Midland Counties Railway – early 1840s.

Wyverns on the centre-piece above the entrance of Charles Trubshaw's 1893 frontage of Derby Midland Station. Now removed to the north end of the car-park.

Engraving of one of the Birmingham & Gloucester Railway's American Norris engines hauling a train up the steep Lickey Bank near Bromsgrove – engraved by J.C.Bourne *c.*1844-45.

The second station at Nottingham was built by the Midland Railway in 1846. Fronting the new Station Street it was designed in a classical Greek character – demolished 1903.

Castle Station, Newark built by the Midland Railway in 1846 in elegant Italianate style, on its new line to Lincoln.

they had signed a formal agreement on 14 January 1845 and were applying to Parliament for an Act to formalise the arrangement. Ellis overhead the conversation on the train (whether by chance or by design is an interesting speculation) between the Birmingham & Gloucester directors, Joseph Gibbins and Edmund Sturge, discussing the proposals for the acquisition by the Great Western Railway. Hearing the reason for their journey to London he then assured them, solely on his own authority, that if the negotiations with the Great Western failed, then the Midland Company would be willing to take a lease on their railways. It was a bold and far-sighted action by Ellis. The two Gloucester Companies were in serious operating difficulties and needed a way out. The GWR declined to meet the Gloucester Company's requested terms, so they turned to the Midland. On 27 January the Midland Railway signed a lease to operate the prospective Bristol & Birmingham Railway for 14 years, and to take on and settle all their financial liabilities.

The Midland thus acquired an important main line expansion to the south-west and for the time being frustrated the Great Western's push to Birmingham. But with the acquisition came a problem. The Gloucester & Birmingham line was laid as standard gauge track, but the Bristol & Gloucester Railway with its connection to the Great Western at Temple Meads, Bristol, had been laid with broad-gauge track, the peculiarity of the Great Western Railway. This meant that for a continuing number of years everyone had to change trains at Gloucester, until by 1854 standard gauge had been laid through to Temple Meads in replacement. The acquisitions placed more demands on Kirtley as locomotive superintendent since the locomotive power on the Birmingham & Gloucester was inadequate, with its unsatisfactory stock of mainly American type Norris engines, needing replacement.

As part of George Hudson's schemes for rapid expansion, and his plans trying to frustrate the proposed Great Northern Railway north from London to Doncaster, the Midland promoted Parlia-

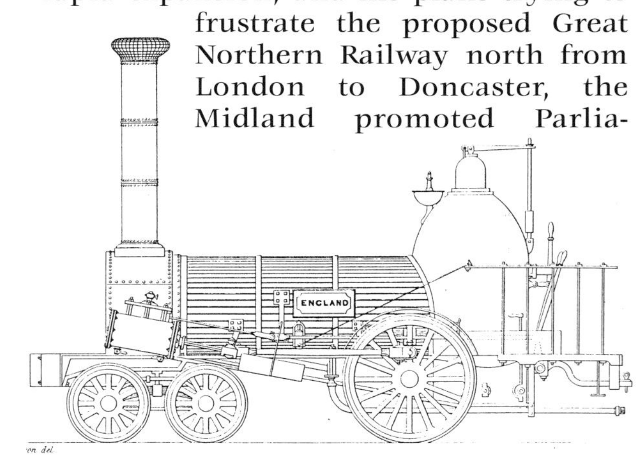

One of the American Norris engines used on the Birmingham & Gloucester Railway and inherited by the Midland Railway from 1845.

mentary Bills in 1845 for two new lines. The first was for a railway extending from the Nottingham station to Newark and Lincoln. There had been a proposal for a Nottingham-Lincoln Railway in 1840, revived in 1842, but not seriously furthered until the Midland Counties began preparatory work in 1844. The projected new line necessitated the modification of the Nottingham terminus of the former Midland Counties Railway by adding two extra platforms on the south side, with through running lines passing over Carrington Street via a level crossing. The line to Lincoln was soon completed and opened in August 1846. But just before this in July 1846 it had become apparent that although extended, Nottingham Station would not be adequate to cater for additional traffic from another direction. The revived Erewash Valley Railway line had been authorised by Parliament on 2 August 1845 to connect to the Midland main line at Long Eaton, and the Leen Valley line to run from Mansfield and connect with the Derby line at Lenton had been given Parliamentary Assent on 16 July 1846. Further, the completely independent project, grandly named the Ambergate, Nottingham, and Boston, and Eastern Junction Railway had also been authorised on 16 July 1846 and would need running powers over the Midland's lines through Nottingham. To meet these new needs the Midland Company decided to abandon the old station, after only six years of use, and to build a new one beyond Carrington Street on the West Croft land. This new station was built to front the new Station Street. It was much larger than its predecessor, with an elegant long classical frontage in keeping with the architecture of many of the Midland Company's other stations to that date. The Lincoln St Marks and Newark Castle Stations were also designed to a refined classical character with Grecian details; although the smaller intermediate stations between Nottingham and Newark were of a tudor character, and those beyond to Lincoln were in a simple Italianate style.

A party of early railway surveyors at work in the field. The first astronomer's transit telescope had been used as a surveyor's level on Strood Tunnel on the Thames & Medway Canal – built 1819-24.

The length of the Ambergate, Nottingham, and Boston, and Eastern Junction Railway's line between Grantham and Nottingham was completed and eventually opened on 15 July 1850, but due to a severe shortage of funds the rest of the line to Ambergate, and everything east of Grantham was not built.

Stamford Station built *c.*1847 by the Midland Railway on their new Syston to Peterborough line, an eclectic style in local stone. Note the fancy valances on the later canopies.

Beeston Station, Notts. A Midland Railway replacement of 1847 with fancy barge-boards and gable-end finials. The shallow hipped ridge and furrow awnings are much later additions.

Also in 1845 a Bill was deposited in Parliament for a line connecting from the Midland line at Syston, north of Leicester, through Melton Mowbray, Oakham, Stamford to Peterborough, for which an Act was granted on 30 June 1845. The building of this line raised more difficulties than the Lincoln line. Its survey and construction met with fierce opposition from Lord Harborough, whose seat was at Stapleford Park near Saxby. His Lordship was a substantial landowner who didn't want a railway on, or even near to, his property. He was additionally concerned that it would be a threat to his interests in the Oakham Canal. His resistance is remembered in the famed fracas on 14 November 1844 between the Midland's surveyors, backed by some 40 burly navvies, and Lord Harborough's estate workers armed with farm implements. Another brawl a few days later, landed several men in gaol for riot. The dispute delayed completion of the Saxby section on the line until 1848.

Stations along this line were a remarkably mixed collection of styles, and the work of several architects. It is known that the architect Francis Thompson turned up again, and had a hand in more than one – possibly Brooksby, Luffenham and Oakham.

There had been a tremendous number of Parliamentary Bills lodged for the 1845 session, 224 altogether, including schemes for Hudson's northern interest – the York, Newcastle and Berwick scheme towards Scotland. Also in was the Great Northern's London to York direct line, and Hudson's

Beeston Station. Elegant iron posts with ornamental cast awning brackets supporting ridge and furrow.

separate schemes linked with the Great Eastern Railway (of which by now he'd become its chairman) by which he intended to thwart the Great Northern project which threatened the Midland routes. George Hudson's manoeuvres to extend his railway interests is complex and a story in itself, but it was one contributory influence in the great speculative boom in railway projects and railway shares from 1845 to 1848, the so-called 'railway mania" when some 650 Railway Acts were passed. The Great Northern Act was eventually passed in June 1846 after a great battle in the committee stages, and became the longest line authorised by one Act of Parliament. Hudson meanwhile, by his rather unscrupulous dealings in this matter, and over his handling of other railways, had entangled himself in a self-created web. This would ultimately lead to his downfall in 1849, following allegations of his having manipulated some companies' accounts and, paid dividends out of capital. At a packed meeting of shareholders at Derby on 19 April 1849, John Ellis as deputy chairman read out a dignified letter from George Hudson resigning from the office of chairman, and by implication, from the board of the Midland Company. The respected John Ellis, whose railway experience went back to the original creation of the Leicester & Swannington Railway in 1829 was then elected as the new chairman.

So passed George Hudson's control and direction of the Midland Railway after six energetic years. It was his shrewd foresight and vision that engineered the amalgamation creating the Midland Railway, and he saw it through the first formative years. His financial trickery was indefensible, but at the same time he deserves some respect for his perception of the sense of larger railways, rather than an extreme multiplicity of little ones. With the creation of the Midland he led the way forward.

Fortunately, Hudson's control of the Midland Company had been more reputable than his management of some other companies, and left fewer problems over its accounts. However, the Midland's finances were at the time seriously overstretched and in a perilous state – partly due to George Stephenson's death in August 1848, then Hudson's personal problems, and not least the necessary programme of rapid expansion.

John Ellis of Beaumont Leys, Leicester, a wealthy Quaker manufacturer interested George Stephenson in the proposed Leicester & Swanington Railway. Deputy chairman of the Midland Railway 1844 and its second chairman 1849-1858.

Fortunately John Ellis was to prove an extremely able chairman, so that by 1851 the company's financial state had been turned round and the position consolidated.

More problems for the company came to a head in December 1849, when all the goods guards and goods porters came out on strike. This put an immediate stop to all goods traffic over the Midland's lines. The situation arose when as an economy measure, the board reduced the wages of these two classes of employees from 19s (95p) to 17s (85p) weekly for the guards and from 17s (85p) to 16s (80p) for porters. The engine drivers and firemen were also on the point of striking when the board tried to force them to work three journeys at the same rate for two journeys. But the directors were forced to back down when faced with the strength of opposition from the men. The directors also had to withdraw the proposed reduction in the pay of the goods guards. But, by taking on numbers of agricultural labourers at a much lower rate of pay the board were able to force most of their goods guards back to work at the reduced rate, although they did temper it by promising to pay more if the price of food rose. The policemen and pointsmen were also restive after their pay had been reduced by five per cent.

In addition to the financial difficulties,

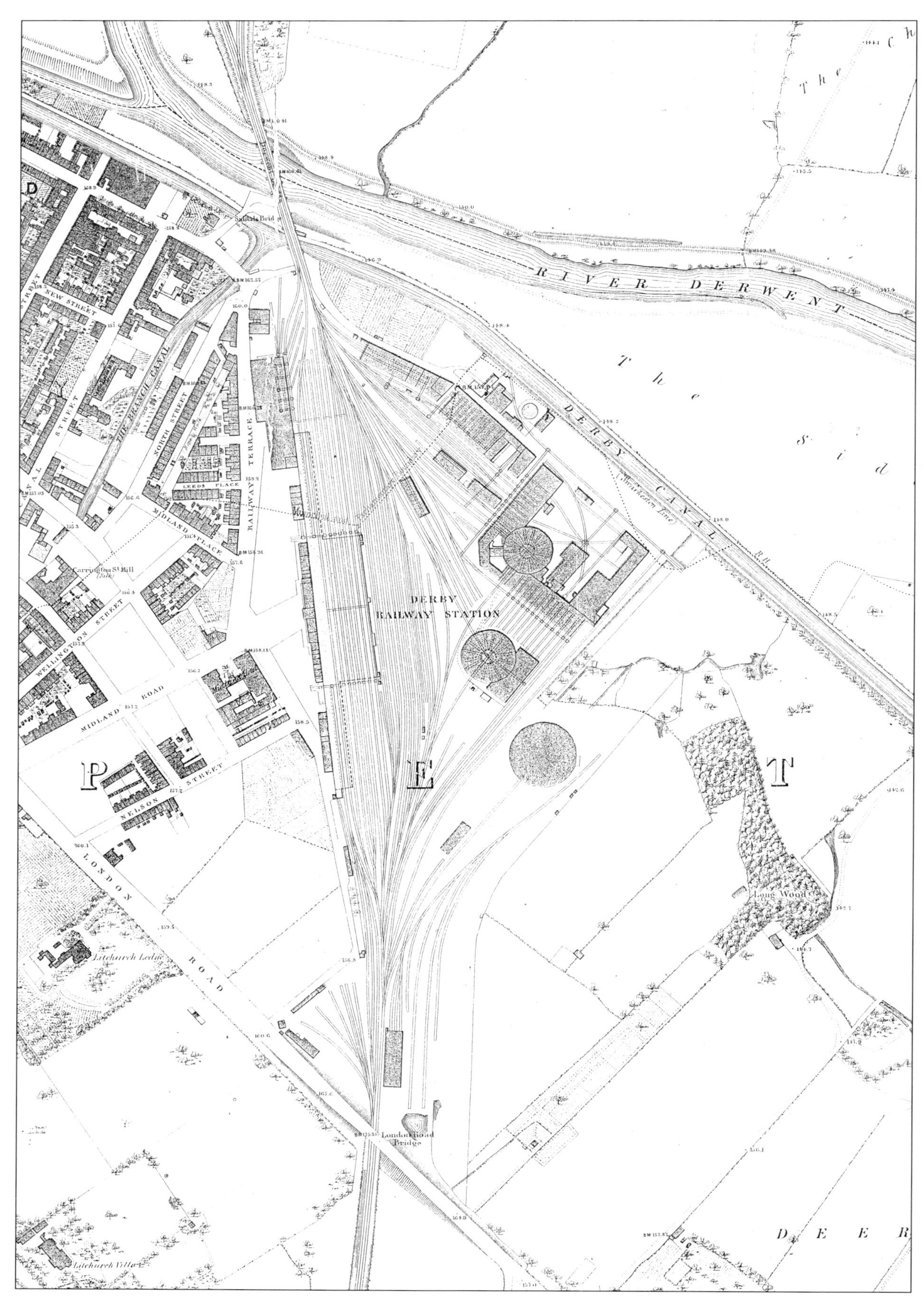

Local Board of Health map of Derby surveyed by the Board of Ordnance – with Midland Railway and works shown. 1852.

Ellis also inherited the problems of the threats to the company's established areas of operation from its rivals around: the London & North Western Railway and the North Staffordshire Railway to the west, the Great Northern to the east and the Manchester, Sheffield & Lincoln Railway from the north. In particular for these

ANNO VICESIMO OCTAVO & VICESIMO NONO

VICTORIÆ REGINÆ.

****

Cap. ccxliii.

An Act to authorize the Construction of a Railway in the Town of *Burton-upon-Trent;* and for other Purposes. [5th *July* 1865.]

WHEREAS by "The *Midland* Railway and *Burton-upon-Trent* Bridge Act, 1859," and "The *Midland* Railway (*Burton* Branches) Act, 1860," the *Midland* Railway Company were empowered to construct within the Town of *Burton-upon-Trent* the Railways in those respective Acts mentioned, one of which Railways was authorized to be constructed across and on the Level of a Street in the said Town called *Guild Street*, and another of which Railways was authorized to be constructed across and on the Level of a Street in the said Town called *High Street:* And whereas the said Railways have for some Time past been completed and opened for Traffic, and by reason thereof a great Diminution in the Passage of Traffic along the Streets of the said Town has been effected, and Obstructions to the Passage of Traffic have decreased, and further Convenience to the Inhabitants of and others frequenting the said Town would result from the Construction of another Railway across *Guild Street*, by facilitating the Transmission of Traffic between the Premises of Messieurs *Bass* and Company on the one Side of the

22 c. 23 c.

[*Local.*] 39 *S* said

Frontispiece of the Act of Parliament 5 July 1865 for various railway lines to be constructed for connecting breweries in Burton upon Trent by the Midland Railway.

railways, was the lucrative coal traffic of the Midland from its Notts-Derbyshire heart, and the Leicester-Derbyshire coalfield. The Midland had an initial monopoly in the area and was content for some years to rely on its early lines, but as the century advanced, the gradual intrusions by the other companies caused the building of a complex web of competing interweaving lines over the Notts-Derby country of the Erewash coalfield, and, to a slightly lesser extent, in the Swadlincote and Coalville areas to the south. The hitherto rural areas became scarred by innumerable coal-pits and waste banks. Extensive sidings containing row upon row of loaded and empty coal wagons decorated the industrial scene. Country villages became extended with regimented terraces of pitmen's cottages. The small border townships of Eastwood, Hucknall, Kimberley, Alfreton, Ripley, Heanor, Ilkeston all became drawn in and soon begrimed through coal-dust and smoke.

The North Staffordshire Railway had built a line to Burton upon Trent in 1848, with a branch from Marston Junction to Willington; and running rights over the Midland lines into Derby Station from 1849. After a request to the Midland Company on 18 October 1849 the North Staffordshire were given the use of the former Birmingham & Derby Junction Railway engine shed near the London Road. After the new Carriage and Wagon works were established off Litchurch Lane in the 1870s, the old shed had to be demolished to give a rail extension into the new works, and the shed was replaced nearby.

The London & North Western Railway also eventually had use of Derby station, with trains running in from March 1872. It also established its own agents at the station and in the town. The LNWR had built its own shed by the Birmingham line at Peartree in the 1860s. And in 1871 it built its own large goods warehouse, called St Andrew's Wharf, adjacent to the railway church of that name, together with a yard and sidings. The North Staffordshire Company were also allowed use of this wharf from 1872.

Burton upon Trent was attractive to the railway companies because of the development of its brewing industry, eventually becoming the largest brewery town in Britain. The Birmingham & Derby Junction Railway was the first there in 1839, and was inherited by the Midland from 1844. The railway connection greatly assisted the development of the brewing industry at Burton by improving its expansion into wider markets and the swifter conveyance of the beers. Ultimately there would be some 20 breweries and malthouses by 1900, but amalgamations reduced this number to 17 by 1911. A complex system of sidings was developed, linked by innumerable branch lines across the town from the various breweries to the main lines. The individual brewery companies each had their own distinctive shunting engines for moving the beer wagons in their yards..

Following the arrivals of the Midland and the North Staffordshire Railways into Burton, the London & North Western also achieved running powers into the town from 1849. The Great Northern finally came in 1878 via its Nottingham – Derby line. All the branch lines to the breweries were built by the Midland Company, and so extensive were these that by 1900 there were some 32 level crossings over the town streets, causing considerable nuisance and delay as road traffic developed

Burton upon Trent Station, with a train of beer barrels on the goods line, evidence of the Midland Railway's important beer transport trade.

through the twentieth century. The internal private railways of the breweries amounted to some 40 miles of track. The Midland Company benefited from the brewery traffic, running fast beer trains in all directions from Burton. It also took advantage of the huge London traffic by building the undercroft of St Pancras Station as a purpose designed vault for Burton barrels.

One of the most notable members of the Burton brewing families was Michael Thomas Bass, grandson of the founder of that company. He became a Member of Parliament for Derby in 1848, representing the town for 32 years. His especial interests included the improvement of the condition of the working classes, and he took up the interests of railwaymen as his constituents and furthered this in Parliament. He caused the Midland Railway to make improvements in the working conditions of its employees. He was a philanthropic benefactor in many

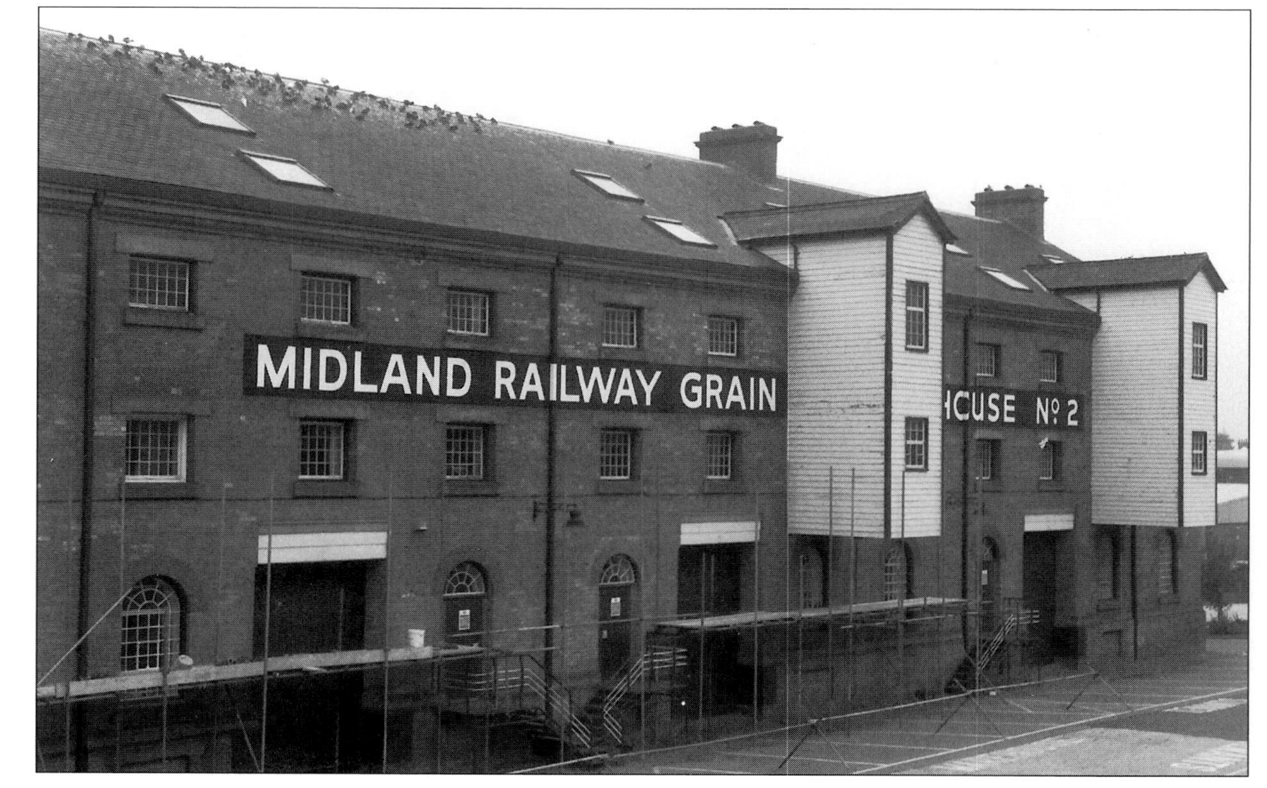

One of a number of nineteenth-century Railway Grain Stores and Bonded Warehouses built by the Midland Railway in Burton upon Trent.

Original Rowsley Station of the Midland Railway 1849 – reputedly designed by Sir Joseph Paxton. The listed building still survives marooned in a contractor's yard.

ways, including the Derby Museum and Library and providing for the establishment of the Railway Orphanage at Derby.

The branch line to Wirksworth was built, principally as a result of railway politics, since the Midland had not originally wanted or needed it. The local worthies of Wirksworth had made approaches way back when the North Midland was being built, for a branch from Duffield, but nothing came of it. The grandly named Manchester, Buxton, Matlock & Midland Junction Railway had opened on 4 June 1849 from Ambergate to Rowsley, and in which the Midland Railway had a major shareholding, and the London & North Western Railway also inherited a lesser holding.

The arrangements also provided for the Midland to work the line for 19 years. In 1863 the Midland opened its own line from Rowsley on to Buxton, and then on to Manchester by 1867. As the Midland was in rivalry with the London & North Western, it became fearful of losing its use of the M, B, M & MJR section in the link and therefore promoted a line from Duffield to Wirksworth and proposals to

Wirksworth Station on the line terminus from Duffield. Midland Railway built 1867. Train of mineral wagons and large number of milk churns on the platform evidence of principal goods traffic. View of *c.*1890.

Invitation for tenders for additions to Goods Warehouses at Derby very early in Midland Railway era – 4 July 1844.

MIDLAND RAILWAY.

TO BUILDERS.

THE Drawings and Specifications for certain additions to the Derby Goods' Warehouses will be ready for inspection at the COMPANY'S OFFICES on and after TUESDAY, July 9th.

TENDERS to be delivered on or before MONDAY July 15th, addressed to Mr. PETER CLARKE, and endorsed "Tender for Works."

The Directors do not pledge themselves to accept the lowest Tender.

PETER CLARKE,
Derby, July 4th, 1844. Superintendant.

extend onwards to Rowsley.

After the Wirksworth branch had been opened in 1867, and the end of the MBM & MJR joint lease approached, the LNWR saw there was little purpose in retaining their share in that line, so from 1 July 1871 the Midland took sole possession of the Ambergate to Rowsley line. The Wirksworth branch enjoyed a moderate passenger traffic and increasing mineral carriage from the limestone quarries. A sizeable traffic in milk transport also built up over the line in the nineteenth century. In 1883, the morning train was taking some 8 to 10 vans, each containing more than 40 churns of local farmers' milk.

Within two months of the creation of the Midland it had been necessary to extend the goods warehouses at the station to meet increasing needs. By 1851 it was reported that trains at Derby were being seriously delayed because there was no provision outside the station to sort goods vehicles. To enable shunting to form a train it was necessary to use the passenger lines with consequent disruptions since there was still only the single long platform from 1840. There was the goods wharf north of the station but this was congested, and the heavy coal traffic caused particular problems. It was therefore proposed that a separate goods yard and coal wharf should be established, north of the Nottingham Road, near to St Mary's Bridge. It was hoped that such a coal wharf, with easier access for users, would provide for coal from the collieries served by the Little Eaton to Ripley branch, and also encourage transfer of coal from the nearby Derby Canal to the railway, altogether generally improving business. The matter was temporarily shelved, but despite certain relief measures at the station the situation continued to worsen. In September 1855 the St Mary's Yard scheme was proceeded with, and opened late the same year. There were several ensuing extensions to the yard throughout the 1860s with the building of coal offices, goods warehouses, corn and potato stores, and stables with the unusual double deck level stables being constructed in 1862. Bonded stores were added together with a fish shed, when the Yard was extended in 1882.

THE WONDER OF 1851!

FROM YORK

TO LONDON AND BACK FOR A CROWN.

THE MIDLAND RAILWAY COMPANY

Will continue to run

TWO TRAINS DAILY

(Excepted Sunday, when only one Train is available)

FOR THE GREAT EXHIBITION,

UNTIL SATURDAY, OCTOBER 11,

Without any Advance of

RETURN SPECIAL TRAINS leave the Euston Station on MONDAYS, TUESDAYS, THURSDAYS, & [illegible]URDAYS at 11 a.m., on WEDNESDAYS and FRIDAYS at 1 p.m., and EVERY NIGHT (Sundays excepted) at 9 p.m.

First and Second Class Tickets are available for returning any day (except Sunday) up to and including Monday, Oct. 20. Third Class Tickets issued before the 6th instant are available for 14 days, and all issued after the 6th are returnable any day up to Monday the 20th.

The Trains leave York at 9-40 a.m. every day except Sunday, and also every day, including Sunday, at 7-20 p.m.

Fares to London and Back:—

1st Class 15s. 2nd, 10s. 3rd, 5s.

The Midland is the only Company that runs Trains Daily at these Fares.

Ask for Midland Tickets!

Children above 3 and under 12 years of age, Half-price. Lugg[illegible]allowed—112 lbs. to First Class, 100 lbs. to Second, and 56 lbs. to Third Class Passengers.

APPROVED LODGINGS, of all classes, are provided in London for Passengers by Midland Trains. The Agents will give Tickets of reference on application, without charge, and an Office is opened in London, at DONALD'S WATERLOO DINING ROOMS, 14, Seymour-street, near Euston Station, where an agent is in regular attendance to conduct parties who go up unprepared with Lodgings.

The Managers have much pleasure in stating that the immense numbers who have travelled under their arrangements have been conducted in perfect safety—indeed in the history of the Midland Lines, *no accident, attended with personal injury, has ever happened to an Excursion Train.* In cond[illegible]g the extraordinary traffic of this Great Occasion the first object is to ensure *safety*, and that object has hitherto been most happily achieved.

With the fullest confidence, inspired by past success, the Conductors have pleasure in urging those who have not yet visited the Exhibition, to avail themselves of the present facilities, and to improve the opportunity which will close on the 11th of October.

All communications respecting the Trains to be addressed to the Managers, for the Company,

John Cuttle & John Calverley, Wakefield;
Thomas Cook, Leicester.

October 2nd, 1851.

T. COOK, PRINTER, 28, GRANBY-STREET, LEICESTER.

Midland Railway advertisement for special trains to the Great Exhibition, London 1851.

Wisbech Sidings 1905. Vast numbers of wagons on the extensive sidings between the Midland Railway and the Midland & Great Northern Joint Railway into East Anglia showing the great goods traffic of the Midland.

Upper level of Midland Railway Bonded Stores at St Mary's Goods Wharf, Derby built 1882.

Land for the Chaddesden Sidings near Derby was acquired in 1860. These were gradually developed alongside the old Nottingham main line, to give a chain of extensive marshalling facilities for goods trains, with hump shunting provisions. At the eastern extremity of these, near Spondon a large carriage shed was provided in 1872, and nearer, by Meadow Lane, Chaddesden, a wagon repair workshop was built in 1873.

Five Arches bridge, Derby Station – widened on this east side in 1862 to carry four tracks over the River Derwent and Derby Canal. View 1994.

The bottleneck of only two rail tracks over the Five Arches Bridge was relieved by widening the bridge and providing two additional lines. The Litchurch relief route, the present main line south to London out of the station was opened in 1867. This avoided the hitherto tiresome need for reversal in the station of trains coming in over the original Midland Counties Railway approach via Chaddesden, and which were going onwards in a northern direction. To build this new relief route the Midland Company bought the rest of the old Castlefields Estate land beyond the Railway Works, down to Deadman's Lane. This area had formerly been the Deer Park of Castlefields House, but a substantial piece of it had been bought from the trustees by William Etches a cheese merchant in Derby.

The Etches were an old established family of cheese factors with a business seemingly started in about 1820 in the Corn Market at St Peter's Bridge. In the late 1840s W.J. & E.Etches moved into a specially built new cheese warehouse,

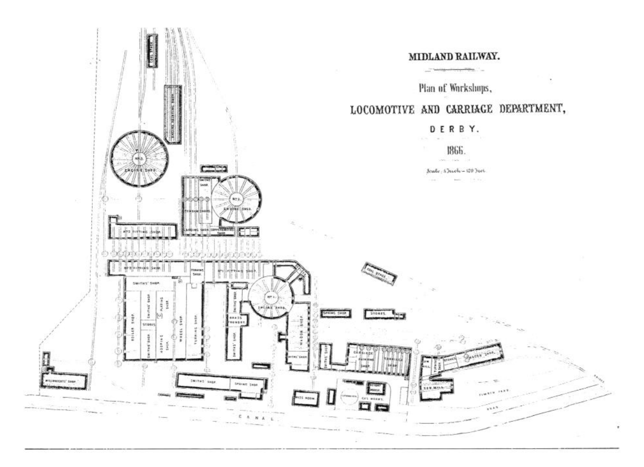

Midland Railway plan of workshops at Derby. 1866.

adjacent to the former North Midland/ Midland Counties Warehouse on Railway Terrace. At about the same time William Etches bought some of the Castlefields Deer Park land from the trustees, together with more there from the estate of the late Henry Cox in 1848. Etches built himself an unpretentious villa on the land, with the grand title of 'The Park', Litchurch. The purchase of this Castlefields land and Etches estate enabled the Midland to not only build the new line, but to extend its works, and to build carriage sheds. This part of the Midland Railway Works has continued to be called 'Etches Park' right up to present time.

In 1855 James Allport the general manager, recommended to the Midland board that an intermediate station should be provided on the north side of the old Nottingham Road, in connection with the Ripley branch to be opened in 1856. This new station was opened in September that year and proved so popular for local use that it had to be extended in 1860 and again in 1867 and 1868. The station was additionally busy on the occasions of the Derby Races which had been transferred from the old Siddals Course to the new Racecourse nearby, in August 1848.

James Allport was one of the exceptional men who served the Midland Railway well over the years of its existence. He was born at Birmingham in 1811 and joined the Birmingham & Derby Junction Railway on its opening in 1839, becoming in turn Chief Clerk and then its general manager. When the Midland was formed in 1844 he became redundant, but George Hudson recognising his abilities, found him a post as general manager on one of his other interests, called the York, Newcastle & Berwick Railway, until it formed part of the North Eastern Railway in 1854. When Hudson fell in disgrace Allport went to the Manchester, Sheffield & Lincolnshire Railway, before finally coming to Derby as general manager of the Midland Company in 1853. He became a director from 1854 to 1857 but returned to the post of general manager from 1857 until 1880, when he retired. On his retirement he was given a seat on the board of directors again, with an honorarium of £10,000 for his distinguished service. He was knighted in 1884 in recognition of his services to the travelling public. Sir James Allport built a large house – 'Springhill' – on Hazlewood Road, Duffield in the mid-1880s, but only lived there for a few of his remaining years. He died appropriately on Midland Company territory on 25 April 1892 in the Midland Grand Hotel at St Pancras.

During the 1850s a series of alterations were made at the Derby Station. In 1850 George Thompson, the builder erected offices for the Goods Dept., at the station's east end. In 1853 Francis Thompson's central office block was raised by a part third storey, by the builder John Wood, and decorated with fashionable jalousies to the windows. Additionally, new offices for the Audit Dept. were built in that year. Then in 1855 the splendid *'porte-cochère'* was added, covering in the main entrance from the elements. This was immediately

James Joseph Allport (1811-1892) born at Birmingham. In1839 at 28 he joined the Birmingham & Derby Junction Railway as traffic agent at Hampton, rising to become manager of the B&DJR. Exceptional general manager of the MR from 1853 until retirement in 1880. Knighted in 1884 in recognition of his services to rail travel.

Front of Derby Station *c.*1891, with the splendid shareholders room of 1857, by John H.Sanders, to the right – the Member's Institute accommodation was downstairs.

followed in 1856 by the start on building the great new shareholders' room. Designed by John Holloway Sanders the company Architect and built by George Thompson it was completed in 1857. This two-storey block was arranged as a wing projecting forward from the south end of Thompson's 1840 station offices. The shareholders room, a splendid large and lofty space was arranged on the upper floor level. Previously, Midland Company shareholders meetings had been held in rather unsatisfactory accommodation. Firstly in the former Midland Counties engine shed next to their old works, but after a shareholder had been accidentally killed crossing the tracks to get to the building, the half-yearly meetings had then been transferred to the ground floor space of the old North Midland/Midland Counties Warehouse on Railway Terrace. The ground floor area of the new block was designed to provide space for the Members Institute, replacing the early use of railway cottages in Leeds Place with a new reading room, library and class-rooms. After 1892 when the fine new Midland Railway Institute building was constructed on the opposite corner of Midland Place the ground floor of the shareholders building was converted for use by the Railway Veterans Club.

The shareholders room was followed in 1859 by an additional three-storey office accommodation to the left of the station entrance to house the general manager and superintendent's offices, and also along in front of Thompson's screen wall to the north side.

A new boardroom, beyond the share-holders room, was added in 1872-73,

Interior of the great share-holders room in 1983 – just before demolition.

Part of general manager and superintendent's offices of 1853 just before demolition in 1985.

admirably fitted out by Gillows of London – the fashionable firm of Designers and Furniture makers. The original North Midland boardroom of 1840 had been in use until then, and was proving inadequate for the substantial Company that the Midland was becoming.

Platform no.1, the original long single one, had been in use as the sole one until 1867, when the old central carriage lines were taken out and replaced with a new island platform nos.2 and 3 and provided with an overbridge. It was 1881 before any further significant alterations were made – then platform no.4 was put in inside the overall roof, with platform no.6 complete with an awning roof being added outside Thompson's original wall. The single bay platform no.5 was put in at the same time. These additions were made because of increasing traffic, but also with the prospect of the Royal Agricultural Show being held in the grounds of nearby Osmaston Hall, with Royal visitors.

Over at the Loco Works Matthew Kirtley had found by 1845 that he urgently needed to provide extra cover for the larger number of Locomotives in use. Building Roundhouse no.2 was authorised providing 16 additional lines, with a Butterley Company turntable, and was in use by early 1847. Although this eased the position for a few years, by the early 1850's there was need for more accommodation. A much larger Roundhouse no.3 was built in 1852, providing 24 lines inside. It was designed by Sanders and built by Geo. Thompson. Finally in 1890 a fourth engine shed was built, rectangular in shape but containing double turntables. Over this same period the Works expanded greatly from the extent of the original North Midland and Midland Counties workshops – with a continuing stream of building – fitting shops, boilers, millwrights, smith's, carriage shops, copper, wheel turning and repair shops, brass foundry and more, to meet the ever increasing needs of the company.

The original Loco offices of the North Midland Company were doubled in size in 1859-60 by the addition of a second floor; while the clock tower was raised in height

Part of the MR's boardroom suite of 1873, prior to demolition in 1985.

Derby Station interior by gaslight on an evening in June 1911. Up-train on Platform 2 with fruit, milk vans and a horse box. Stephenson/ Thompson's train shed was swept away 1954, to be replaced with concrete awnings.

at the same time, and a footbridge link was built from platform no.1 on the station, over to this new floor, and down to ground level. Finally in 1893 a third floor was added to these offices. The tower remained unaltered except for the clock faces being raised in to the top turret.

By the early 1850s, the Midland Company was experiencing considerable difficulties and delays to its freight traffic on to the LNWR lines at Rugby, down to London. In 1852 some 325,000 tons of coal

Midland Railway locomotive roundhouse No.3 of 1852, providing 24 lines inside. Outside can be seen a Samuel Johnson 2-4-0 locomotive, No.131 and an 0-6-0 tank engine No.1720. This building was damaged by bombs in a Zeppelin air raid on Derby in January 1916.

Midland Railway Erecting Shop No.8 in the great days of steam power, filled completely with Kirtley and Johnson locomotives – 1895.

Derby Works – tool shop *c.*1910, and with shop foreman's glazed cabin.

had gone on to the LNWR line down to Euston and the south. The LNWR line was grossly overloaded. Plans for improving the situation had even included an amalgamation with the London & North Western Railway, with a Bill being introduced into Parliament for the 1853 session. But this was stopped because a House Committee was still considering whether any further large amalgamations were desirable. The Midland next turned to considering an extension line from Wigston, Leicester down to a junction with its old enemy the Great Northern at

Derby Works – shop foremen's group *c.*1872, in front of Kirtley 0-6-0 No.321 built in 1859.

Derby Work's offices – ground floor stage North Midland Railway of 1839 with their engine workshop beyond – first floor added by Midland Railway in 1859 and the second floor level in 1893 – photograph *c.*1900.

Hitchin, so as to gain an alternative route into London via Kings Cross – which had spare capacity. Various routes were considered and that via Bedford was adopted, and relations with the Great Northern were mended. The Bill went before Parliament in 1853 and receive the Royal Assent on 4 August. The main contract was awarded to Messrs Brassey, Peto and Betts, that great amalgamation of Victorian railway contractors. Work started expeditiously, but the course of the

Above: **Derby Work's and Station area looking north c.1890. Coaling shed to the left, track centre leads into the old NMR roundhouse.**

works were bedevilled with problems, the most serious being a continual shortage of men and disruptions particularly at harvest times which drew the navvies away. The contract overran into 1857, and the Leicester to Hitchin extension line was finally opened for mineral and goods trains in April, with passenger traffic from 7 May.

Kettering and Wellingborough stations of 1857 on the Leicester-Hitchin line were designed by the architect Charles H.Driver. They were particularly significant for the first appearance of the Midland's subsequent extensive use of glazed ridge and furrow awnings over platforms. It was that great architectural and horticultural innovator John Claudius Loudon who introduced the philosophy of glasshouses. Joseph Paxton is usually credited with the idea of ridge and furrow glazing with its introduction on the building of the Great Conservatory at Chatsworth House in 1836-40. But while this may be so, the detailed creation and execution of such a mathematically complex design as the Great Conservatory was by the classical architect Decimus Burton (1800-1881). The principle of glazed ridge and furrow roofs was also used very effectively on stations of the Derby to Manchester extension line (1863-67), with its dramatic route through the

Right: **Express locomotive 2-2-2 type No.130 built 1852 for the MR by Robert Stephenson & Co of Newcastle upon Tyne.**

Far right: **Joseph Paxton and Decimus Burton's Great Conservatory at Chatsworth which inspired the ridge and furrow glazed platform awnings of the Midland Railway.**

The original North Midland Railway station by Francis Thompson at Chesterfield in 1867-68, with the addition of ridge and furrow canopies. 'Jenny Lind' express type locomotive No.728 built at Derby in May 1855.

Peak District, and its fine lofty stone viaduct crossing Monsal Dale, memorably execrated for its impact, by the art and architectural critic John Ruskin. Edward Walters a Manchester architect, and friend of the Midland's Consultant Engineer William H.Barlow, designed a number of fine stations on this line with the new Rowsley, and Bakewell Stations being particularly handsome for smaller stations, probably because they respectively served the Duke of Devonshire for Chatsworth, and the Duke of Rutland for Haddon Hall.

The use of the Great Northern's London terminus at King's Cross in place of the London and Northern Western's Euston was not to prove a lasting solution. By the early 1860s the line between Hitchin and London also became seriously congested. There was only one pair of lines, and these were being called upon to cope with the expanding goods and passenger trains of two major companies. This meant that it was frequently necessary to shunt lengthy heavy mineral and goods trains off the lines to make way for the faster timed passenger trains. In the continuing congestion the Midland Company was finding that its trains were rather naturally being relegated in preference to the Great Northern's. A number of serious accidents on the line and the collapse of negotiations with the Great Northern helped the Midland decide that its only recourse was for the company to build its own London terminal, with a new route into the metropolis from Bedford southward through Luton and St Albans. In 1861 the Midland board had begun serious steps, firstly with a sanctioned goods station at Agar Town, Kentish Town, London, and then with the purchase in the December of lands fronting Euston Road in St Pancras Parish. The Midland Railway (Extension to London) Bill went before the Commons Select Committee on 3 March 1863. There was extensive examination of the Midland's case with the evidence mainly turning on the enormous increases in the Midland goods and coal traffic to London; especially the latter:-

Trent Station at the junction of the Nottingham, Derby and Erewash Valley lines. Located in the 'middle of nowhere' without proper road access it was built in 1862 purely as an interchange station. Both sides of the island platforms had a fine range of ridge and furrow canopies supported on cast-iron bracketed posts – closed December 1967.

The new lounge/tea room at the Midland Grand Hotel, St Pancras 1912. A scene of refinement among the sprouting potted palms.

The Midland Railway's termini for London traffic. The extensive Somers Town Goods Station alongside the soaring spires and pinnacles of Sir Gilbert Scott's St Pancras Hotel and Station, with William Barlow's great train shed behind, pictured in May 1922.

	Goods and Coal	Coal alone
1857	676,000 tons	492,000 tons
1862	1,111,000 tons	818,000 tons

Also because of the congestion on the Great Northern's line, and the high dues being paid on that route, four times as much coal was being sent via Rugby over the LNWR's lines. The Bill was finally approved and the Royal Assent given on 22 June 1863. The planning and execution of the extension scheme was one of the most difficult and complex civil engineering ventures undertaken by the Midland, notwithstanding the herculean demands of the Settle-Carlisle line. The primary objects of the scheme were the needs of the company's goods, and coal traffic, since the core of the Midland Railway's income came from freight receipts. This is usually unremarked because of the overpowering majesty of Barlow's great train shed, and Sir Gilbert Scott's splendid gothic hotel at St Pancras – two integrated masterpieces – and which reflect passenger traffic rather than more mundane freight. The station was completed in 1868, with the hotel starting building in that same year, and being finally opened for public use in 1873.

The frontage of St Pancras drawn with the extra storey planned by Sir Gilbert Scott, but omitted from the final building.

It was as well that the Midland carried through its own London line at that time. By the 1880s some 18,000 wagons would be received and dispatched during summer months at Toton sidings, rising to as many as 26,000 in winter months. In summer there would be thirty or forty horses on shunting duty, but sometimes two or three horses would be needed to move one wagon in winter when axle boxes froze up.

The Midland Railway was a considerable user of horse power. They were used

Interior of William Barlow's soaring vault over the St Pancras train shed. Photographed pre-1876. There are rows of early Midland Railway four and six wheel carriages with roof luggage racks and roof mounted compartment oil lamps. There are horse boxes in the foreground and an early signal cabin like a small sentry box at the end of platform 1.

A Kirtley straight framed '240' class 0-6-0 locomotive No.2300 (built in 1850 as No.240) at Chesterfield in July 1911 hauling a Toton-Cricklewood destined coal train.

Vast lines of loaded Midland Railway and private owners coal wagons at the Toton marshalling yards in 1910 awaiting sorting and assembly into trains, mainly for London. Large numbers of shunters were employed to do the work, which could be hazardous.

Midland Railway cartage horses at London Road stables, Derby 1905. There were more, extensive stables at St Mary's Goods Yard.

for shunting goods vans and wagons, also for road haulage of parcel and goods vehicles, carts, wagons and, horse omnibuses in London. At the end of the Midland in 1922, the company employed 3,007 horses for the haulage of 7,283 road vehicles, and

96 horses for shunting duties.

In the 1860s in addition to the great ventures of the line to Manchester, and the London Extension to St Pancras the Midland also decided to extend its lines to the most northern extent.

The Settle & Carlisle Railway of 72 miles length, was an unlikely route for an all weather main-line to Scotland. It runs over and through wild hills and bleak moorlands, in remote stretches of the Pennines where the population is sparse and the rainfall high. For the 22 miles from Edenvale to Aisgill the climb is gruelling and the engineering problems awesome – so much so that the resilient general manager James Allport rather understandingly remarked after walking over much of the route – "I shall never forget, as long as I live, the difficulties surrounding the undertaking..."

The project of the line arose from a continuing determination of the Midland from its Hudson days, not to be confined to being a mere regional railway, but to expand into all parts of Britain. Its main rivals, the LNWR and the Great Northern group already controlled the west and east coasts traffic routes to Scotland. The Midland was not content to sit back to this situation. During the earlier 1860s the Midland had established a route up via Leeds to Skipton and then on via the so-called 'Little North Western Railway' to Ingleton on the Lancaster-Carlisle Railway. But the latter was controlled by the LNWR, so the Midland was only allowed a low priority for its passengers and goods from Ingleton to Carlisle. The Midland's frustrations led to the promotion of a Bill before Parliament in early 1866, supported by its Scottish allies the Glasgow & South Western, and the North British Railways. The Royal Assent for the Carlisle & Settle Railway was granted on 16 July 1866.

Although the Midland board now had the authority and the will, there were the obstacles of the diffi-

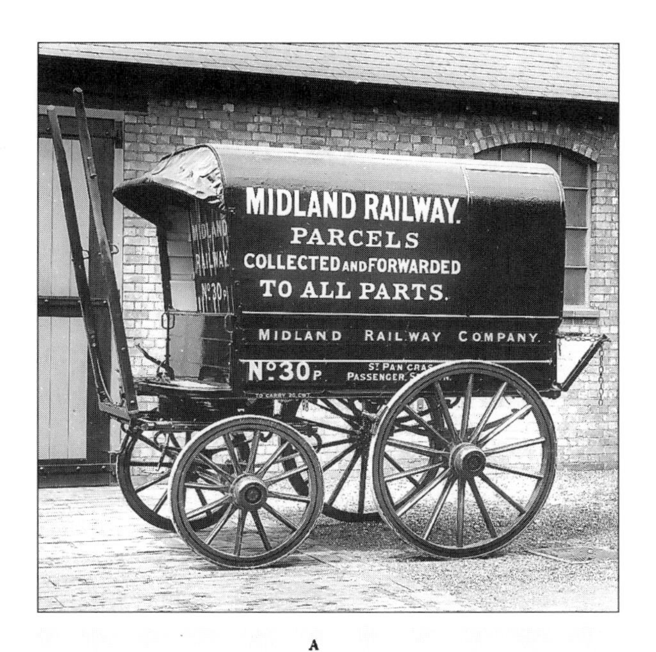

One of the numerous Midland Railway horse-drawn parcel vans allocated all over their system. This one was based at St Pancras Station.

A

BILL

For enabling the MIDLAND RAILWAY COMPANY to construct RAILWAYS from SETTLE to HAWES, APPLEBY and CARLISLE; and for other Purposes.

[The words printed in *Italics* are proposed to be inserted in Committee.]

WHEREAS it is expedient that the Midland Railway Company should be empowered to construct Railways from Settle to Hawes, Appleby and Carlisle, and to raise additional capital for such purpose:

5 And whereas Plans and Sections showing the lines and levels of the proposed Railways and the lands which the Company are by this Act empowered to acquire for the purposes thereof, and Books of Reference to such Plans containing the names of the owners or reputed owners, lessees or reputed lessees and occupiers of such lands, have been 10 deposited with the Clerks of the Peace for the West and North Ridings of the county of York and for the counties of Westmoreland and Cumberland respectively:

And whereas it is expedient that the Company should be empowered to work over and use the Hawes and Melmerby Railway and the 15 stations, works and conveniences connected therewith, and also the

Front page of Parliamentary Bill for the Midland Railway Company proposing to build a railway from Settle to Carlisle in 1865.

Engraving showing constructing Arten Gill Viaduct in the Vale of Dent – 660 feet long and some 117 feet high of 11 stone arches – in wild countryside on the Settle & Carlisle line opened in 1876.

Engraving of Dent Head Viaduct north of Blea Moor tunnel on the Settle & Carlisle line – 600 feet long and some 100 feet high, of ten arches.

cult terrain to overcome; and not least to raise a very substantial capital sum for the work. The Midland finances were already over stretched by its other schemes. Then on 11 May 1866 the London financial markets were shaken by the catastrophic collapse of the old established bank of Overend Gurney & Co, with known debts of £10 million. Overend Gurney with others had been major financiers of railways and contractors. The respected Thomas Brassey lost £1 million in the collapse and survived, but Peto and Betts folded, and Sir Morton Peto was ruined. Even the Midland Railway had to pay its contractors in shares in place of cash during the worst time of the disaster.

The Midland tried to delay its start on the Settle-Carlisle line but a Parliamentary condition of approval was that the work should be completed in five years. Although preliminary work commenced in 1869, full construction did not get under way until 1870. The works involved 20 big viaducts including the magnificent Ribblehead viaduct of 24 spans with a maximum pier height of 100 feet, together with 14 tunnels including Blea Moor Tunnel, 2,629 yards long with a maximum depth below the moor of 500 feet. Both these greater constructions took from 1870 until 1875 to complete. The Midland built 19 stations along the route, and despite the company's financial restraints, these were all of substantial construction. Built mainly in stone with slate roofs. J.S.Crossley's designs largely followed the by then standard Midland form for a country station of twin wings with central booking hall link and a glazed porch to the station side (c.f. Butterley Station at the Midland Railway Trust).

The line was eventually opened in 1876, and the first passenger train was hauled by a modest sized rebuilt Kirtley 2-4-0 locomotive. From 1879 the superb carriages of the Midland Company's Scottish joint stock came into service giving luxury travel to Scotland.

With the completion of the Settle & Carlisle line the final form of the Midland system was virtually complete. It would add the Dore & Chinley Railway in 1888 with its long tunnel of 3.95 miles between Dore and Grindleford stations. The longest railway tunnel in Britain, other than the Severn Tunnel, it was extremely difficult to construct because of the incredible flow of water out of the natural rock. Lowburn Tunnel on the same line is 2.18 miles long and the third longest on the Midland system. It was also a tough

Kirtley class 2-4-0 No.158A built at Derby in 1866 – double-framed and re-boilered by Johnson – in ownership of the National Railway Museum, York.

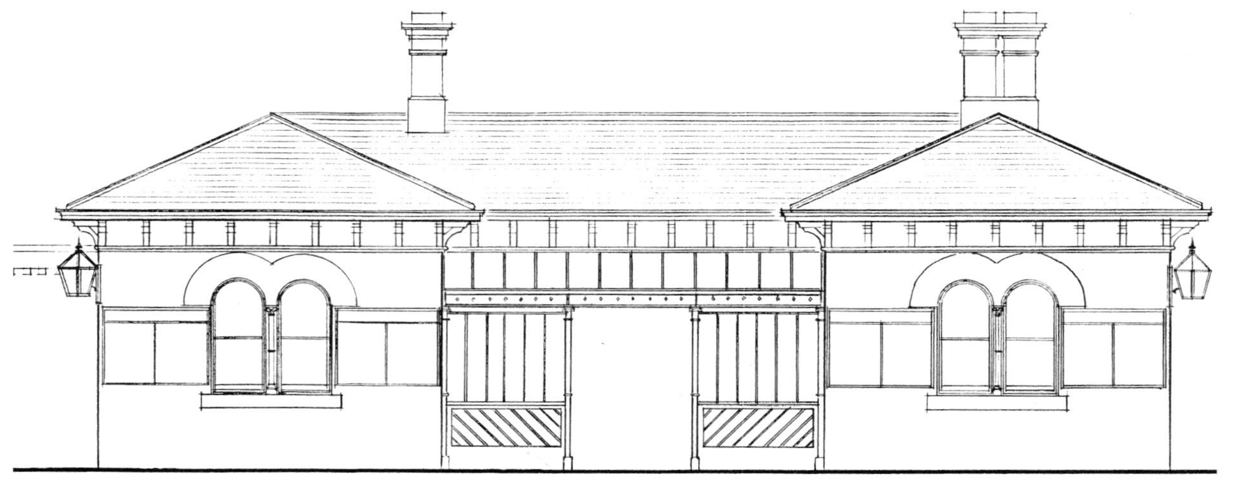

Whitwell Station, Midland Railway – standard pattern of 1875 by John S.Crossley – relocated to Butterley by the Midland Railway Trust in 1983-85 to replace the original station demolished by BR.

tunnel to drive because of the hard rock, but it was dry. The line was opened through for goods traffic in November 1893 and for passenger in May 1894.

A conclusive final extension for the Midland system came with the addition of the London Tilbury & Southend Railway on 1 January 1912. The LT&S was a much different railway from the Midland. Its goods traffic was minimal but in relation to its track mileage its passenger traffic was enormous. In 1910 alone it carried over 32 million passengers, some 46,500 being season-ticket holders. It was an intense and highly organised commuter service into London run by a fleet of 72 distinctive 4-4-2 type tank engines.

It was the end of another era when Matthew Kirtley the first Locomotive Engineer of the Midland Railway died on 24 May 1873. His excellent engines were soundly built, and giving good performance many achieved remarkable longevity; some dozen even survived through World War Two to pass into British Rail ownership in 1948.

Following Kirtley's death his nephew William, the workshop superintendent, temporarily took on his late uncles duties until the new locomotive superintendent, Samuel Waite Johnson arrived at Derby to take over the post from 1 July 1873. Samuel Johnson had a wide experience on several railways in his career to that date, the last of which was with the Great Eastern, and he was to prove a more than worthy successor. An extremely able man, he was to take the Midland locomotives forward into the twentieth century. He was a totally different character to Kirtley's jovial workmanlike manner. Johnson was of a more refined nature, meticulous and, almost treated engine design as an art. This is reflected in his locomotive designs, in the clean elegant lines of his famous single driver express engines, his fine 4-4-0 engines – simples

Open third class four-wheeled coach No.471 built by outside contractor, the Gloucester Carriage & Wagon Co, for the MR in 1865.

Samuel Waite Johnson (1831-1912) MR locomotive superintendent from 1873 to 1903. Successor to Kirtley, he came from the Great Eastern Railway – a meticulous designer of elegant locomotives.

Johnson Tank engine 0-4-4 No.1636 built at Derby 1883 – the last Midland locomotive to come out painted in the old green livery.

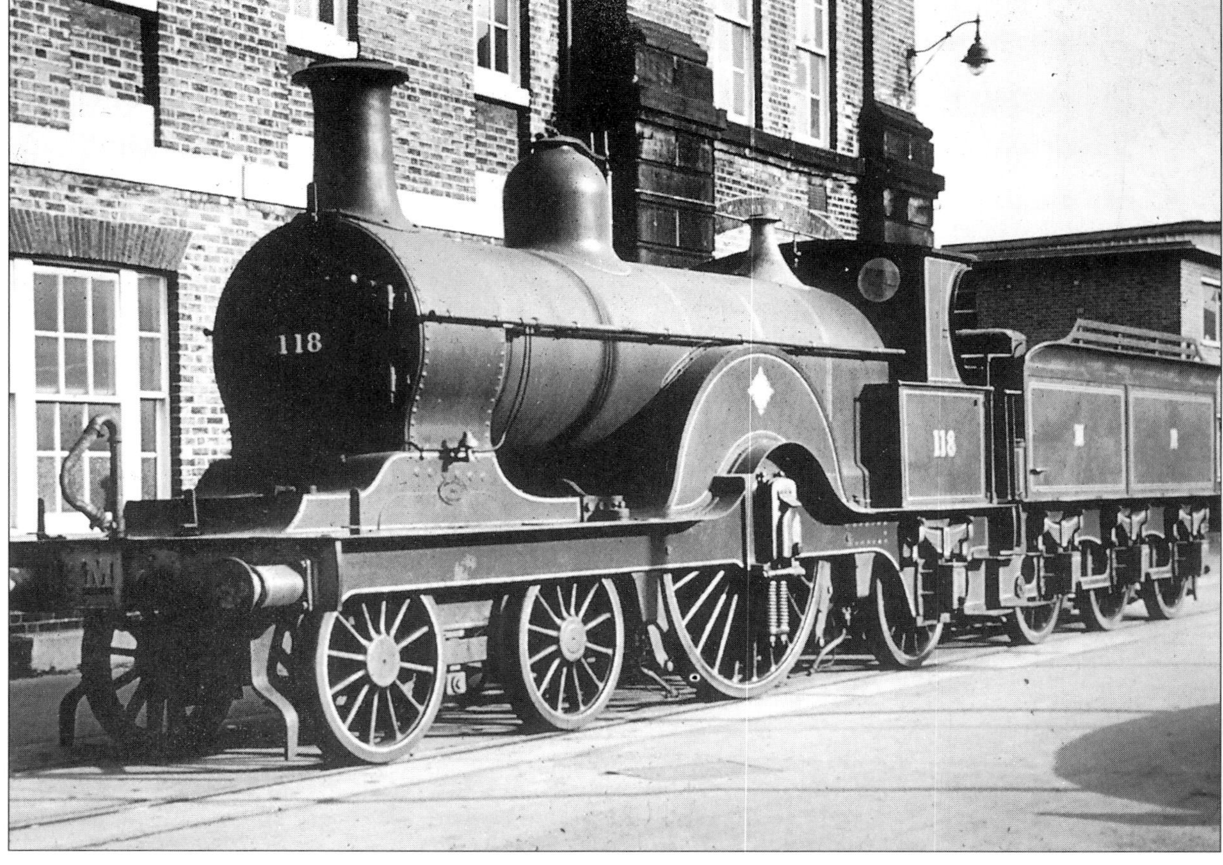

One of the splendid Johnson 2-2-2 express locomotives, commonly known as "Spinners". There were originally 95 of these engines, built in five series between 1887 and 1900. All had been broken up by 1928, except No.118 (673) which survives in the National Railway Museum collection.

and the compounds, and sound little tank engines.

It was during Johnson's tenure that the famous 'Midland Red' colour was evolved and adopted. This notable colour was the third livery to be adopted for the company's engines. Kirtley had them painted dark green from the beginning in 1844. This was then changed to a blue green, with black edging and white lining. During 1876-77 a much lighter green was used. Then after an experiment with a duller red in 1881, the splendid crimson was evolved and used from 1883 as the locomotives' livery, with yellow and white linings.

The carriages of the company had been painted a claret or dark red from July 1844, but from 1883 they also were painted the same crimson as the engines. Carriage stock and locomotives were turned out in an immaculate state, and were kept so in daily use. The paint specification grew more detailed to achieve the high standard demanded, requiring some five undercoats, a top coat of colour, then finished with three coats of varnish. Labour was very much cheaper in the Victorian age.

It had been decided before Kirtley's death that the Locomotive, and Carriage and Wagon departments needed to be separated because of the greatly increased scale of the work. Thomas Gethin Clayton came from the Great Western Railway and took up the new separate post of Carriage and Wagon superintendent at the same

Far right: **Osmaston-by-Derby Hall (1696) in *c.*1862 photographed by Richard Keene and J.A.Warwick, bought by the MR in 1888 to extend their Carriage and Wagon Works. Used by the Midland for a while as offices and records store, it was eventually sold to Derby Corporation in 1938, and promptly demolished.**

Right: **Litchurch Lane, Osmaston Hall and Estate before Midland Railway expansion into this area. Rogerson's map, 1819.**

Map of Derby – showing expansion of the Midland Company and the new Carriage and Wagon Works off Litchurch Lane. 1876.

time as Samuel Johnson came. Clayton started with just three clerks from out of the old locomotive department and then added to these with a base of workmen who had previously worked on the carriages. Some 50 acres of land was purchased in late 1873 for the new Carriage and Wagon Works to be located off Litchurch Lane. Plans were approved in early 1874 and the Way and Works Committee was authorised to immediately proceed with machine and fitting shops, a foundry and other necessary facilities. A new wagon shop, carriage

New MR carriages under construction at Derby in 1921 – 54-foot long, bogie brake thirds non-corridor designed by Robert W.Reid, the company's last Carriage & Wagon superintendent.

building shop and paint shops followed in early 1875. By 1878 there was some 13½ acres of workshops and these were in full production.

Clayton from his arrival at Derby had set to work to modernise the archaic carriage stock of the Midland. He abolished the old four wheel coaches and established six wheel ones as the norm. Then after Allport's visit to America in 1873 came the large Pullman cars with bogie wheels in kit form, from Detroit. Gradually, four and six wheel bogied carriages were designed and introduced, including the splendid 54 ft long vehicles for the Settle & Carlisle line joint stock in 1879, with the Midlands own following in 1883. Clayton's development and improvement of Midland carriage stock was radical and set high standards – these would be continued and built upon by his able successor David Bain after 1903.

The Carriage & Wagon Works also built large quantities of wagons, vans and trucks, of all sorts. In July 1888 the Midland purchased most of the adjacent Osmaston Park Estate for further extensions, and converted the fine hall of 1696 to office use. Only the small part of the park used for the Royal Agricultural Show was left. The last show there was in 1933.

Unloading traffic at the show-ground sidings and platforms specially provided by the MR for the Royal Agricultural Show in June 1906 on some 84 acres of the grounds of Osmaston Hall – rail access was through the Carriage & Wagon Works site. St Osmund's Church on London Road at left, recently completed in 1904.

MR first-class dining carriage No.361 the pinnacle of luxury and passenger comfort on the Midland in 1896. This particular coach was specially fitted out by Gillows of London and trimmed with green silk to specially impress.

In 1938 this remaining area of the Park with the Hall was acquired by Derby Borough Council, and the distinguished Hall building was promptly demolished, one of the earlier ones in the tragic procession of local halls and buildings of note, swept away by the unenlightened Derby Town Councils of yesterday.

By 1898 the Carriage and Wagon Works had grown to employ 3,450 men, and some

One of a pair of office blocks built by the MR in Nelson Street close to the Derby Station – designed by John Holloway Sanders the company architect. The near block pictured, was built in 1872 to house the accounts staff. The larger block behind of 1873 was for the goods manager and staff.

Map of the Midland Railway and its connections. Late 1870s.

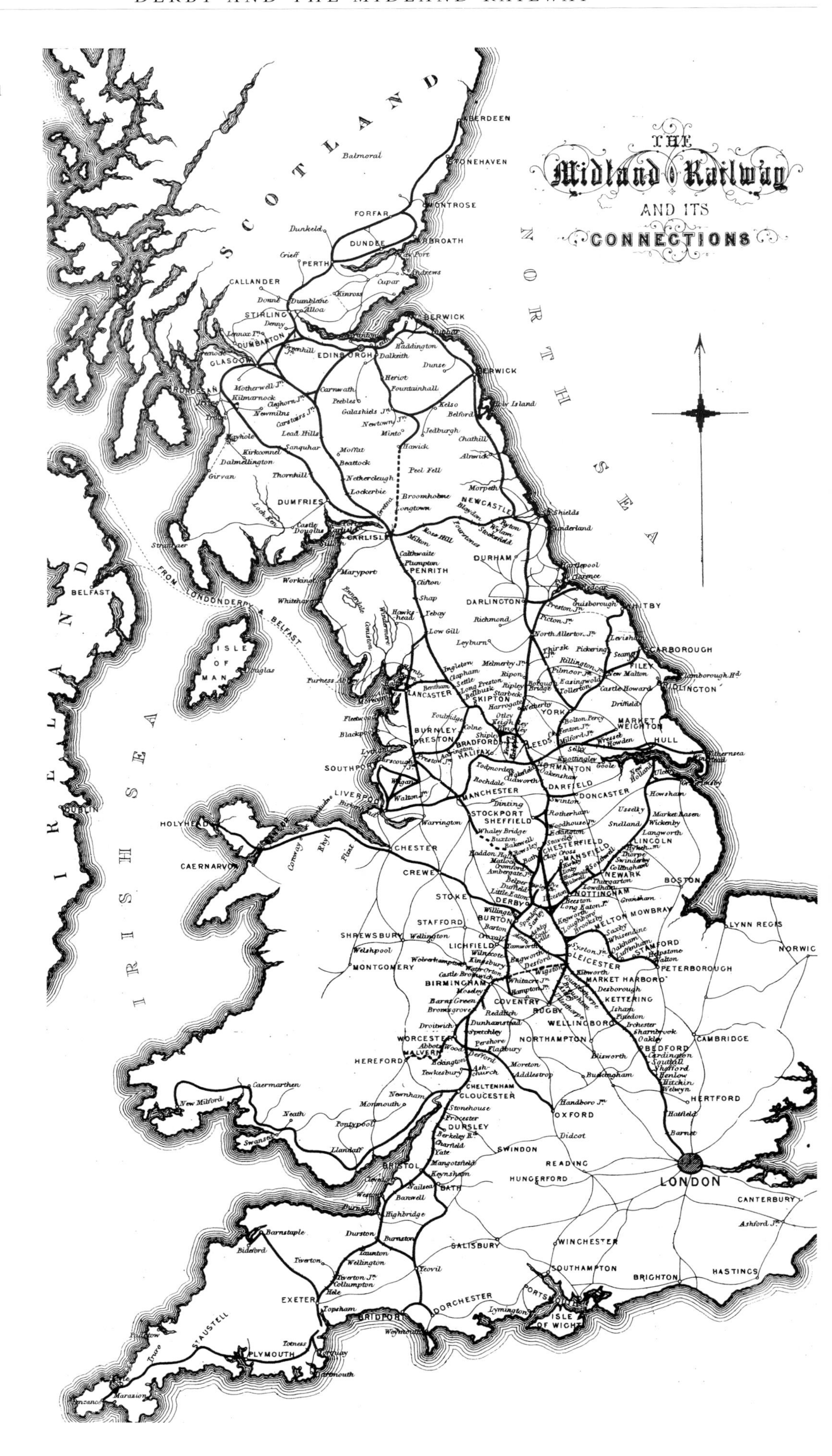

150 women in upholsterers and sewing rooms. Eight passenger coaches were being built there each week, and 180 wagons. The Midland Company's carriage stock amounted to 4,786 vehicles and 116,330 wagons.

In 1872 the company had incurred more expenditure with the necessary building of a new office block for the MR accountant and his staff. This was immediately followed with an adjacent similar, but larger block for the goods manager in 1873. These two blocks of similar design, by the company's architect J.H.Sanders, were built in Nelson Street adjacent to the station – the smaller one nearer the station being for the accounts staff. Although close together the blocks always remained unconnected until only recently, when they were refurbished for Inter-City – joined with an elegant glazed link, and renamed 'Midland House'.

In 1872 also, the company built an enginemen's lodging house near the station, at the end of the old Siddals Road. A substantial building of three storeys, in an imposing style, and also probably designed by J.H.Sanders. It provided dormitories, with washrooms, and dining facilities for engine drivers and firemen needing overnight accommodation between working trains in and out of Derby. The company built others at a number of the larger towns and centres on its routes. The building still survives, now used by an old established firm, as a shop and depot for garden machinery.

The Midland Railway's Signal Department had been developing significantly since the first days of the three early railways at Derby. The early rudimentary control of train movements by 'policemen' using their arms and flagmen standing by the rail tracks, had gradually been replaced with semaphore arms and crossbars on posts – but a man still had to be positioned at the foot to operate it. If he was fortunate he might have a little sentry type box to give him some protection from the weather, between trains.

At some places it had been found convenient to elevate the early semaphore signals on a tower for visibility to the train crews. A rare surviving example of this is the stone tower of 1839-40 on the Chevin Ridge above the Milford tunnel, built by the North Midland Railway Company. The earliest 'signal box' in Derbyshire, it is unclear whether it was still in use when the Midland Railway came into existence in 1844, but it is quite likely. This development probably originated from the earlier Admiralty overland semaphore signalling system. By around 1860 the early boxes had become a timber

MR enginemen's lodging house of 1872 near the Station on Siddals Road. A substantial building in imposing style, designed J.H.Sanders.

Chevin Ridge signal tower built by the North Midland Railway in the late 1830s above the Milford Tunnel. It survives today, the listed building remains of a remarkably early railway signalling tower.

Midland Railway – engraving of the 1850s of Clay Cross Junction and industry on the old North Midland line. An early signal box on trestles can be seen with semaphore arms on posts, and a signalman hanging a flag out.

Level crossing at Long Eaton in September 1911. Plenty of typical MR detail, signal box, signal posts, gates, fencing, and gas lamp post.

cabin with a gallery, on a tall trestle structure, with semaphore arms working on tall posts – there was such an example at Clay Cross junction.

The expanding demands of fixed signalling caused the Midland Company to establish a separate signal works division within the main works in 1860. The introduction of the tumbler lever frame in conjunction with block instruments led the Midland to introduce the policy of standard design signal boxes from 1869-70. With this development the signal section soon outgrew the space available in the works, so that in 1872 a special separate Signal Works was established on a site north of the Five Arches Bridge, between the river and the main line north. Eventually this became a substantial works in its own right on an area extending to nearly seven acres – with drawing office, work-

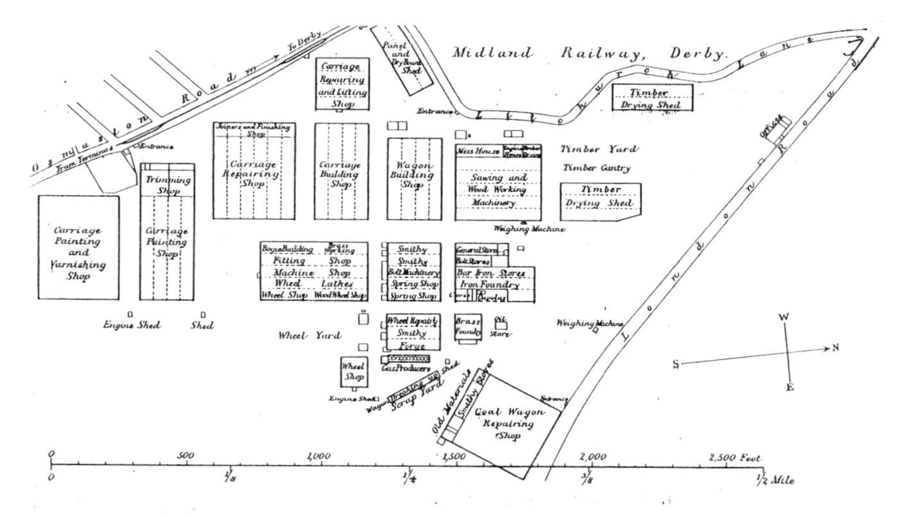

Plan of the Carriage & Wagon Workshops of the Midland Railway – Derby. 1898.

Burton & Ashby Light Railway, tramcar No.10 – owned and operated by the Midland Railway 1906-1927.

Midland guards in uniform 1906-22, but the styles had been introduced in the late 1800s. Passenger guard right, and goods guard on the left – each has a Wyvern device cap badge.

Rows of Midland locomotives 'on shed' outside No.2 roundhouse (built 1847) photographed in the late 1880s. They are mainly Kirtley types but with a few of the new Johnson locomotives among them.

shops and outside working areas. Here all the signalling equipment was made for the entire Midland system and on the joint lines it operated. By 1900 the signal works at Derby employed some 450 carpenters, smiths and fitters, with about 500 employed there altogether. Another 150 or so were employed as outdoor instal-

Derby Works – boiler shop *c.*1911 – fundamental parts before the additions of the finery of outer casings.

Final frontage of Derby Midland Station in 1903 after the forward extensions of 1893 by Charles Trubshaw – company architect, horse-drawn Broughams wait for customers in and outside the re-erected *porte-cochère*. A Derby Corporation horse-drawn tram also waits.

lation and repairmen. An average of 30 new prefabricated timber signal boxes with their distinctive pattern, and handsome roof finials as on the signal posts, were built at the works every year. And, there was a continuing maintenance of some 1,700 signal boxes over the whole Midland system, plus thousands of signals and points. The works was modernised in 1912 and continued in operation into the LMS era from 1923, before being closed in 1932 when stock, staff and operations were transferred to Crewe.

An unusual operation of the Midland Railway was the Burton & Ashby Light Railway – popularly known as the 'Sixpenny Switchback.' In reality this was a conventional electric tramway run by the Midland Company as a wholly owned subsidiary. It was originally promoted privately in 1899 but met objections. The Midland took over the idea and with the only modification of including the township of Newhall in the route it was approved with a Light Railway Order. The tramway linked Ashby-de-la-Zouch to Burton upon Trent and ran via Woodville and Swadlincote, with branch spurs to Church and Castle Gresley. Although the route almost duplicated Midland Railway lines to these places the railway traffic was primarily industrial to serve the coal-mines, clay-pits and the wide range of clay-ware goods manufactured in the Swadlincote-Gresley locality. The tramway was opened throughout in mid-1906 and operated by 20 double-deck open top tramcars. These were all painted in standard Midland lined out crimson lake livery to the waist and end panels. Central on the waist panels was the full Midland arms topped with the Wyvern. The lower waist bore the legend Burton & Ashby Light Railways. The glazed saloon was well fitted out with panels and mouldings. The route length from Ashby to Burton was just over ten miles, and the fare was 6d (2½p) in 1906, increased to 9d (4p) in 1919 – much less than the railway fares. There were reduced workmen's fares for artisans, mechanics and labourers. Most of the route was along town streets and country

The first-class booking hall of 1893 at Derby Station in 1983, long since disused and awaiting demolition.

An animated Edwardian group of passengers on Derby Midland Station adjacent to the Bristol train – *c.*1902.

Faded grandeur – the elegant stairs put in 1872-73 to serve the shareholders room and the Midland Company's new boardroom – seen in 1983.

roads, but there were also fenced sections across fields.

The route was a hilly one with several gradients of 1 in 12 so good brakes were essential. The steep route caused disaster in October 1919 when one tramcar slipped back on the hill at Winshill, overturning on the bottom corner and catapulting 15 passengers over into the garden of a house. Tragically one women passenger and the conductress died from their injuries. The tramway passed into LMS ownership in 1923, but with falling passenger receipts from the competition with new bus services, the last tramcar finally ran into Swadlincote Depot on 19 February 1927.

Theatrical companies always moved from one town's theatre to another across the country on Sundays – "Derby was the great meeting place of the profession. I always liked a Sunday wait at Derby where every train had its labelled theatrical carriages and where theatrical specials were shunted and assembled and divided. As each train came up you turned to read its labels and call on any member of the company with whom you had previous acquaintances" – *Cecily Hamilton.*

In 1851 we find Mary Chalters and her daughter Catherine of London, together with one Ann Murphy from Wellington. All described as 'Theatrical Visitors' and lodging at 4 Railway Terrace with William Pearce and family before moving on by the railway to another town theatre.

In 1892-3 the Midland Railway Company emphasised its position as a superior railway line by providing improved facilities for its passengers at Derby Midland Station, and drew together all the elements of the extensions from the original Thompson 1840 building, with a splendid new and final frontage designed by Charles Trubshaw. Three storey pavilions in elegant classical style, with pediments, balustrades, and pepperpot domes in the corners were built in front of the wing extensions of the shareholders room block, and the three storey office block on the north side.

In between, the old forecourt was filled in with separate splendid new first and third class booking halls, and an arrivals hall. Thompson's building being left virtually intact behind. These new works were linked across at first floor level with offices, capped with repeat balustered balustrades, and pediments. As the central

Staff of Derby Station *c*.1900. All grades are represented from porters to the station-master, with the only exception of young lads who were clearly too immature to be seen with their betters.

The faded Victorian splendour of the MR board-room, Derby of 1872, converted to the new main train control room in 1908-09. The great route map display case robbed of its charts. Seen in 1983 prior to demolition.

feature there was a station clock surmounted and flanked by wyverns. In front of this the 1855 *porte-cochère* of John Holloway Sanders was re-erected for a fine entrance.

By the early years of the twentieth century there was severe congestion on the Midland's lines, causing considerable delays to goods and mineral trains. To overcome these problems a train control system was developed and introduced, which successfully achieved a considerable reduction in delays and wasted standing-time of trains. The Main Control Office was set up in 1908-09 in what had been the boardroom suite, next to the shareholders room.

The Midland Railway Institute was officially opened on 16 February 1894 by George Ernest Paget, the Midland Chairman. Built on the corner of Midland Place and Railway Terrace, it is an imposing building, in brick with terracotta detailing. To build it necessitated the removal of 15 of the old North Midland houses to make space, including the house that had accommodated the highly respected George Rickman the first station master and, the estimable Matthew Kirtley. The Institute was another design by Charles Trubshaw, the company architect. It generously provided a lecture and concert hall to seat 500 people, three classrooms, a library with some 14,000 volumes, a magazine and newspaper

The imposing Midland Institute, Derby of 1892 built on the site of 15 of the former North Midland Railway houses on the corner of Midland Place/ Railway Terrace.

Top left: Neat worked-in sign for the original café entrance, Midland Institute 1892. Right: Nottingham's third station off Carrington Street, built by the Midland in 1904, designed by A.E.Lambert in confident Edwardian style. Lambert had also happened to design the new Great Central Railway's Victoria Station, 1898-1900, in the city.

room, games rooms, café and a coffee room. Membership was open to all employees, and with only a small weekly subscription charged. The library ran a lending service of books, which were sent out in special containers via passenger trains for collection and return at all stations. This followed on the example of Charles Mudie's highly successful circulating Lending Library from London, which began to exploit the growing railway network from 1842, sending out books with bright yellow labels in brass bound boxes.

In the Edwardian era and the four years before World War One, the Midland Railway had reached the zenith of its powers and importance. Its lines reached out to all corners of England and South Wales, and had connections into Scotland.

Midland Institute Library in 1896, with some of its stock of over 14,000 volumes.

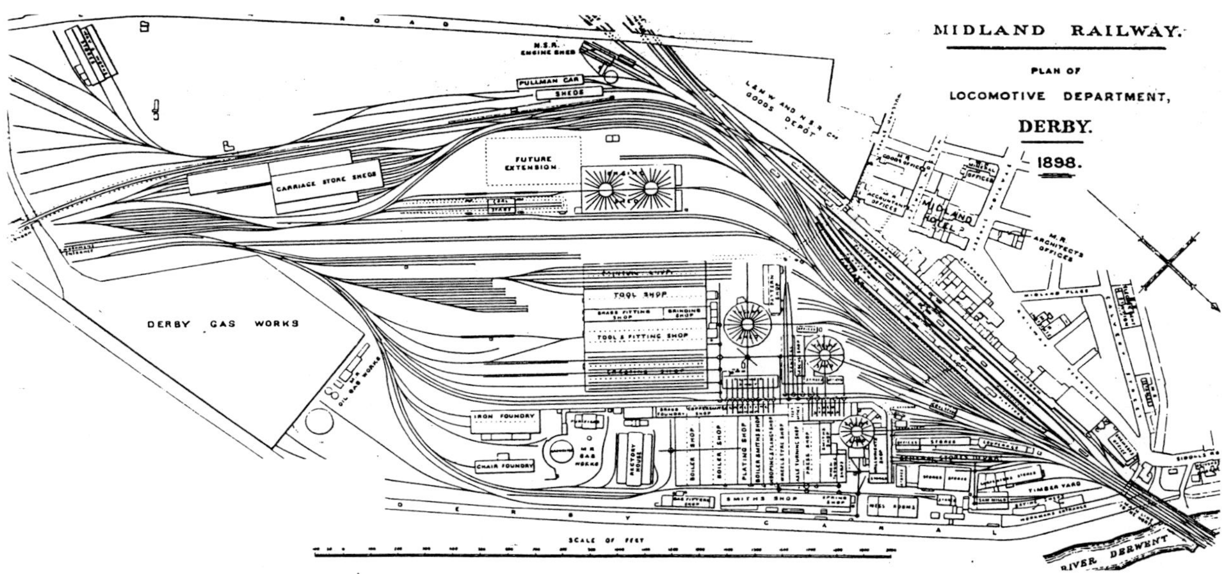

Plan of the Locomotive and other departments of the Midland Railway – Derby. 1898.

It had even acquired railways across in Ireland, and sailed steamers over the Irish Sea to connect with them. Its trains were immaculate, their splendid crimson colour seen everywhere. By 1900 the company had a total of some 2,530 locomotives and 15,500 men employed in the locomotive department alone. The Derby works was building about 40 new engines and re-boilering around 120 each year.

Decline came with the punishing war years of 1914-18, with all the railway companies struggling to maintain their services, while sustaining the heavy demands of continual troop trains, and carriage of war material. The Carriage & Wagon Works produced ambulance trains, general service army wagons, other war vehicles, and parts for rifles. The Derby Locomotive Works turned to manufacturing gun cradles, field gun carriages, and limbers. It was also heavily involved in recycling 18-pounder brass shell cases for continual new ammunition. With the war, female workers came into railway service to replace the huge numbers of

Midland enquiry office at the Royal Agricultural Show, Derby 1906, particularly advertising the Midland's new boat service from its harbour at Heysham across to Belfast.

Sir Guy Granet, last chairman of the Midland Railway (served 1918-1923) and second chairman of the new London Midland & Scottish Railway from 1924-27.

men called away to armed service. The women were mainly employed on dirty mundane jobs such as engine cleaning and coal stacking, and also in the workshops re-servicing the shell cases. This was the first real advent of female labour into the railway, apart from the 150 who had been working in the carriage works from the late nineteenth century. Those earlier 150 had either to have been railway workers widows, or the daughters of railway employees. Some 2,870 Midland Railway employees paid the ultimate price in that terrible war and never returned. Their names are inscribed in bronze on the Portland Stone walls of the solemn Midland Railway memorial and cenotaph, designed by Edwin Lutyens, on the edge of the Midland Hotel garden.

Construction of locomotive No.1000 at Derby 1905. The first of the famous 4-4-0 compounds designed by Richard Deeley. Shown nearing completion in the erecting shop. Now in the National Railway Museum Collection.

Women carrying out the arduous task of stacking locomotive coal in front of No.4 shed, Derby in 1917. Loss of men to the military forces led to the widespread use of female labour on the railways.

Fine large art nouveau style wrought-iron gates at Nottingham's Midland Station, 1904 and Midland Railway's T.T.S. Londonderry built 1904 for the new Irish service from Heysham harbour (constructed by the Midland in 1896). The Midland had been empowered in 1902 to run is own steamship service to Ireland and the Isle of Man.

After the war the railways found it difficult to regain their pre-war state and there was also the ever-increasing competition from motor road transport. Very soon they all, including the Midland Railway, lost their separate identities in the great merger of 1923 when virtually every British railway company was amalgamated into the 'big four'. One of the earliest of all the railway amalgamations had created the Midland Railway Company on 10 May 1844 and the Midland Railway Company itself ceased to exist when a second great amalgamation came about on 1 January 1923. However, its standards and character were to continue in its successor the London Midland & Scottish Railway.

The Growth of Derby from the Railways

The principal trade is that of malting, with which many good estates have been raised.
William Woolley, 1712

Derby is a fine and beautiful town . . .a town of gentry rather than trade.
Daniel Defoe, 1724-26

THE coming of the railways to Derby made a distinctive lasting contribution to the development and expansion of the town in the Victorian age. In 1841 the population was almost 33,000. It had doubled in the previous 20 years, showing a quickening expansion. The population then stabilised for a while before steadily increasing to 50,000 by 1871. There was then a period of appreciable growth over the next 20 years with the population doubling to 100,000 by 1892. However, part of this expansion was accounted for by the authorised extension of the Borough's boundaries in 1877, which took in the developing residential areas of Litchurch and Normanton.

The township of Litchurch was an ancient manorial estate lying just south of the town boundary beyond St Peter's Parish. It had been a royal manor since at least the Domesday Survey of 1086 where it was mentioned as Ludecerce, and with the reigning monarch as Lord of the Manor. The Survey recorded 1 freeman and 9 villagers. It is uncertain whether it ever had a church or chapel of ease. William Woolley recorded in 1712 that it had "no house, only three or four cottages. It consisted of meadow and pasture land" Its population was always sparse and had hardly grown at all by 1801 when 35 inhabitants were recorded. These were mainly in the hamlet in Litchurch Lane. From that date there began a steady increase in its population, as an adjunct of Derby. There were 93 people in 1821, 516 in 1831 and 855 in 1841 by the time the railways had come. This last figure including those railway employees who were moving into the part of the NMR Railway houses which lay within Litchurch. But, much of the increase in this last decade was accounted for by the building of the new Derby Union Workhouse on the Osmaston Road in 1839 (converted in 1878 to the use of the new Royal Crown Derby Porcelain Co), which accommodated 138 people in 1841. By 1861 the population of Litchurch had swollen rapidly to 6,560, almost entirely due to the consequence of Derby becoming a major railway town; although initial expansions in Derby Borough and the Litchurch Township between 1831 and 1851 was also accounted for by increasing extension of the silk, hosiery and narrow fabrics industries in the town.

It was only after 1851 that the Midland Railway establishment really began to grow to become the huge company it eventually achieved at its zenith in the Edwardian era before World War One. At the turn of the century the Midland Railway was the largest employer in Derby. Some 15,500 men were employed in the locomotive department of the company, another 3,450 men and 150 women in the Carriage & Wagon Works, plus 450 within the Signal Works. Many more were employed in the extensive offices at Derby – controlling, planning and administering the running of this enormous national enterprise, at the stations and along the lines.

The opening of the railways in 1839-40

Matthew Kirtley with his wife Ann, and daughters Elizabeth and Emily outside their home at Litchurch Grange in the late 1860s.

Arboretum Street houses of the 1830s with 1860s houses in Arboretum Square beyond, and the Arboretum Lodge and Orangery in Italianate style by Henry Duesbury of 1850.

began a need for more houses in Derby to accommodate the inflow of workers drawn to work initially for the three separate companies and after 1844 for the Midland Railway. At first, needs were not excessive since quite a number of the new employees were Derby born and already lived there. Unskilled men were needed as well as skilled artisans. From what evidence survives it seems that in the main the skilled men came from elsewhere, while most of the unskilled were local men simply changing from one sort of job to a new one. Of nine men employed at the station as porters in 1842, all lived in the adjacent Castlefields Estate area. No less than four of these still claimed to be Burgesses of the town (although how this could be so after the Municipal Corporations Act of 1835 is an interesting point). Two more of these employees were Freemen of the Borough. So, all these were local men. Another four railway employees in Castlefields, plus two more in the newly built railway houses were 'policemen at the station'. Of these one was a Freeman and the other a Burgess. As already intimated these were not policemen in the civic sense but rather flagmen and train movement controllers along the lines and at the station.

The all-important engine drivers mainly came to these new railways from existing ones elsewhere, and from where they had obtained their experience. In 1842 the North Midland employed 20 enginemen and 20 firemen to drive its locomotives. Of these men it is only possible to identify three – Edward Roffey living in Canal Street, John Greenah at 30 North Street, and William Horsley living at 12 Leeds Place. Three more men living in the railway houses worked in the Locomotive Department but in what capacity is unclear. Another six Locomotive Department men lived rather further away, but still on the station side of town, in Wilmot and Sacheverell Streets off Osmaston Street – Leonard Street near the Arboretum, Devonshire Street off London Street, with three more men in Green Lane. It is likely that all these employees were incomers to the town and obtained accommodation where

Three-storey houses built in pairs *c.*1830-40s by speculative builders – also the Prince Regent public house on Regent Street, Litchurch.

there happened to be a vacant house. When the 93 new railway houses were built by the North Midland Company this must have greatly eased the early problems of housing – at least for that company's employees.

By 1842 housing existed more or less up to the town boundary on its south-east side near the station. Between Normanton Street and Siddals Lane expansion had started to fill in the open estate land southward since the earlier part of the nineteenth century. Westward of Normanton Street there was only the Little City area at the top of Green Lane, a group of cheap houses on narrow streets, run up in about 1818 adjacent to Thomas Madeley's Haarlem Mill.

The Parliamentary Boundary Commissioners Report of 1831 describes Litchurch still "as a small place, strictly agricultural". But the more prosperous citizens of Derby had been gradually building comfortable villas in large grounds along the London and Osmaston Roads, attracted by the rural surroundings. Even in November 1848 there was an advertisement in the *Derby Mercury* of a market garden on Osmaston Road for sale as building land, describing its rural nature as "the situation of this land on a brow of a gentle hill is peculiarly beautiful and salubrious." Of the large villas all set in small parks, there was Litchurch Grange a seven-bedroomed house in some eight acres, occupied in 1844 by the Reverend Horsfall and family. Matthew Kirtley would eventually move into this house from The Mount on Burton Road in the early 1860s, ending his days at Litchurch Grange on 24 May 1873.

The large villa called Field House had been built in the 1820s and was occupied by Henry Boden. He was a proprietor of Boden and Morley lace manufacturers, whose large steam operated four-storey factory in Castle Street of 1825 was the largest in the country at the time. Litchurch Villa had been built in *c.*1830 for the brothers James and Thomas Bateman of Hartington Hall, as a town house. There was also Woodville House (now La Gondola restaurant) and Holly House. Douglas House was an early nineteenth-century house built for Alderman Douglas as a town house, later given a Victorian treatment, probably about the time it was bought by Henry Swingler the ironmaster of Swingler and Eastwood. Litchurch Lodge on the London Road, opposite to where St Andrew's Church would stand, had been built in *c.*1800 for John Brookhouse a prosperous plaster and stucco manufacturer in the town. Eventually these would all be surrounded by encroaching streets as a growing tide of development advanced around them.

Litchurch Villa, Osmaston Road, built *c.*1830 for the Bateman brothers of Hartington Hall, as a town house.

A few new streets were beginning to be built in Litchurch and these were in the vicinity of the Arboretum Park, opened in 1840. Litchurch Street and Regent Street ran up from the London Road to Osmaston Road and were almost built up with small terraced houses by 1842. Round the corner on the Osmaston Road were two terraces of larger houses – Litchurch and Strand Terraces. Francis Thompson architect to the North Midland Company was lodging at no.163 Litchurch Terrace in 1841, and J.O.Baiger the superintendent of the Railway Coaching Department of same Company was at a nearby house in 1842.

The set of six houses nos. 183 to 191, part of Strand Terrace may well have been designed by Thompson since they bear an uncanny similarity to his houses on Midland and Railway Terraces. On the opposite west side of Osmaston Road, Arboretum Street and Square were laid out in 1850 when Henry Duesbury's Entrance Lodge and Orangery was built as a main entrance to the Arboretum. Nearby Morleston Street was being built up, and

The Rutland Arms public house and former 1840s artisans' houses in Nelson Street, Litchurch.

Small pairs of houses of *c*.1850-60s in High Street, Litchurch – with the High Street Tavern. Virtually every street in Litchurch, as in other areas of the town, had one or more public houses.

the Arboretum Hotel (renamed The Olde Avesbury in 1978) had recently been erected to benefit from visitors to the park. Adjacent, catering for poorer souls was the Derby Union Workhouse of 1839.

By 1852 more of the old Castlefields Estate land in Litchurch, between the station and London Road had begun to be filled up. Park Street had been extended through to Midland Road. Wellington Street had been put in, and where Carrington Street had been extended through to Midland Road there had already been an extent of infill building. The George Inn on the corner of Carrington Street/Midland Road was built, as were adjacent houses, but the Crown & Cushion pub on the corner of London Road was not to be built until a later date. There was also now a group of small terraced houses along Wellington Street, next to Midland Place. Beyond Midland Road only Nelson Street was in place by 1852. This street had groups of small terraced houses on its north side, running round into the extension of Carrington Street. The Rutland Arms pub had opened for trade, with another short terrace of small houses opposite. Further down Nelson Street another terrace of these small houses backed on to the end of the Midland Hotel.

There was not yet any sign of further infill in the rest of the triangle of land beyond Nelson Street to the railway bridge, but this would follow and culminate in St Andrew's, the so called 'railwaymen's church'. There was similarly no building yet on the land immediately in front of the station building. This would follow, with the York Hotel being built on the corner of Midland Road soon after, around 1850. The York would subsequently extend round the corner into two more properties. Adjacent, on Railway Terrace, a neat row of houses were built along to Midland Place, the corner one eventually becoming 'Wright's Vaults' a beerhouse converted from an off-licence. Both the Wright's Vaults and the York Hotel have unfortunately had their venerable names rather unnecessarily changed to new ones in recent years.

All of the land in front of the station up to the London Road was bought piecemeal for development from the trustees of the Castlefields' Estate. Despite a sketch plan that survives from 1840 and suggests to the contrary, none of this land was ever acquired by the North Midland Railway (apart from the railway 'village' site), nor was it acquired by its successor the Midland Railway.

In March 1853 there was a notice inviting tenders for new streets, sewers, and gullies on London Road and in front of the railway station which 'is about to be laid out in building lots.' A similar notice appeared in December 1854, for laying out streets in Rose Hill between the Osmaston and Normanton Roads.

The 1851 census recorded three farmers still in Litchurch, one of whom had 200 acres and still lived in old Litchurch Lane. By 1862 the population of Litchurch had grown to 6,560 and to all intents it had become a small town itself, immediately outside the Derby Borough's administration. From 1860 until incorporated into Derby in 1877, Litchurch had its own Council and services, including an 11-man fire brigade.

In Derby Borough the industrial development of the town, first in textiles in the 1700s and on into the nineteenth century, was also beginning to see an expansion

Litchurch Township fire brigade in 1873 outside St Andrew's School and Church.

into engineering. By 1789 there were 12 silk spinning mills, plus William Strutt's cotton calico mill of 1793. By 1823 there were two iron foundries and four lead works, but these had been preceded by the iron slitting and iron and copper rolling mills of Brigham Humpston established alongside the Derwent Navigation in the Morledge back in 1734. Pigot lists five iron-founders in 1835. Thomas Wheeldon had established the first foundry in the town in the late 1790s, later called the Derwent Foundry. This was followed by Weatherhead Glover & Co who in 1818 formed the Britannia Foundry in Duke Street – later taken over in 1847 by Andrew Handyside who expanded the company into large scale structural engineering so that by the 1870s it had become world famous. Falconer and Peach's Union Foundry was opened in 1822 in City Road and there was also James Haywood's Phoenix Foundry off the Nottingham Road. By 1843 all these companies were benefiting from the arrival of the railways at Derby and were manufacturing a wide range of railway material – engine wheels, rails, carriage wheels, engine castings, turntables, columns, girders and bridge-works. There were also several firms making machinery such as slide lathes, planing, milling and slotting machines – including the fine lathe making firm of James Fox of City Road established back in 1785.

Superb quality cast-iron window frame – Midland Counties Railway workshops, Derby – 1839. Castings of this standard were most probably from Weatherhead, Glover & Co.'s Britannia Foundry in Duke Street – late known as Handysides Foundry.

This tide of engineering expansion encouraged by the establishment of the railway workshops also flowed over into Litchurch. John Smith's brass foundry was established in Cotton Lane in 1844. James Eastwood, who had been in the town, relocated as the 'Railway Iron Works' in around 1852. Thomas Swingler who had been making wrought-iron axles, cranks and other items also moved, setting up the adjacent Victorian foundry by the Birmingham railway line on the Osmaston Road, making railway points and crossings. Eventually the two firms joined as Eastwood Swingler & Co making railway bridges and general

ANDREW SMITH, MILLWRIGHT, Engineer, &c., (late of Belper), begs to inform the Millowners, Manufacturers, &c., of Derby and its vicinity, that he has recently removed his establishment, to his newly erected manufactory, in Liversage-street, London-road, Derby. He is conscious of possessing the means of giving entire satisfaction in all branches connected with Mill or Engine Work; and begs to assure those who may intrust him with any portion of their work, of meeting with all that a thorough practical knowledge, connected with the strictest punctuality and despatch, can supply. During the period that A. S. has been engaged in business, he has supplied Planing Machines, Slide Lathes, and Machinery of the finest descriptions, requiring the utmost nicety in fitting, to most parts of this Kingdom, as also to the Colonies, and to the United States.

Inventor and Manufacturer of the Patent Locomotive Cylinder Printing Machine, which requires no more time in preparation and obtaining register, than the common Press, while the speed is of the double action, from 25 to 31 impressions per minute, and of the single action, from 14 to 17. The Demy and Double Crown single action Machines, may be worked by two hands. Prices at the manufactory (exclusive of roller moulds) single action, Demy, £60. Double Crown, £80. Double Royal, £110. Largest sized News, £170. Double action Demy, £80. Double Crown, £130. Double Royal, £150. Largest sized news, £190. Terms of payment, Bill at three months, on delivery.

N. B. Liversage-street is within a very short distance of the Railway Station.

Advertisement of Andrew Smith, millwright, who had recently moved into Litchurch Street from Belper – shows industry developing in this area in 1843.

constructional engineering material. The Rolls-Royce foundry continues on the site.

In 1849 John Jobson came from Sheffield and set up an iron foundry in Cotton Lane, Litchurch, eventually taking over the old Derwent Foundry – finally moving to Sunny Hill beyond Normanton in 1929 under the name of Qualcast. George Fletcher, a one time apprentice of George Stephenson, moved his firm to Derby in 1860 and established his sugar-processing machinery at Masson Works in old Litchurch Lane. Nearby, Francis Ley in 1874 set up a foundry fabricating malleable iron castings, and following this with Ewart Chain Belt on adjacent land.

Other firms followed into greater Derby after the 1877 extension, drawn by its industrial potential, its railway carrying facilities, and its growing core of engineers and skilled machine operators; not least Rolls-Royce moving into the Litchurch/Osmaston-by-Derby area in 1907.

Two other non-engineering firms directly owed their development to the Midland Railway. William Bemrose had begun in business in Wirksworth in 1826 but in the following year he removed to Derby, setting up as a stationer, bookseller and printer. The latter side developed so that by 1840 when the railways came he had 12 printing staff. He first became printer to the North Midland Railway, then secured continuing contracts with the new Midland Company, eventually producing timetables, stationery and publicity leaflets in great profusion and variety. From these early beginnings Bemrose grew into the technically advanced printing firm of today, from its early factories in Midland Place by the Station to new ones at Wayzgoose Drive, Derby and at Spondon. James Smith began in business as a tailor in Bridge Gate, Derby in 1830. In 1844 he obtained a contract to supply staff uniforms for the Midland Railway, and continued to do so through the MR's existence, going on to

Bemrose's new printing works in Midland Place in 1874 – opposite Thompson's railway houses. Bemrose became established in Iron Gate in 1827. He printed for the North Midland Railway as early as 1840, and then became major printers to the Midland Railway.

St Andrew's Church, Litchurch – the so-called 'railwaymen's church' built in stages 1862-1881. View taken *c*.1890. Demolished in 1971.

supplying military uniforms in bulk to the Government, and to Police Forces, the GPO, and other large establishments. The steady growth of James Smith & Co eventually led to a factory in Drewry Lane, Derby and others at Staveley, and Rhymney in South Wales.

In 1854 Derby applied to Parliament for an extension of its boundary to include Litchurch, but this was strongly opposed by Litchurch inhabitants and was refused. It was not until 1877 that a further application was approved and Litchurch absorbed. By that date the township had grown even further and had been divided into new parishes. The big church of St Andrews was consecrated in 1866, with St James on Dairy House Road following in 1867, and, St Thomas the Apostle on Pear Tree Road shortly after in 1881.

The driving force behind the new church of St Andrews to serve the growing Litchurch area was the energetic Revd John Erskine Clarke, vicar of the old town church of St Michael's. As early as 1851 there had been complaints that Litchurch had no church despite it containing 'a swarm of industrious workmen' at the station. Clarke took on the task of promoting the new church, since many of the new railwaymen preferred his church to the others in the town. He formed a building committee to promote the project and Gilbert Scott (later Sir Gilbert) was appointed the architect, seemingly on the suggestion of his brother the Revd Melville Scott then Vicar of All Saints, Ockbrook. In June 1862 Scott's design was approved and a building contract was let. However due to a mistake in the builder's tender the firm had underestimated and they went broke. In consequence the

Douglas Street, Litchurch houses *c.*1850-60s leading to development expansion into New Normanton and Peartree. View, with Derby Corporation open top electric tramcar taken *c.*1907.

committee could only then afford to build the body of St Andrews. The dominant steeple took until 1881 to complete following the initial Consecration and opening in 1866. In 1863 plans for schools adjacent were produced and had been built by April 1864.

By the following year the buildings were providing for church 'Sunday Schools' and for junior and senior boys and girls 'National Schools' on weekdays. For this provision parents paid 3d (1p) each week. To complement the needs of the community a branch infants school was opened in one of the railway houses in March 1869, at 19 North Street.

By the end of 1869there were 500 children were being taught in the St Andrew's schools, rising to 700 by late 1873 and, even more to 800 by the beginning of 1879. The need for education was further advanced by starting evening classes for adults in November 1864 on two nights a week, at first for men only, and then for women on two other nights. Initially only the three 'R's were taught in the evenings, but in 1869 drawing and science subjects were added. Ultimately the classics – Latin and Greek were added in 1878. Also by 1867 a Lending Library had been introduced at 3d (1p) per month for adults and ½d for children.

When the church and schools project was first initiated, Revd Clarke approached C.B.Borough of Chetwynd Park for a gift of the necessary land. Borough replied that the land could only be sold to them as it was in trust, but he personally promised to give £1,000 towards the purchase if church, parsonage and schools were all built. The building committee also approached the Midland Railway Company for financial support through Michael Bass MP – but from the company's half yearly General Meeting in 1862 they got the reply that 'the board did not consider itself justified in aiding, from the company's funds, any religious body.' Bass then as a major shareholder himself appealed to the other individual shareholders for support. Within three weeks £1,100 had been contributed.

By 1863 Nelson, Hulland and Noble Streets had been built adjacent to the church site, and were largely occupied by railway employees. On the other side of London Road – Oxford Street, High, Bloomfield, Clifton and Barlow Streets were filling up towards Bateman Street. Beyond the London Road, building was starting at Rose Hill next to the Arboretum.

A rolling expansion of Derby into New Normanton, Pear Tree, Osmaston and Sinfin followed, and then on into all the present suburbs of the town.

The coming of the railways to Derby in 1839-40, and especially the creation of the Midland Railway at Derby in 1844, were primary propagators of the expansion of Derby in the later nineteenth century and early twentieth century.

Endpiece

AS PROVIDED for under the Railways Act 1921 came the great amalgamation of virtually all the railways in Britain from 1 January 1923. They were regrouped into four big groups. From then the Midland Railway ceased to exist as an entity and became part of the new London Midland and Scottish Railway. Also into the group passed its hitherto great rival, the London & North Western Railway, together with other former competitors the North Staffs Railway, and the Lancs & Yorks, the Furness, the Maryport & Carlisle, the Caledonian, Glasgow & South Western, the Highland Railway and other small railways creating a railway with over 230,000 employees.

The headquarters of the LMS was located at Euston, and this marked the beginning of decline of Derby as the heart of a railway. The illusion nevertheless continued awhile and World War Two also served to cover the gradual decline for a further period. The nationalisation of the big four and all lesser railways still outside this on 1 January 1948 into British Railways, marked a further stage in the slow decline. The concentration of research facilities for the LMS system with the new Scientific Research Department headquarters built at Derby in 1933 further helped conceal the decline, and ultimately led to the establishment of British Rail's Railway Technical Centre at London Road, Litchurch in the 1960s. This brought together all of the British Rail Board's National Research Division for mechanical, electrical, and civil engineering work. Additionally it provided for centralisation of all mechanical and electrical design and development. Test facilities were also included for vehicles. There was centralisation of other departments such as Central Purchasing. Back in 1936 the LMS had also built its School of Transport at Wilmorton, a training college for its non-engineering staff.

The abandonment of the use of steam locomotives by British Rail in the late 1960s brought more change at Derby. The last steam locomotive was built at Derby in 1957 – a standard class 5, 4-6-0 no.73154 and was put into traffic use on 14 June that year. The last steam locomotive to come out of Derby works as an 'official repair' was no.75042 a Standard Class 4 engine, although there were one or two more, until class 9, 2-10-0 engine no.92102, the last ever, was repaired in early 1964.

In April 1967 the last new diesel locomotive no.D7677 came out of the works. This was destined to be the last of all locomotives built at the Derby Loco Works – apart from six Advanced Passenger Train power units produced in 1977.

In 1968 the Locomotive, and the Carriage & Wagon workshops were renamed British Rail Engineering Ltd. This was sold off under a privatisation scheme in 1989 to a partnership of British and Swedish engineering firms. The Swedish Company ABB bought out its partners share in 1992. Employees in the works had declined to 7,500 employees in 1977, then to 2,300 in 1994. Uncertainties over the future leave a question mark over whether the works can survive through the harsh economic climate of nowadays.

Derby station's train shed was damaged in January 1941 by a direct hit from a World War Two bomb. British Rail swept away the rest of Robert Stephenson's overall platform roof in 1954 and replaced it with ugly individual platform canopies of concrete. The old Midland Railway superintendents offices to the north side of the station entrance went at around the same time, to be replaced by a car-park.

The splendid, historic station building of the North Midland, and Midland Railway Companies survived longer. But in 1983 British Rail produced designs for a replacement station building. Despite widespread objection, but with no resistance from the city and the county councils, even though it stood at the heart of the newly-created Railway Conservation Area, British Rail proceeded to demolish the old building in 1985. It was replaced with the present undistinguished building for the not inconsiderable sum of £3½ million. The historic shareholders room, the old boardroom, and the Midland Railway's Goods and Mineral Traffic Main Control Office were all swept away at the same time. The extensive Signal Works established by the Midland Railway was removed to Crewe in 1932 and the site eventually cleared. It is now occupied by the modern plant of the *Derby Evening Telegraph* – a continuity of communications in a different form.

Present-day interior of the old North Midland Railway roundhouse-showing its intricate roof construction.

The extensive St Mary's Goods Yard became redundant as mixed traffic goods and the conveyance of domestic coals dwindled. The site has been cleared apart from a few buildings which have been given Listed Building status. These latter have been rehabitated and converted to private commercial uses. The rest of the old Goods Yard area is currently being overbuilt with new mixed housing, and commercial redevelopment. Likewise, the extensive Chaddesden Sidings area and the old Midland Counties route into Derby has all become redundant. The Wyvern shopping centre is built on part of the land, while gravel extraction has been taking place on the western end, to be developed as part of the Derby Pride Project. The Wagon Repair Workshop has been in private commercial use, but a recent serious fire destroyed half the building and severely damaged the rest.

At the old railway works site the Midlands Counties engine shed was demolished a few years ago. The substantial surviving parts of the Midland Counties Workshops were recently made listed buildings, to accompany the previously listed parts of the North Midland Works, including the historic No.1 Engine Roundhouse, the old Works Offices and clock tower. All these buildings are currently vacant and have passed into the hands of the Derby Pride Venture. A rehabitation and conversion scheme is in course of execution under the management of Derbyshire Historic Buildings Trust for Derby Pride Venture, with anticipated occupation by Waterman Railways as their headquarters and repair workshops for their historic locomotives and stock. The Midland Railway works buildings, extensive repair and fitting shops, foundries, erecting shops, roundhouses nos. 2, 3 and engine shed no.4 are now almost gone. Demolition began at the end of the steam age by British Rail, and was continued by ABB and Derby Pride.

The whole of the Midland Railway's 'bottom yard' part of the works, cleared away 1994 – boiler shops, plating, hooping, flangeing, wheel & tyre, axle turning, press and smiths' shops. The end of 155 years of a great railway works.

The splendid Nelson Street offices languished shabbily for some years but have recently been rehabilitated and imaginatively linked at last in a fine scheme. Now as Midland House they accommodate the Inter-City St Pancras-Derby rail route control and administration, together with some associated cross-country routes.

The Midland Institute was renamed the LMS Railway Institute in 1923, becoming the LMS Club in 1938, until renamed again in 1948 to the Derby Railway Institute. The significant library within was closed in 1963 and the collection sold. The Institute was then made into a British Railway Staff Association Branch on the lines of a social club. In recent years the Institute building was sold off to a property investment company who leased it to the Post Office Social Club. That use failed and the club closed. The building has since been vacant. A new use for this fine building has been elusive. Plans in 1994 to convert it into a major arts complex were eventually dropped, but there are now serious proposals to convert it into a large pub with extensive function rooms.

The Midland Railways' loco-men's overnight lodging house on Siddals Road survives, albeit long out of railway use.

The township of Litchurch disappeared long ago, when the Carriage & Wagon Works, and George Fletcher & Co moved there in the 1860s-1870s. The ancient name survives still, in the old winding lane between London and Osmaston Roads, and as a City Council ward. St Andrew's Church and the adjacent schools went between 1969 and 1971. The steeple, longer in the building than the church body, also proved more obdurate in its demolition. The church's support had gone with the clearance of the little houses in Castlefields, nearby Nelson and Hulland Streets, and terraced street dwellings between London and Osmaston Roads – these latter to make way for Derbyshire Royal Infirmary extensions and new housing.

The heart of a great railway has gone, but the memory of its achievements lives on. The impetus created by the establishment of railway headquarters at Derby in the 1840s continues as the city evolves into the future.

Bibliography - References and Further Reading

The Midland Railway its rise and progress - F.S.Williams, Bemrose & Co, 1877.

History of the Midland Railway - C.E.Stretton, Methven, 1905.

The Midland Railway - C.Hamilton Ellis, Ian Allen, 1953.

The Rise of the Midland Railway - E.G.Barnes, Allen & Unwin, 1966.

Derby Works and Midland Locomotives - J.B.Radford, Ian Allen, 1971.

Midland Style - George Dow/R.L.Lacey, Historical Model Railway Society, 1975.

Sixpenny Switchback (Burton & Ashby Tramway) - P.M.White & J.W.Storer, J.M.Pearson & Son, 1983.

Brewery Railways - Ian B.Peaty, David & Charles, 1985.

Regional History of Railways of Great Britain (Vol 9 The East Midlands) - Robin LeLeaux, David & Charles, 1976.

The Cromford & High Peak Railway - Alan Rimmer, Oakwood Press (1956) new edition 1985.

The Wirksworth Branch - Howard Sprenger, Oakwood Press, 1987.

Rail Centres - Derby - Brian Radford, Ian Allen, 1986.

Settle to Carlisle - W.R.Mitchell & David Joy, Dalesman Books, 1989.

The Railways of Great Britain and Ireland (1842) - Francis Wishaw, David & Charles, reprint 1969.

The Railway King - George Hudson 1800-1871 - Richard S.Lambert, Allen & Unwin, 1934.

Birmingham & Derby Junction Railway - C.R.Clinker, Avon Anglia, 1982.

The Midlands Counties Railway - Railway & Canal Historical Society, 1989.

The North Midland Railway Guide - (orig. publ. 1842) - introd. O.F.Carter, Turntable Enterprises, 1973.

The Nottingham & Derby Railway Companion 1839 - re-published by Derbyshire Record Society, 1979.

The Leicester & Swannington Railway - C.R.Clinker, Avon Anglia 1977.

The Birmingham and Gloucester Railway - P.J.Long and Revd W.V.Awdry, Alan Sutton 1987.

The Chevin Signal Tower - Peter Billson, Wyvern Journal No.72, 1988.

Victorian Stations - Gordon Biddle, David & Charles, 1973.

The British Railway Station - Gordon Biddle & Jeoffry Spence, David & Charles, 1977.

Railway Station Architecture - David Lloyd & Donald Insall, David & Charles, 1967.

London's Historic Railway Stations - John Betjeman, John Murray. 1972.

An Introduction to Railway Architecture - Christian Barman, London Arts & Technics, 1950.

Railway Architecture - Save Britain's Heritage edit Marcus Binney & David Pearce, Orbis, 1979.

Early Victorian Architecture in Britain - Henry Russell Hitchcock, Yale University, 1954.

The Golden Age of British Hotels - Derek Taylor & David Bush, Northwood, 1974.

British Railway Hotels - Oliver Carter, Silver Link Publishing, 1990.

Dinner in the Diner - railway catering - Neil Wooler, David & Charles, 1987.

Victorian Pubs - Mark Girouard, Yale University 1984.

The North Midland Railway and its Enginemen 1842-43 - Michael Robbins, Journal of Transport History, May 1960.

The Railway Builders - Victorian Railway Contractors - R.S.Jobey, David & Charles, 1983.

The Railway Navvies - Terence Colman, Hutchinson, 1965.

Early Victorian Britain 1832-51 - J.F.C.Harrison, Fontana/Collins, 1979.

The Age of the Railway - Harold Perkin, Panther, 1970.

Liverpool & Manchester Railway Operations 1831-1845. Thomas Donaghy, David & Charles, 1972.

Railway Carriages in the British Isles 1830-1914 Hamilton Ellis, Allen & Unwin 1965.

Our Iron Roads - F.S.Williams 1852 Bemrose & Sons.

Encyclopaedia of Cottage, Farm and Villa Architecture and Furniture - Supplement to the 1844 edition - J.C.Loudon, 1835.

The Canals of the East Midlands - Charles Hadfield, David & Charles, 1966.

Pigot and Co's Commercial Directory of Derbyshire 1835 - Derbyshire County Library fasc. reprint 1976.

Glover's Derby - History and directory - 1843 (and 1850 and 1858 editions) - Breedon Books facs reprint 1992.

Samuel Bagshaw - Gazetteer and Directory of Derbyshire - 1846.

Freebody's Directory of Derby - 1852.

Drake's Commercial Directory of Derby - 1862.

Kelly's Post Office Directory - 1864.

Boundary Commissioners Report on the Borough of Derby - 1831.

Minutes of the North Midland Railway - Public Record Office, Kew.

Minutes of the Birmingham & Derby Junction Railway - Public Record Office, Kew.

Minutes of the Midland Counties Railway - Public Record Office, Kew.

Minutes of the Midland Railway - Public Records Office, Kew.

Midland Railway Locomotive and Carriage & Wagon Works - Journal of the Society of Mechanical Engineers, July 1898.

A Biographical Dictionary of Railway Engineers - John Marshall, David & Charles, 1978.

The Derby Mercury

Derby & Chesterfield Reporter

Derbyshire Courier

Leicester Journal

Nottingham Mercury

York Courant

Census Records of - 1841, 1851, 1861, 1871, 1881 and 1891.

Appendices

Appendix A – Chairmen and Officers

Midland Counties Railway 1836-1844

Chairman	1836	Matthew Babington
	1836-1844	Thomas Dicey
Secretary	1836-1844	John Fox Bell
Locomotive Superintendent	1839-1844	James Kearsley
Traffic Superintendent	1839-1844	William E.Hutchinson
Resident Engineer	1836-1843	Thomas J.Woodhouse
	1843-1844	William Henry Barlow

Birmingham & Derby Junction Railway 1836-1844

Chairman	1836-1843	Henry Smith
	1843-1844	Samuel Beale
Secretary	1839-1844	Thomas Kell
General Manager	1842-1843	John Dixon
	1843-1844	James Allport
Locomotive Foreman	1839-1841	Matthew Kirtley
Locomotive Superintendent	1841-1844	Matthew Kirtley

North Midland Railway

Chairman	1836-1841	George Carr Glyn
	1841-1842	J.W.Childers MP
	1842-1844	William Leaper Newton
Secretary	1836-1842	Henry Patteson
	1842-1844	Peter Clarke
Chief Locomotive Engineer	1839-1842	Robert Stephenson
	1843-1844	Thomas Cabrey
Locomotive Superintendent	1840-1843	William Prime Marshall
	1843-1844	Thomas Kirtley
Superintendent of the Line	1839-1841	Ashlin Bagster
	1841	Robert Stephenson (temp acting)
	1841-1844	William Hanson
Superintendent Coaching Dept	1840-1841	William Hanson
	1841-1844	J.O.Baiger
Traffic Superintendent	1840-	William E.Hutchinson
Assistant Engineer	1836-1844	Frederick Swanwick
Company Architect	1839-1842	Francis Thompson

Midland Railway Company 1844-1923

Chairman	1844-1849	George Hudson
	1849-1858	John Ellis
	1858-1864	Samuel Beale MP
	1864-1870	William E.Hutchinson
	1870-1873	William P.Price
	1873-1879	Edward Shipley Ellis
	1879-1890	Sir Matthew W.Thompson
	1891-1918	Sir Ernest Paget Bt.
	1918-1923	Sir Guy Granet
Secretary	1844-1853	John Fox Bell
	1853-1856	Joseph Sandars
	1857-1868	G.N.Browne
	1868-1899	James Williams
	1899-1906	Alexis L.Charles
	1906-1923	W.N.Bancroft
General Superintendent	1844-	Peter Clarke
General Manager	1853-1854	James Allport
	1857-1860	W.L.Newcombe
	1860-1880	James Allport
	1880-1892	John Noble
	1892-	G.H.Turner
	-1905	John Mathieson
	1905-1918	Guy Granet
	1918-1922	Frank Tatlow
Locomotive Superintendent	1844-1873	Matthew Kirtley
	1873-1903	Samuel Johnson
	1904-1909	Richard Deeley
Chief Mechanical Engineer	1910-1922	Henry Fowler
(Acting)	1915-1919	James Anderson
Chief Motive Power Superintendent	1907-1909	Henry Fowler
	1910-1913	James Anderson
General Superintendent	1907-1919	Cecil Walter Paget
General Foreman of Workshops	1855-1863	John Fernie
Workshops Superintendent	1864-1874	William Kirtley
(General Foreman re-styled)	1874-1893	Francis Holt
Works Manager	1893-1901	John Lane
(Works Superintendent re-styled)	1902-1903	Richard Mountford Deeley
	1903-1907	Cecil Walter Paget
	1907-1909	Henry Fowler
	1910-1913	James Edward Anderson
Works Assistant (Works Manager re-styled)	1913-1923	James Edward Anderson
Carriage & Wagon Superintendent	1844-1873	Matthew Kirtley
	1873-1902	Thomas Clayton
	1902-1919	David Bain
	1919-1922	Robert Whyte Reid
Resident Engineer (Civil)	1844-1857	William Henry Barlow
	1858-1875	John Sydney Crossley
Ass. Resident Engineer	1844-	Frederick Swanwick
Consultant Engineer (Civil)	1858-1904	William Henry Barlow
Joint Consult. Eng. (Civil)	1875-1879	John Sydney Crossley
Company Architect	1845-1884	John Holloway Sanders
	1884-1905	Charles Trubshaw
General Chief Draughtsman	1854-1860	Charles Little
Chief Locomotive Draughtsman	1874-1890	Robert John Billington
	1890-1901	Thomas Gill Iveson
	1901-1906	John William Smith
	1906-1913	James Edward Anderson
	1913-1923	Sandham John Symes
General Manager Hotels & Catering Service	1884-1914	William Towle
Joint Assistant Managers	1898-1914	Francis William Towle
	1898-1914	Arthur Edward Towle
Joint General Managers	1914-1916	Francis Towle
	1914-1917	Arthur Edward Towle
General Manager Hotels & Catering Service	1920-1923	Arthur Edward Towle

Appendix B
Resolution of Derby Town Council Towards a Joint Station

Borough of Derby 2 February 1836

At a meeting of the Council of this Borough held at the Guild Hall on the 2nd day of February 1836 -

Joseph Strutt Esq.
Mayor in the chair.

It was resolved that the consent of this council be for the present withheld from the lines of Railways as now proposed to pass through the corporation lands near Derby, by the Derby and Birmingham, by the North Midland and by the Midland Counties Railway Companies, and that a Committee of five in number of the Council should be appointed to confer with the Gentlemen to be appointed by the respective Railway Companies to induce them to adopt other lines (as shown upon the Plan made by order of the Committee) which this Council believe to be more advantageous to the Inhabitants of the Town, and also more beneficial to the Railway Companies themselves -
That a copy of these resolutions be sent to the agents of the respective Railway Companies, and that the Directors of each Company be requested to appoint Gentlemen to confer with the Corporation Committee at the earliest convenient period –
Resolved that the following Gentlemen be appointed a Committee to carry with effect the above Resolutions with power for three or any more of them to act viz -

Mr John Sandars
Mr Fras. Jessopp
Mr John Johnson
Mr Robert Longdon
Mr Jas. Thomason

Addressed to -

To The Agent
of the
North Midland Railway

Appendix C
Letter from Derby Town Council Railway Committee objecting to the decision to site the joint station in Castlefields.

7 April 1838
Railway Station, Derby

To the Directors of the North Midland Railway Company

Gentlemen,

The Railway Committee appointed by the Town Council of Derby, beg to call the attention of your body to the proposed change of the Railway Station, and for fixing the same in Boroughs Field.

In February 1836 the consent of the council was requested by the three Railway Companies to the Bills then before Parliament empowering the several companies to pass over certain lands belonging to the Corporation of Derby, or lands over which the Freemen had rights of commonage, for whom the Council were Trustees. The Council at that time declined to give their consent, but after an explanation given by one of its members of certain improvements which would be contingent upon fixing a suitable place for the Station, a long-discussion took place and the Council unanimously (with only one disentient) appointed a Committee to further enquiries into the proposed scheme and to ascertain the most eligible place for an united Station and which Committee was directed also to confer with the several Railway Companies relative there to – In order to expedite the negotiations Messrs Sandars and Johnson were appointed a Deputation to proceed to London to confer with the Directors of the several Companies.

Messrs Sandars and Johnson proceeded to London accordingly, and on the 1st and 2nd March 1836 well as at other times had conferences with the several Directors, and those Directors pledged themselves to Messrs Sandars and Johnson, that they would take the subject into early consideration and that the "Derby Station should be fixed in a situation most convenient and advantageous to the Inhabitants of the town of Derby." Relying upon the good faith and honourable fulfilment of this pledge the Council at all times gave every support in their power by Petition and otherwise to the Railway Bills then before Parliament. If such pledge and assurance had not been given the Council would have felt if their duty as Trustees for the public, to have used all the means in their power to have had the stations for Derby fixed by Parliament and no reasonable doubt can be entertained that they would have succeeded.

Upon the faith of those promises this Committee caused the most rigid enquiry to be instituted by conferring with persons well acquainted with the localities of the Town and neighbourhood, also by causing plans and estimates to be prepared at considerable expense for carrying the proposed object into effect, they have also negotiated with persons whose consent would be necessary for completing the approaches to the proposed Meadow Station, and which negotiations are in a forward state and may be soon completed.

At a conference on the 6 August 1836 at which Sir Oswald Mosley Bart., and Messrs H. Smith - G.C.Glynn - W.L.Newton – C.Vignoles and J.Bell were present, the proposals of the Council were fully discussed, and this Committee was afterwards informed that the plan of making the Station in the Holmes would be too expensive on behalf of the Railway Companies, but "if the Corporation would make better approaches to the Holmes, and a road across the same - the Railway Companies would then build a Bridge over the River Derwent opposite such a new road and fix their Stations in the Old Meadows" – upon that proposition this Committee immediately proceeded, and several thousand loads of earth have been already deposited in the Holmes towards forming the intended new road; and the committee beg to say that they will do all in their power to carry this Plan into immediate effect, feeling no doubt that the Council will unanimously second their efforts.

The Committee have been informed that a legal difficulty exists in crossing the Nottingham Road by the North Midland Company in as much as the Trustees of the said Road refuse to give their consent to any deviation from the plan proposed by the North Midland Company on the 4 February 1836. This Committee will therefore immediately submit a case upon this point to Counsel – and they have no doubt that the Commissioners of the Derby Improvement Act will follow up their Resolutions which were unanimously passed at a large meeting of the Commissioners held on the 22 January last, a copy of which has already been forwarded to you.

This Committee have been informed that it will be necessary for the levels of the North Midland Railway to be raised considerably in order to cross the Nottingham Road; this will inflict a very serious injury in the Town, and in the opinion of the Committee cause a very great increase of expense to the Railway Companies as compared with the present levels and the Old Meadow station.

It is the opinion of this Committee that it is unnecessary to raise further objections at this time against the change in question as they may be considered Engineering questions. But being convinced that the proposed alteration will in every respect prove injurious to the interest of the Inhabitants of Derby generally, they must earnestly protest against the removal of the station from the Old Meadows; and in strict conformity with the important duties committed to their charge respectfully request that the pledge given by the several Railway companies may be strictly and honourably fulfilled - namely – that "the Station be fixed where it will be most convenient and advantageous for the Inhabitants."

Derby April 7 1838

John Sandars
Chairman
(of the Railway Committee
of Derby Town Council)

To:
G.C.Glyn Esqr.
Chairman of the North
Midland Railway Company
Lombard Street
London

Appendix D
North Midland Railway Conditions of Employment and Application Form

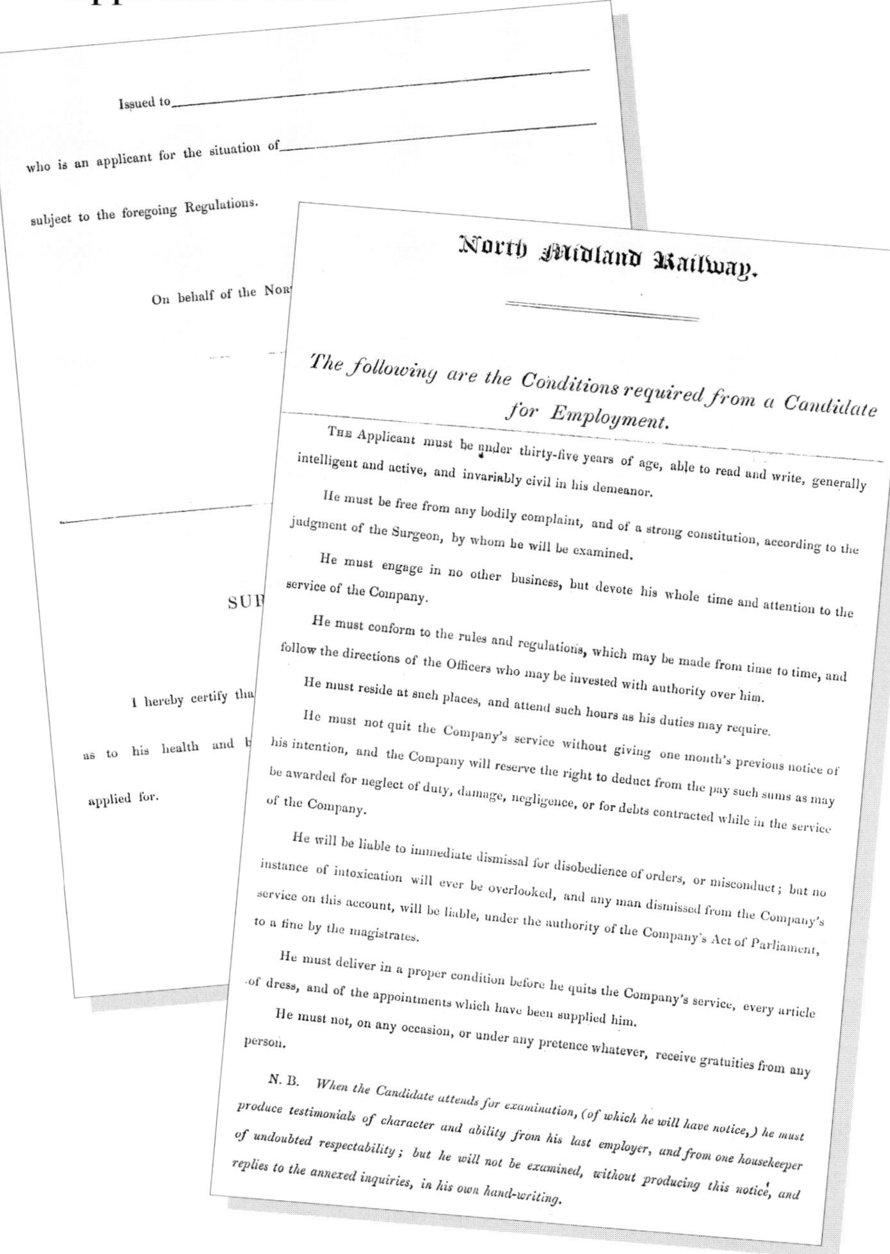

Issued to________

who is an applicant for the situation of________

subject to the foregoing Regulations.

On behalf of the Nor[...]

SU[...]

I hereby certify tha[...]

as to his health and [...]

applied for.

North Midland Railway.

The following are the Conditions required from a Candidate for Employment.

The Applicant must be under thirty-five years of age, able to read and write, generally intelligent and active, and invariably civil in his demeanor.

He must be free from any bodily complaint, and of a strong constitution, according to the judgment of the Surgeon, by whom he will be examined.

He must engage in no other business, but devote his whole time and attention to the service of the Company.

He must conform to the rules and regulations, which may be made from time to time, and follow the directions of the Officers who may be invested with authority over him.

He must reside at such places, and attend such hours as his duties may require.

He must not quit the Company's service without giving one month's previous notice of his intention, and the Company will reserve the right to deduct from the pay such sums as may be awarded for neglect of duty, damage, negligence, or for debts contracted while in the service of the Company.

He will be liable to immediate dismissal for disobedience of orders, or misconduct; but no instance of intoxication will ever be overlooked, and any man dismissed from the Company's service on this account, will be liable, under the authority of the Company's Act of Parliament, to a fine by the magistrates.

He must deliver in a proper condition before he quits the Company's service, every article of dress, and of the appointments which have been supplied him.

He must not, on any occasion, or under any pretence whatever, receive gratuities from any person.

N. B. *When the Candidate attends for examination, (of which he will have notice,) he must produce testimonials of character and ability from his last employer, and from one housekeeper of undoubted respectability; but he will not be examined, without producing this notice, and replies to the annexed inquiries, in his own hand-writing.*

Appendix E
Staffing of the North Midland Locomotive Works in 1842

Enginemen	20
Firemen	20
Foremen	5
Clerks	3
Timekeepers	2
Boilermakers	2
Brass founder	1
Coppersmith	1
Engine turners	4
Fitters, erectors, millwrights	26
Storekeepers	2
Joiners	4
Patternmakers	2
Labourers	14
Painter	1
Planer	1
Drillers	2
Smiths	10
Smiths fittings	5
Spring maker	1
Stationary enginemen and pumpers	8
Strikers	14
Turners	5
Cleaners	20
Cokemen	9
Labourers on traffic	4
Boys "paid at 2s (10p) per day and under"	11
Total	197

Total weekly wages of the locomotive Department £261 13s 10d (£261.69p)

Appendix F
Midland Railway and Other Engines and Wagons

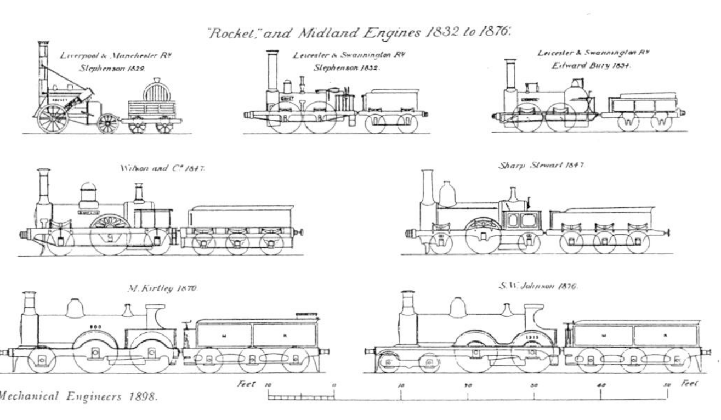

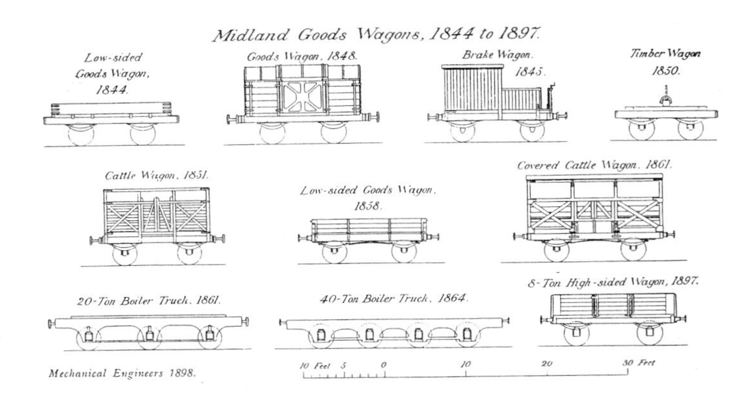

Appendix G
Midland and Associated Carriages and Rails

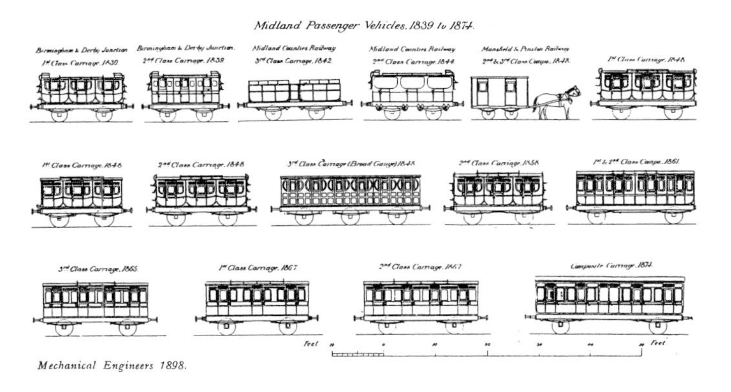

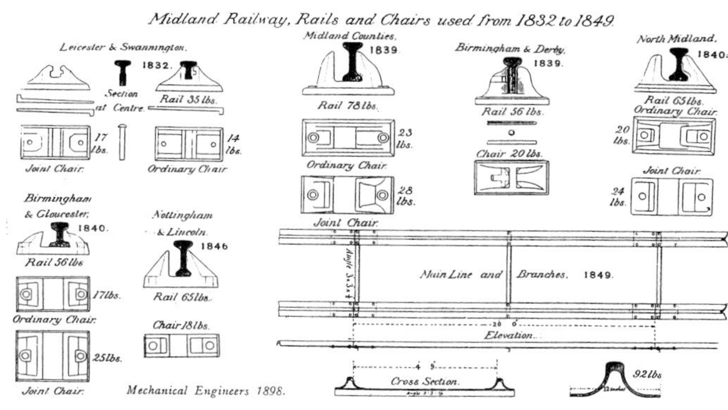

Appendix H
Companies absorbed into the Midland Railway up to the re-grouping 1923

1844 - Midland Counties Rlwy
- North Midland Railway
- Birmingham & Derby Junct. Rlwy

1845 - Sheffield & Rotherham Rlwy
- Erewash Valley Rlwy

1846 - Birmingham & Gloucester Rlwy
- Bristol & Gloucester Rlwy
- Leicester & Swannington Rlwy
- Ashby De la Zouch Canal & Railways
- Oakham Canal

1848 - Mansfield & Pinxton Rlwy

1851 - Leeds & Bradford Rlwy

1861 - Dursley & Midland Junct. Rlwy

1871 - Manchester Buxton Matlock & Midlands Junct. Rlwy
- Chesterfield & Brampton Rlwy
- North Western Railway
- Cromford Canal

1874 - Redditch Railway
- Wolverhampton Walsall & Midland Junct. Rlwy
- 'Old' Midland & South Western Junct. Rlwy
- Hereford Hay & Brecon Rlwy

1875 - Birmingham West Suburban Rlwy

1876 - Tewkesbury & Malvern Rlwy
- Wolverhampton & Walsall Rlwy
- Swansea Vale Rlwy

1877 - Manchester South District Rlwy

1878 - Stonehouse & Nailsworth Rlwy

1881 - Keighley & Worth Valley Rlwy

1882 - Evesham & Redditch Rlwy

1885 - Bedford & Northampton Rlwy

1886 - Hemel Hempstead Rlwy

1888 - Dore & Chinley Rlwy

1897 - Kettering Thrapston & Huntingdon Rlwy

1899 - Barnoldswick Railway

1912 - London Tilbury & Southend Rlwy

1914 - Tottenham & Forest Gate Rlwy

Companies vested in and worked jointly by the Midland Railway with other Companies

1863 - Furness & Midland Rlwy - with the Furness Rlwy

1865 - Cheshire Lines Committee - with the MS&LR and GNR

1869 - Sheffield & Midland Joint Lines - with the MS&LR

1875 - Widnes Rlwy - with the MS&LR

1871 - North & South Western Junct Rlwy - with the LNWR and NLR

1872 - Halesowen & Bromsgrove Branch Rlwy - with the GWR

1875 - Somerset & Dorset Railway - with the LSWR

1882 - Forth Bridge Rlwy - with NBR, the GNR and the NER (Midland largest shareholder)

1885 - Portpatrick & Wigtownshire Joint Committee - with the LNWR, CR and G&SWR

1890 - Bristol Port Rlwy & Pier - with the GWR

1893 - Midland & Great Northern Jt Committee - with the GNR - included the Eastern & Midlands Rlwy, Peterborough, Wisbech & Sutton Rlwy, Norwich & Spalding Rlwy, Midland & Eastern Rlwy

1894 - Severn & Wye & Severn Bridge Rlwy - with the GWR

1902 - Tottenham & Hampstead Junct Rlwy - with the GER

Abbreviations

MS&LR = Manchester Sheffield & Lincolnshire Railway (renamed Great Central Railway in 1897)
GNR = Great Northern Railway
LNWR = London & North Western Railway
NLR = North London Railway
GWR = Great Western Railway
LSWR = London & South Western Railway
NER = North Eastern Railway
NBR = North British Railway
CR = Caledonian Railway
G&SWR = Glasgow & South Western Railway

Appendix J
Midland Railway Stock and Vehicles at Re-Grouping 31 December 1922
Route Miles 1,521 excluding joint and leased lines

a. Locomotives

Passenger tender engines	674
Passenger tank engines	266
total passenger locomotives	940
Goods tender engines	1,598
Goods tank engines	386
total goods locomotives	1,984
Banking engine (Lickey Banker)	1
total steam locomotives	2,925
Battery electric locomotive	1
total of all locomotives	2,926

b. Coaching Stock

Dining carriages	80
Sleeping carriages	22
Other passenger carriage and train stock	5,917
Electric motor cars	48
Electric trailer carriages	49

c. Goods, Wagons, Vans, Brakes etc.

107,617

d. Service Vehicles **8,098**

London Tilbury and Southend Section
(London Tilbury and Southend Railway was absorbed by the Midland Railway in 1912)

Tank passenger engines	72
Tank goods engines	10
Tender goods engines	2
total locomotives	84
Electric motor coaches	37
Electric motor trailers	37

Burton and Ashby Light Railway

Light railway electric tramcars	20

Midland Railway Road Vehicles

Parcel and goods road vehicles	195
Carts and road wagons	7,066
Miscellaneous vehicles	12
Horse omnibuses	10
London inter-station petrol motor buses	
Rural petrol motor buses	

plus:

Horses for road haulage	3,007
Horses for shunting goods vans and wagons	96

Midland Railway Steamships

Heysham - Belfast route	- T.S. Manxman
..	- T.S. Donegal
..	- T.S.Antrim
..	- T.T.S.Londonderry
Barrow - Belfast route	- T.S. Duchess of Devonshire
..	- T.S.City of Belfast

Local Ferry Services

Heysham - Fleetwood	- T.S. Wyvern
Tilbury - Gravesend	
(across the R.Thames)	- T.S.Edith
..	- T.S.Gertrude
..	- T.S.Carlotta
..	- T.S. Catherine
..	- T.S. Rose
..	- Tilbury (paddle steamer)

The Midland also had a one fifth share in the Larne to Stranraer Steamship Joint Committee, operating ships to Ireland.
The Midland also had a vested interest in the Somerset & Dorset Joint Railway which it worked jointly with the London & South Western Railway from 1875. This had operated a cross channel service between Burnham and Cardiff up to 1888. Following the opening of the Severn Tunnel by the Great Western in 1886 the service declined. By the end of 1922 the S&DJR still had three ships but confined to working from the harbour at Highbridge and the wharf at Bridgwater. These were:
SS Alpha, SS Julia and SS Radstock.

Appendix K
Prospectus for the Erewash Valley Railway, 1843.

EREWASH VALLEY RAILWAY,

Commencing at the Long Eaton Station of the MIDLAND COUNTIES RAILWAY and terminating at Pinxton, where it will communicate with the MANSFIELD and PINXTON RAILWAY.

Length of the Line, 15 miles.—Capital, £70,000, in Shares of £50 each.

PROVISIONAL COMMITTEE:

EDWARD MILLAR MUNDY, Esq., M.P., Shipley Hall, Derbyshire.
EDWARD T. COKE, Esq., Mansfield Woodhouse, Nottinghamshire.
FRANCIS WRIGHT, Esq., Lenton Hall, Nottinghamshire.
GEORGE WALKER, Esq., Eastwood Hall, Nottinghamshire.
JAMES SALMONDE, Esq., Mansfield Woodhouse, Nottinghamshire.
WILLIAM JESSOP, Esq., Butterley Hall, Derbyshire.
JOHN SANDARS, Esq., Derby.
CHARLES VICKERS HUNTER, Esq., Kilbourn, Derbyshire.
Mr. WILLIAM GOODWIN, Birchwood.

BANKERS—Messrs. CROMPTON, NEWTON, and Co., Derby.
SOLICITOR—JOHN BARBER, Esq., Derby.
SECRETARY (PRO TEM.)—FRANCIS SANDARS, Esq.

PROSPECTUS.

The Railway is intended to pass along the valley of the River Erewash, which presents peculiar facilities for its construction, and, being kept upon a low level, will not require either large embankments, excavations, or other expensive works; and being intended to be made a Single Line of Railway, the comparatively small Capital above stated will be fully sufficient for its completion.

The great Mineral district of Nottinghamshire and Derbyshire, abounding in Coal, Iron, and other products, will, by means of this Railway, in connexion with the Midland Counties Railway, convey its produce not only to the present markets, but by the reduction on the expense of transit greatly enlarge them, and open new and extensive sources of traffic.

The Towns and Villages from Mansfield, and along this Line, contain a population of Sixty Thousand, intimately connected in occupations with the staple Trades of Nottingham, Derby and Leicester, with which places there is great intercourse which will afford a considerable Passenger Traffic.

An extensive trade in Coal to the London Market may be established, the impediments to which have hitherto been the reluctance of the Canal Committees in this locality to meet the liberal views of the Grand Junction and Union Canal Companies, as well as the delays and hindrances by floods and other causes, on the River Trent and the Soar Navigation at that period of the year when Coal is most in demand.

The present amount of the Coal Trade on the local Canals is upwards of 500,000 Tons annually—if only 200,000 Tons be calculated to pass on the Railway for 12 miles, at one shilling per ton, it would alone pay ten per Cent. on Capital, above all expenses, but this quantity will certainly be greatly exceeded.

The Traffic from existing sources may be stated as follows:—

Coal, 250,000 Tons, at 1s.	£12,500	
Merchandize—Iron, Timber, Corn, Lime, Bones, Stone, Foundry Sand, Earthenware, and Coke	4,000	
Passengers and Parcels	1,500	18,000
Deducting 1-3rd for expenses of working and maintenance		6,000
Leaves a nett profit of nearly 17 per Cent.		£12,000

In the above statement the increase from extended markets and from a London Coal Trade is wholly omitted, as it is difficult to estimate its amount, but it will certainly be very considerable; and as nearly the whole traffic will be carried to or from the Midland Counties Railway, that line must derive a most important accession of revenue, probably to an amount of £30,000 annually.

The gradients of the Railway are most favourable, varying from 9 to 14 feet in the mile, and the descent is in the direction of the heavy traffic.

A considerable part of the Capital will be contributed by local Proprietors. Application for the remainder to be made to the Committee under cover to FRANCIS SANDARS, Esq., Derby, on or before the 31st of December instant, after which the distribution will be made, and a deposit of Ten per Cent. will be required agreeably to the standing Orders of Parliament.

If on the Act being obtained, the Proprietors prefer a certain fixed amount of Dividend, responsible parties will take a Lease of the Line for a period of Ten years, paying Six per Cent. on the Capital, beyond the expenses and maintenance of the Road.

Plans have been deposited, and the necessary steps taken for applying for an Act in the ensuing Session of Parliament.

FORM OF APPLICATION FOR SHARES TO THE COMMITTEE.

GENTLEMEN,

I desire to have Shares in the Erewash Valley Railway, and I agree to take such Shares as may be allotted to me, and to pay the Deposit of 10 per Cent. and execute the Parliamentary Contract and Subscribers' Agreement when required.

I am, Gentlemen,

Name ....
Residence..............................
Trade or Profession.................